Imagining the International

The Cultural Lives of Law
Edited by Austin Sarat

Imagining the International

Crime, Justice, and the Promise of Community

Nesam McMillan

Stanford University Press

Stanford, California

Stanford University Press

Stanford, California

Printed in the United States of America on acid-free, archival-quality paper

Library of Congress Cataloging-in-Publication Data

Names: McMillan, Nesam, author.
Title: Imagining the international : crime, justice, and the promise of
    community / Nesam McMillan.
Other titles: Cultural lives of law.
Description: Stanford, California : Stanford University Press, 2020. |
    Series: The cultural lives of law | Includes bibliographical references and index.
Identifiers: LCCN 2019053656 (print) | LCCN 2019053657 (ebook) |
    ISBN 9781503602014 (cloth) | ISBN 9781503612815 (paperback) |
    ISBN 9781503612822 (ebook)
Subjects: LCSH: International crimes. | International criminal law. |
    Criminal justice, Administration of. | International criminal courts.
Classification: LCC KZ7000 .M38 2020 (print) | LCC KZ7000 (ebook) |
    DDC 345—dc23
LC record available at https://lccn.loc.gov/2019053656
LC ebook record available at https://lccn.loc.gov/2019053657

Cover design: Rob Ehle

Typeset by Westchester Publishing Services in 11/13.5 Adobe Garamond Pro

Contents

Acknowledgments

At its heart, this book is concerned with the ethical significance of suffering in the world, interrogating the social and legal frames through which suffering and social connection are imagined. In this sense, it is also a book being written by others in different forms and one that I will continue writing for some time yet. I hope that all of the diverse works and conversations that have enriched and furthered my thinking are evident throughout my text, and I apologize for any omissions or errors. As it is a book that has largely been written on the land of the Wurundjeri people of the Kulin nation, I would also like to acknowledge the Traditional Owners of this land and pay my respects to their Elders past, present, and emerging and acknowledge that their sovereignty was never ceded.

There are many people to thank for their generosity and support. I am indebted to all those who read the manuscript and gave feedback when I presented it. Thank you in particular to Jennifer Balint, Nicola Henry, Sara Kendall, Maria Elander, Rachel Hughes, Lia Kent, Natalia Hanley, Julie Evans, Michelle Burgis-Kasthala, Ilana Feldman, Fiona Haines, Dave McDonald, Joris van Wijk, Barbora Holá, Charlotte Mertens, Douglas Guilfoyle, Alex Jeffrey, Annika Björkdahl, Jeremy Farrall and Wayne Morrison. Many of these people also provided the invaluable personal and collegial support that enabled this book to come to fruition. I am also appreciative of the incisive feedback I received from participants after presenting this work at the Criminology Research Group, Redress and the Ethics of the International workshop at the Australian National University, Centre for Critical International Law at the University of Kent, Department of Criminology at Birkbeck, University of

London, Regnet at the Australian National University, Centre for International Criminal Justice at Vrije Universiteit, International Criminal Justice workshop at the University of Oslo, Leuven Institute of Criminology, and finally, the Affective States of International Criminal Justice workshop at the Melbourne Law School—and to those who made these presentations possible: Sappho Xenakis, Luis Eslava, Hilary Charlesworth, Stephan Parmentier, and Peter Rush, in addition to those already mentioned. Thank you also to Jennifer Balint, Patricia Grimshaw, Marianne Constable, Julie Evans, and Gerry Simpson for your ongoing mentorship during this period.

I am immensely grateful for the support and encouragement I have received from the editorial team at Stanford University Press—in particular, that of Michelle Lipinski, whose expertise, enthusiasm, and flexibility from the book proposal stage to the final editing has been very much appreciated. Thank you also to Brian Ostrander and Jeanne Ferris for their close copyediting of my manuscript. I feel extremely fortunate to have had the opportunity to have my book proposal and manuscript reviewed by such dedicated and interested scholars, whose insights I hope are reflected in the pages that follow.

This book would not have been possible without the research assistance of Charlotte Mertens, Matt Mitchell, Felicity Gray, Bethia Burgess and Rebecca Bunn, who now know the manuscript as well as I do. Charlotte's work has also given shape to the arguments in it.

I am thankful to the universities that provided the space in which to write this book: the University of Melbourne, Vrije Universiteit (Amsterdam) and the RMIT University (Melbourne). My time as a visitor at the Centre for International Criminal Justice at the Vrije Universiteit (facilitated by Joris van Wijk) was particularly rich. I was surrounded by excellent and always generous criminological and international criminal justice scholars and practitioners, and the position enabled my visits to the International Criminal Court and other justice institutions, and related interviews. This book has also received generous financial support from the University of Melbourne and the Australian Research Council (through its funding of the related Minutes of Evidence project), and I have enjoyed collegial support from the Criminology Discipline at the University of Melbourne.

Earlier versions of Chapters 1 and 2 have been published as "Imagining the International: The Constitution of the International as a Site of Crime, Justice and Community," *Social and Legal Studies* 25, no. 2, (2016): 163–80, and "Remembering 'Rwanda,'" *Law, Culture and the Humanities* 12, no. 2 (2016): 301–28, respectively, and I thank SAGE Publications for their permission to reproduce revised versions of these texts.

My deepest gratitude to Remi for all his support to me and this project, while our life continued outside of it. Thank you to my sister Shanti for her unwavering positivity regarding my work and to all my amazing friends who keep me going. To Eva and Kris and the Kowalski family and to John and Rich, I am so appreciative of your care for me and the kids. And last but not at all least, thank you to Lucy and Benjamin for always grounding me in time and place, and making me smile along the way.

Imagining the International

Introduction

The Ideas of "International" Crime and Justice

IN HIS OPENING STATEMENT AS CHIEF PROSECUTOR at the Nuremberg trials, Robert Jackson proclaimed that "the privilege of opening the first trial in history for crimes against the peace of the world imposes a grave responsibility. The wrongs which we seek to condemn and punish have been so calculated, so malignant, and so devastating, that *civilization cannot tolerate their being ignored, because it cannot survive their being repeated.*"[1] Through these poignant words, Jackson sought to underscore the broader significance of the suffering inflicted by Nazi Germany. It was so abhorrent, he explained, that it constituted an offense not only against its direct victims but also against civilization as a whole. Over sixty years later, at the first trial at the permanent International Criminal Court, Benjamin Ferencz expressed a similar sentiment. Referring to his own Nuremberg address, he claimed that "once again, 'the case we present is a plea of humanity to law'. . . . Let the voice and the verdict of this esteemed global court now speak for the awakened conscience of the world."[2] Although Jackson and Ferencz drew on different generalized subjectivities ("civilization," "humanity," and "the world"), their claim was the same: that certain harms are of wider import, affecting and offending against a broader international constituency and requiring a global response.

The notion that certain events and categories of harm are of broader, global significance is now commonplace. From campaigns such as Stop Rape Now, which seeks to promote global condemnation of sexual violence in situations of war, to Save Darfur, which sought to spark international action in response to the atrocities committed in Darfur, there is now a sense that particular harms should be of concern to a general global community.[3] Meanwhile, particular atrocities are known in shorthand as "Rwanda" or "the Holocaust" and widely understood as devastating international events that have significance beyond their cultural and geographic specificities.[4] Specific crimes, although committed against certain people in certain places at certain times, are now seen to constitute "crimes so serious that they are the concern not only of their victims, survivors or the state in question, but of humanity as a whole."[5] And there are now specifically international courts and tribunals tasked with the prosecution and judgment of those responsible for such crimes. A permanent International Criminal Court sits in The Hague, framed by advocates such as Ferencz as being able to "speak for the awakened conscience of the world."

This book critically engages with these ideas of distinctly *international* crime and distinctly *international* justice and interrogates their ethical and relational effects. It focuses on two main concerns. First, it examines how (that is, on what grounds) certain forms of crime and justice are figured as international and distinctive, of broader global import and status. I demonstrate how these forms of crime and justice (and their international character) are portrayed in socio-legal representation. Second, this book explores the ethical and relational effects of dominant approaches to international crime and justice by interrogating what subjectivities and communities they bring into being and how they make it possible to conceptualize, respond, and relate to suffering and injustice in the world. Through a focus on three case studies—post hoc responses to the now global event of the Rwandan genocide; the International Law Commission's debates regarding the definition of *crimes against the peace and security of mankind* (problematically gendered terminology); and dominant representations of international criminal justice—I demonstrate the specific claims to global character and significance that are made in concrete circumstances and the very particular modes of understanding global interconnection that are enabled, and foreclosed, through dominant approaches to what constitutes a distinctively *international* crime or mode of justice.

My interest is thus in the ethical and relational significance of these ideas of distinctly international crime and international justice and the sense of global interconnection with which they are associated. I argue that the sentiment that certain experiences of harm concern the whole of humanity or threaten "civilization" has the potential to connect people and communities—cognitively, emotionally, and materially—with the suffering of others. It serves to situate these harms as globally and historically signifi-cant, affecting and implicating "us" all. In this way, the productive framing of particular forms of crime and justice as somehow worldly or international in character can foster a sense of ethical proximity to suffering that might otherwise be geographically distant—making it feel closer and more mate-rial to others elsewhere.[6] Claims of the international character of certain harms, such as the Rwandan genocide or the Holocaust, situate them as somehow globally located and resonant: as events in broader international social and legal history whose significance extends beyond their immediate cultural, political, and geographical context.[7] As international events, they are seen to affect and implicate a global "we," rather than their significance being confined to their geographically, culturally, and socially immediate communities. Claims of internationality can also enable the portrayal of certain geographically, historically, and politically located institutions—like the permanent International Criminal Court—as intrinsically worldly or cosmopolitan in character, somehow transcending their particularities and being globally representative and accessible. At a time of broader con-cern in scholarship and practice with the potential indifference of Western populations to the "distant suffering" of geographically far others,[8] ideas of international crime and justice seem to enable a sense of ethical proximity and humanitarian connection that transcends physical space.

As I will show in this book, these are indeed the sorts of qualities that are associated with notions of international crime and international justice. As the quotes from Jackson and Ferencz above demonstrate, the concepts of international crime and justice are powerful ideas associated with a rich and vivid imagery of heinous suffering and an injured humanity seized to act. International crimes are portrayed as crimes that are of "concern to the international community as a whole," that "deeply shock the conscience of humanity," and that "threaten the peace, security and well-being of the world."[9] Meanwhile, international criminal justice is portrayed as serving "the cause of all humanity," a progressive and enlightened global movement dedicated to the redress of harm and human suffering.[10] The work of identi-fying, prosecuting, and punishing individual perpetrators for international crime is depicted as a "global fight," a "global justice" project that seeks to "bring justice to victims."[11] Rather than simply being seen as another field of positive law—law that is valid and binding because it has been legislated so—international criminal justice is understood to symbolize something more.[12] International justice is described by advocates as a "dream" that has been realized and as an evolving global enterprise that is currently invested with much hope and "faith."[13] Importantly, given the focus of this book, international criminal justice is currently framed as inherently humanitarian in nature and operation—an ethical enterprise that is dedicated to the acknowledgment and redress of suffering everywhere and is undertaken in the name of the victims of mass harm.[14]

Yet the ethical possibilities inherent in notions of international crime and international justice depend on the nature and form of dominant approaches to them. Postcolonial and anticolonial theorists have focused attention on the problematic and unethical forms of international relations that have been inaugurated through purportedly inclusive and humanitarian notions of a "common humanity" or global community.[15] Claims to a universal subjectivity have been powerfully used to deny the voice of some and downplay the diversity of lived experiences in and understandings of the world.[16] Meanwhile, the idea of "humanity" was also a key and legitimating referent in the global project that preceded international criminal justice: the colonial civilizing mission. The notion of humanity was invoked to envision a hierarchy of peoples across the world and justify the exploitation and tutelage of non-Western people and communities.[17] Meanwhile, throughout history attempts to represent and relate to the lives and cultures of others and enact a sense of global responsibility for injustice elsewhere have been grounded in hierarchical and culturally discriminatory images of the West as agentic, heroic, and superior—in contrast to the image of the non-West as passive, victimized, and barbaric.[18]

In this book, I take seriously the humanitarian claims associated with international crime and international justice and consider what ways they make it possible to apprehend suffering and violence around the world and understand its broader significance for others. Yet I also regard contemporary claims to global community to be forever shaped by the divisive and discriminatory colonial enterprise that came before them, which was also an internationally oriented project that envisioned an interconnected world.[19] As a foundational, globally focused endeavor, past colonial practices have shaped present geographies and legalities and modes of international relation.[20] As Ann Laura Stoler, Charlotte Mertens, Antony Anghie, and others have shown, colonial discourses, arrangements, and practices continue to exert "force" in the present, meaning that colonialism is as much an active presence in contemporary life as an enduring legacy.[21] Anghie's work in particular demonstrates how colonialism was both "central to the development of international law" and continues to shape contemporary international institutions and practices.[22] I am also attentive to the ethical implications of attempting to found a global community and claim humanitarian intention through processes of criminalization, prosecution, and punishment. As criminologists and sociologists have emphasized, law provides a particular and limited way of relating to suffering, and criminalization is an inherently punitive practice that should not be assumed to be ethical.[23] The production of community through crime and justice resonates just as much with the harsh law and order policies currently popular in many Western countries as with sentiments of benevolent and altruistic humanitarian practice. Meanwhile, a focus on the criminalization and punishment of so-called international crimes remains open to the same critiques leveled at dominant approaches to criminalization in domestic contexts—namely, that such a focus may not adequately acknowledge the underlying causes of harm or may even tend to obfuscate them.[24]

Hence, *Imagining the International* interrogates exactly *how* international crime and justice are configured and conceptualized. Through a close reading of contemporary and archival texts, I provide a detailed picture of how notions of international crime and justice are given content in practice. I demonstrate how international crime and international justice are both figured as distinctive and privileged, despite persisting ambiguity and debates about exactly what makes them "international" or markedly different from other forms of crime and justice (Chapters 1, 3, and 4). Regarding international crime, I show how it is consistently defined as a higher scale phenomenon—constructed as *the most* serious of all offenses (in an implied hierarchy of harms); as large-scale, mass harm; and as crime affecting generalized states and subjectivities, such as humanity or the peace and security of the world (Chapter 3). Similarly, international criminal justice is portrayed as higher and better than national justice, as an idealized form of best-practice redress (Chapter 4). Indeed, I contend that distinctly international justice is defined almost exclusively through its contrast with national justice and localized harm. It is only through this contrast that international justice emerges as unique and inherently transcendent, defined against the culture, politics, history, and even geography associated with the national and local spheres.[25]

Furthermore, this book draws out the ethical and relational potentiality of dominant understandings of international crime and international justice. I contend that ideas of international crime (as crimes against all of humanity that transcend national borders) and of international justice (as representing humanity and its interests in the face of systematic mass harm) productively imagine an interconnected social world. I demonstrate how these ideas produce a sense of a new social and legal sphere—the international—in which crime can be committed; justice can be dispensed; and, importantly, community can be found. Thus, far from being second-ary considerations to the actual practice of international criminal justice, dominant ideas of international crime and justice actively write space and subjectivity, figuring a global community and an international sphere in which people around the world are connected through their shared repu-diation of internationalized crimes (see Chapter 1). From this perspective, events and experiences of international crime are seen to constitute an assault against humanity as a whole and offer an opportunity for an international community to be visualized through its antithesis (inhumanity)—as well as, in the words of Alison Young, its expulsion.[26]

However, throughout the book I also offer a critique of dominant approaches to international crime and justice. This critique has three main strands. First, I argue that dominant approaches to international crime and justice serve to create *ethical and relational distance* between those who suffer and those who do not, at any given moment in time.[27] That is, when portrayed through a scalar frame as "the top of the hierarchy" of harms, the phenomenon of international crime is spectacularized as "especially horrible, cruel, savage and barbarous."[28] Although such representations appear to do justice to the devastating nature of international crimes, they also serve to exceptionalize these harms, disconnecting them from the lived and the everyday. International crime is conceptualized as the "head of the parade of the hideous monstrosities", perpetrated by *hostis humani generis* ("enemies of mankind") and victims are regarded to have experienced the worst of the worst.[29] As a consequence, it arguably becomes more difficult for external parties to see the lives of victims, survivors, and perpetrators of internationalized crime as multifaceted and ultimately livable.[30] Further-more, such frameworks of understanding downplay the complex individual, social, and structural dynamics of events of genocide and mass harm (in which, for example, perpetrators and victims might be the same people).

Moreover, this scalar approach to international crime also entails a sort of "zooming out," whereby such injustice is generalized as affecting groups or populations, the broader international community, and global peace and security. In such statements, the international significance of certain crimes is not found in the local and lived—that is, it is not understood as emanating from the significance of particular lives, people, and their experiences.[31] As one special rapporteur explains, "if such a crime affects the individual, it does so indirectly."[32] In this way, rather than enabling concrete, specific, and engaged connections between peoples across the world, I show how the claim that particular events of harm have an international character in fact obstructs such connections. A similar dynamic also marks dominant approaches to international criminal justice, whose distinctive and international character is literally grounded in the claim that it is inherently and irreducibly separate from the particularity of life on the ground. Through its contrast with national justice and local suffering—in its portrayal as "an international rather than national or local court" that is "not on the doorstep of those most affected by the cases it hears"—international criminal justice is figured as constitutively other to life as it is lived throughout the world.[33] In this way, it is also fundamentally disconnected from any particular context or community, particularly individuals and communities that have experienced international crime.[34]

In a second strand of critique, I contend that such dominant understandings of international crime and justice have a *power dynamic*. Notions of international crime, for example, rely on an appropriation, whereby a harm or event becomes international through its refiguring as somehow belonging elsewhere and to others.[35] Part of becoming international (or being internationalized) involves the reconceptualization of very particular injuries that are experienced by particular communities and individuals as belonging to others (as crimes against humanity as a whole) and existing elsewhere (as contravening an international order). Meanwhile, defining international criminal justice as constitutively separate from the rest of the world serves to instantiate it as its own subject, with its own interests. Representations of international crime and justice as consistently higher, better, worse, or more important than national crime and justice serve to privilege international forms of harm and justice as particularly special, significant, and worthy of support. And this valorization of international crime and justice affords these ideas with significant social, legal, and political power (authorizing the establishment of tailored justice institutions, as well as areas of scholarship and professional expertise)[36] and leads to their exclusivity and regulation—for example, in claims that the genocide label should not be used too expansively.

Finally, a third intervention of this book is, therefore, to query the *social, political, and legal valorization* of international crime and international justice. For while it may be important to retain a sense of the qualitative characteristics of crimes such as genocide, crimes against humanity, and war crimes and to support the potential utility of justice processes suited to them, I am not convinced that there is a need to declare these harms and initiatives to be somehow better or more important than others.[37] This is emphatically not to deny the broader significance of suffering in the world or the responsibility of others regarding it. Rather, my concern is with how the valorization of ideas of international crime and justice can serve to reinforce their disconnect with the everyday and the lived—thus arguably militating against the forms of ethical human connection with which they are associated. The valorization of certain harm can also, in practice, be used to downplay the wider import of other (noninternationalized) harm.

Overall, then, I argue that there are significant, perhaps insurmountable, problems with the very ideas of international crime and justice. It is not just that these ideals are not properly realized in practice due to political interests or legal deficiencies. These very ideas are captivating and affectively resonant, but also concerning and ethically problematic. This relatively fundamental critique of the ideas of international crime and justice is not one I expected to make when I started this research, and it is one that sits uncomfortably with the dominant sense that the categories of international crime and justice—content aside—give voice to something crucial and incontestable. Yet my aim in critiquing both the content of these categories and their social, legal, and political valorization in this way is to raise the possibility of alternative and truly radical modes of cross-cultural engagement.[38] For me, such modes of engagement might be more grounded in contextual relations between particular peoples and communities. They might also be better placed to both recognize and respect the specificity and significance of those distinct individuals and communities who have experienced international crime and their centrality to any justice-based collaboration. In this respect, I hope that my discussion complements the call from other scholars to refocus attention on the specific and the lived and on (in Evans's words) "lives lived with law on the ground."[39]

My book is also aligned with interdisciplinary scholarship that has refused to take the discourses and practices of humanitarianism at face value, instead demonstrating their proclivity to objectify, dehumanize, and create social and relational distance between external parties and those who suffer, as well as to connect people across the world.[40] This body of work also focuses on how experiences of harm and suffering are culturally represented and socially, historically, and politically responded to, and it emphasizes—as I do here—the significance of how suffering is depicted to the ethics, politics, and effects of different modes of engagement with it.

I bring this body of work together with established analyses and critiques of international law and international criminal justice specifically.[41] My book complements the existing emphasis on the problematic production of international justice as divorced from the local;[42] purportedly apolitical, yet intrinsically political in nature and effect;[43] allegedly universal, yet culturally particular;[44] legitimated through the image of the victim, yet not always responsive to the needs and wishes of those individuals affected by international crime;[45] and, increasingly, a project that is self-interested and invested in its own power.[46] Some of this work is concerned, as I am, with international criminal justice as a representational project and with analyzing its productive effects as well as how it is discussed and portrayed.[47] In joining these critiques, this book seeks to clarify the salience of the ideas of international crime and justice to any evaluation of the ethics and desirability of this field of discourse and practice. It also positions international criminal justice as an inherently discursive project and offers a close reflection on both the ethical and relational limits and potentials of the ideas of international crime and justice, interrogating how (on what terms) they make it possible to understand, connect with, and respond to suffering in the world.

However, my work is distinctly interdisciplinary in the sense that—as indicated in the book's conclusion—I have no intrinsic commitment to the overriding importance of ideas and practices of international crime and justice. The analysis I offer is instead criminological in orientation, given my interest in the way categories of crime and justice function and my ultimate lack of faith in the processes of criminalization and criminal justice as proper avenues to pursue and enact a sense of transnational community. In their belated engagement with international crime and justice, some criminologists have cautioned against the expansion of the concepts of legality and illegality in the international sphere, given the limited and inherently punitive nature of those concepts and practices.[48] Despite the common demarcation between national and international crime and justice, criminologists and others have begun to connect discussions of local and international criminal justice in order to better evaluate the merits (or otherwise) of the current push toward criminalization in the latter.[49] To add to this emerging criminological and critical legal body of work, this book provides an analysis that emphasizes the significance of representations and ideas of international crime and justice to any consideration of the ethics and politics of international criminal justice, connecting existing criminological thought with critical humanitarianism scholarship (discussed above).

Imagining the International: A Cultural Approach

What are international crimes, and what is international criminal justice? What makes a certain form of crime and justice distinctively international, and what does its internationality signify? These are some of the questions that are answered in this book. However, given the powerful and yet often elusive nature of notions of the global and the international, it seems important to begin by tying them down and specifying my particular approach to understanding and exploring them.

First, I consider ideas of international crime and justice—like crime and justice more generally—to be socially, politically, historically, and legally located and produced. Notions of international crime and justice are constructed, contested, and sociopolitically negotiated. In Chapter 3, which focuses on definitions of international crime, I discuss attempts by the International Law Commission to construct an authoritative definition of international crime (or what the commission refers to, in highly gendered language, as "crimes against the peace and security of mankind").[50] I also discuss how the idea of international crime is contested: there is no one definition of international crime, and approaches have shifted across time and space. Although the current focus is on three to four core international crimes (namely, genocide, crimes against humanity, war crimes, and aggression), past approaches have been more expansive, regarding crimes against the environment or the crime of colonial domination as key international crimes. The category of international crime, as well as what behavior is placed in this category, is thus a product of sociopolitical processes of criminalization. As Nils Christie has argued, "acts *are* not, they *become*," underscoring the importance of asking "what are the social conditions that encourage or prevent giving . . . acts the meaning of being crime?"[51] Justice is also a term that has no consensual and fixed definition, and the very attempt to position a single understanding of what justice is (namely, individualistic, legalist, and retributive justice) as international criminal justice has been criticized for occluding the diversity of approaches to what justice might look like in different places and at different times.[52]

Second, and importantly, in interrogating the socio-legal construction of distinctively international crime and justice, my analysis does not proceed from a fixed or preexisting idea of what internationality means or what the international is; nor from a commitment to a particular philosophy of internationalism, humanism, cosmopolitanism, or globalism, or from a belief that certain forms of harm and justice are (or should be regarded as) inherently international.[53] This is largely because I am interested in how these privileged, idealized, and ethically and affectively moving notions of international crime and international justice are actually made to mean, rather than in pursuing a normative line of argument about what they should mean. Nor am I focused, like others such as Anthea Roberts, on the empirical universality of international law and demonstrating its practical variability in different contexts.[54] Rather, my analysis is concerned with the very construction of internationality and is methodologically inductive: I consider how the internationality (or even sometimes just the distinctiveness) of international crime and justice is figured through representation. I tend to also refer to the internationality or the distinctiveness of international crime and justice interchangeably for two main reasons: first, because *internationality* is the term used to characterize these forms of crime and justice as special and distinguish them as different from other (national and local) forms of crime and justice; and second, because in practice dominant depictions of international crime and justice seem to engage with how and why they are special or distinctive and how and why they are international as meaning the same thing (sometimes with a focus on the former). I am also flexible in my terminology, as my focus is less on how these forms of crime and justice are literally named, and more on charting and unpacking the meanings attributed to those categories of harm that are portrayed as somehow distinctive and special and whose uniqueness is somehow linked to claims of their worldliness or broader significance. When approached in this broader sense, international crimes are also referred to—elsewhere and in this book—as crimes against humanity or against the peace and security of humankind, and distinctively international justice is also referred to as global justice.

I thus conceptualize notions of international crime and justice as cultural products and understand their distinctive or international character to be an attribute that is actively negotiated through social, legal, and political processes of meaning making. On this view, the construction of a particular phenomenon as distinctively global or international in character is a social, legal, and political act—one that relies on dominant discourses about internationality and productively affirms certain definitions of what internationality does, and should, mean. My conception of internationality as a cultural construct is indebted to the insightful anthropological work of Liisa Malkki on societal and political understandings of internationalism.[55] In her work on "imagining the international," she charts and critically interrogates diverse social and cultural representations of the international and internationalism, drawing out some of the ways in which they are given content. Her focus is primarily on internationalism, which she conceptualizes as a "transnational cultural form for imagining and ordering difference among people, and as a moralizing discursive practice"[56]—a definition that testifies to the contemporary significance of notions of the international as a lens through which to approach transnational social relations, as well as alluding to some of its limits. Like me, Malkki critiques modes of imagining global community that serve to generalize and gloss over important human differences and specificities, and she calls for forms of solidarity that can be attentive to and grounded in difference. Her work, like that of other anthropologists such as Ilana Feldman, importantly establishes ideas of internationality as social, political, and cultural constructs, directing attention to the importance of investigating "how universals are made."[57]

My focus in this book, however, is not on the construction of internationality or the international per se, but on socio-legal understandings of international crime and international justice and their distinctiveness. Thus, I do not provide a stand-alone analysis of what internationality could and should mean or develop a typology that clearly fixes and delineates the relative meaning of the international as opposed to the global, universal, or transnational. What I do provide is a detailed and substantiated account of how the quality or attribute of internationality is made to mean, in an internally consistent way, in the context of notions of international crime and justice (as associated, for example, with scalar height, social distance, and distinct places and professions). Ultimately, I offer an account of internationality as a quality that is multiply configured—subjectively, spatially, historically, socially, and legally.[58] As it is imagined in and through representations of international crime and justice, internationality is an attribute associated with particular peoples and places. It is configured in ways similar to colonial approaches to internationality, as well as currently ascendant mainstream approaches. And it is declared through legal acts as well as social practices.

In particular, in relation to international crime and justice, I draw out a spatial dynamic to contemporary approaches to internationality. I am influenced in this respect by the work of cultural geographers, legal theorists, and others who have underscored the centrality of spatial ideas to the imagination of the world and of global relations.[59] Notions of international crime and justice rely on spatial ideas (scale; height; a new international level), as well as productively imagining new social and relational space (a community of humanity and a higher international legal sphere). I also show how the construction of an event as international is an inherently spatializing move. Within current modes of understanding, to be apprehended as distinctively international, an event, crime, or form of justice must be resituated elsewhere, among other more generalized and abstracted social and geographic contexts. It must be reconceptualized as a crime against *humanity* unfolding in broader legal and social history, contravening an international legal order, and offending against an international community. Internationalization thus requires, as Annelise Riles argues, that those directly affected by specific harms and events have to understand them as "occurring also on an international plane."[60] It is in this way that configuring crime and justice as international is a dynamic sociopolitical process that entails various intersecting shifts in subjectivity, geography, and signification. As such, an attentiveness to the spatiality of notions of international crime and justice is crucial to appreciating how these ideas create social and relational distance between those most affected by international crime and the (separate) international community and legal order that act in their name.[61]

The Power and Productivity of International Imaginings

In no way does a focus on international crime, international justice, and internationality as cultural constructs suggest that these concepts are meaningless. To the contrary, as I have emphasized, notions of international crime and justice are often valorized and imbued with great cultural significance, and they are socially, politically, and legally consequential and powerful ideas. More broadly, the very notion of internationality is also idealized. Despite the material inequalities and new forms of coercive and discriminatory power produced through processes of globalization,[62] there is still a sense of emancipatory politics and sociality associated with ideas of the international and the global. My point is not to argue that globalization has been a positive or negative development but to highlight the enduring romanticization of the international, despite scholars' and practitioners' efforts to emphasize its inequalities and injustices. As Riles notes, the international is conceptualized as an "utopian space," and I have already noted the sense of humanitarianism and progress associated with the establishment of forms of international crime and justice.[63] Furthermore, claims to represent the international, or that a crime is internationally significant, are powerful: they do things, they have effects. They can attract social, political, and legal attention and resources—as occurred, for example, in the aftermath of the Rwandan genocide. They can also work to authorize forms of coercive intervention, such as in cases of "humanitarian" military intervention or when the jurisdiction of the International Criminal Court is mandated by the United Nations Security Council, despite a particular nation's lack of consent. Those who speak in the name of the international or of "humanity" therefore wield significant power.[64] Thus, recognizing the constructed and indeterminate nature of these terms is not equivalent to suggesting that they have no meaning or force. Rather, it highlights the salience of exactly how they are given meaning in light of their power and significance. This is a task made more pressing by the elusiveness of their use in everyday practice, where they are invoked in a variety of ways, and their definition is frequently taken for granted rather than openly discussed.[65]

Understandings of international crime and international justice are also important because they are productive. They are the embodiment of social, political, and legal negotiations about what kinds of suffering matter and what a commitment to globally engaged justice might involve. However, they also produce meaning themselves, shaping which events of harm come to external attention, which are seen to be important, and who and what they are seen to affect and implicate. Representations of international crime and justice determine the vectors for thinking about global significance and have consequences for how the world and the relations between people within it are conceptualized. Like broader theories of internationalism, cosmopolitanism, universalism, humanism, and globalism, notions of international crime and justice are implicated in the intellectual work of imagining an interconnected world and providing some grounds upon which global interrelation might be based. Ideas of international crime and justice, in particular, provide an image of a global sphere and constituency defined by their repudiation and redress of crime. As I argue in Chapter 1, they construct the international as a crimino-legal sphere, in which human interconnection is grounded in the spectacle of extreme suffering as well as a vision of a broader community that is touched or threatened by such criminality and committed to address it.

In addition to their being powerful and productive, ideas of international crime and justice are also important because they currently constitute a globally ascendant framework for thinking about injustice in the world and global responsibility for it.[66] As Ann Sagan notes, there is now an emphasis on perceiving experiences of injury across the world as legally proscribed crimes (rather than simply injustices and harms), while the language of criminality and illegality is frequently invoked to delegitimize certain acts— from the Iraq War and the conflict in Syria to the Australian government's treatment of asylum seekers.[67] There are calls for the establishment of special tribunals to try those deemed responsible and, more frequently since the establishment of the International Criminal Court, there are campaigns to invoke the jurisdiction of the court in relation to contemporaneous instances of conflict and violence (such as campaigns regarding North Korea, Syria, and Myanmar).[68] In this way, notions of international crime and justice are used as a powerful and authoritative discursive framework for recognizing and responding to injustice in the world.

Interrogating Internationality: The Chapters to Come

As noted above, I focus in this book on three key case studies. My first case study is the Rwandan genocide—an instance of harm that was constituted as inherently international in its aftermath, being belatedly constructed as an event in global social, legal, and political history. Second, I focus on the category of international crime, analyzing how it is imagined in the debates of the International Law Commission tasked with formulating a "Draft Code of Offences Against the Peace and Security of Mankind." And third, I consider representations of international criminal justice by focusing on key portrayals of the first permanent International Criminal Court, including the court's informational material, its statute, and statements at the Rome Conference that established it.

At a time when many understandings of the international are abstracted, generalized, and universalized, this book therefore focuses on specific and grounded sites where notions of international crime and justice have been given content. In discussing these case studies alongside each other, my focus is on what each of them illustrate—on their own terms—about how international crime and justice are understood. In one sense, then, I provide quite a specific reading of how the quality of internationality is configured in texts concerning the Rwandan genocide, the formulation of a draft criminal code, and the first permanent international criminal court, and my arguments emerge from and relate most directly to these empirical sites. However, these are influential representations of international crime and justice that are indicative of contemporary approaches to these ideas. My case studies are thus different from each other and not representative or generalizable: the window they provide on ideas of international crime and justice is shaped by their discrete nature; political dynamics; and broader social, cultural, and historical context. But they nevertheless demonstrate some consistent and concerning tendencies regarding how international crime and justice are conceptualized. Collectively, I use these case studies to urge a rethinking of how internationality and international interrelations are being configured and performed in dominant discourse, to facilitate ways of understanding global interconnection that may be more particularized, contextualized, and historicized.

In Chapter 1, I start by demonstrating the importance of the ideas of distinctively international crime and justice and drawing out their ethical potentialities. I show how international crime and justice are embedded in a rich and dramatic discursive regime, where they are marked out as different from their national and local counterparts as somehow new forms of crime and justice that belong to a different social and legal order. I argue that such representations of international crime and justice are both central to the project of international justice and importantly productive, imagining a new social and legal sphere in which crime is committed, defendants are prosecuted, and justice is delivered. In this sense, then, I argue that notions of international crime and justice have ethical possibilities—connecting people across the world through a shared repudiation of heinous atrocity. Yet I caution that the ethical promise of these notions depends upon the specific ways in which concepts of international crime and justice are given content.

Chapter 2 continues this line of inquiry by demonstrating the limits and potentials of internationalization in relation to the Rwandan genocide. I trace the post hoc construction of this event as a globally significant occurrence: a key moment in global legal, political, and social history. Although the post hoc internationalization of the Rwandan genocide is commonly regarded as an ethical move—an apt recognition of the significance of this crime—here I also discuss some of the problems embedded in the way it is produced as distinctively global. Ultimately, I argue that the Rwandan genocide emerges as an international event through its construction as an event affecting others: a moment of failed Western and international responsibility that is used to underscore what a global non-Rwandan "we" should do when confronted with an event of African suffering. The Rwandan case study thus demonstrates the significance of being attentive to how and why an event or form of crime and justice is constructed as international, or said to matter to all of "us." It draws attention to the salience of the specific terms upon which lived experiences of suffering are internationalized (or, conversely, not internationalized), as these shape the ethical potentiality of such a move.

The remaining two substantive chapters then turn to analyzing in detail how notions of international crime and international justice are given content. Chapter 3 analyzes the debates of the International Law Commission in its attempt to define international crime and develop an international criminal code. Although this code was never enacted, the commission's approach has influenced the eventual constitution of the permanent International Criminal Court and still represents an important attempt to articulate a global criminal code and a single and authoritative definition of international crime. I show how the commission problematically linked internationality to a sense of (higher) scale in its framing of international crime as more important than other crime; as large-scale, mass harm; and as harm that affects generalized subjectivities and states (humanity and global peace and security). I argue that such a scalar approach distances external parties from specific experiences of injury and perpetration, which are portrayed as exceptional and extreme. Such an approach also necessitates a zooming out, whereby the focus shifts from specific peoples, communities, and experiences to abstract and generalized notions of human society as a whole or international peace and security writ large. Thus, scalar understandings of international crime—in a way similar to post hoc portrayals of the Rwandan genocide—appropriate lived experiences of harm and injury and locate them elsewhere and as affecting others.

Chapter 4 considers how a sense of externality and otherness also characterizes mainstream approaches to international criminal justice. Through a focus on key representations of the first permanent International Criminal Court, I demonstrate how the court is figured as culturally, politically, and even geographically transcendent through its contrast with images of a more located, politicized, and contextualized national and local. Using the work of Peter Fitzpatrick,[69] I argue that this ideal of international criminal justice should be acknowledged as mythic, formed only through negative contrast and reliant on a disregard for the way in which the court is grounded, political, connected to the national, and a distinctive legal institution. This is an intervention designed to make visible the power effects of current ideals of international criminal justice (which authorize the building of institutions, new disciplines, and new professions), as well as to provide the conceptual space in which to think about how else a cross-cultural or transnational mode of justice-based engagement might unfold.

Together, the case studies that I discuss in Chapters 2, 3, and 4 reveal consistent tendencies regarding the bases on which certain crimes and forms of justice are configured as distinctly international and the ethical and relational effects of these dominant approaches. Crucially, they also elucidate how some of the problematic tendencies of contemporary understandings of international crime and justice relate quite specifically to how their internationality or global significance is often understood. Assertions of internationality are thus argued to be ethically complex, demanding close attention and analysis. Yet they are also constructed and contingent: there is nothing natural or inevitable about these ways of defining internationality, and alternative internationalisms and modes of global interrelation are possible. For example, David Featherstone writes of "solidarities from below" that come into being through very concrete engagements between different peoples at different times, while Malkki raises the possibility of "ways of conceiving solidarities, and even world citizenship, that would be more respectful of contingencies and particularities, while still reaching out for broader connections."[70] In fact, as is evident in the existing coalitions between various groups of victim-survivors of mass harm across time and space—such as the solidarities expressed between Indigenous Australians and asylum seekers, and the transnational Women in Black movement, mentioned in Chapter 4—more particularized and contextualized modes of human interconnection unfold constantly throughout the world.

I should note, however, that in advancing a critique of the disconnect between ideas of international crime and justice and everyday life, my analysis starts with the categories of international crime and justice, largely as they are conceptualized in official and dominant representations. This means that my focus is on the general socio-legal conceptualization of international crime and justice, rather than the political, social, historical, and cultural life of these ideas or their practical application to concrete sociohistorical circumstances. In problematizing the distance charted between international crime and justice and the lived, I ground my discussion in a detailed exploration of different representations of international crime and justice, but I do not always discuss specific local contexts and experiences. I hope that my analysis of the ideas of international crime and justice can be read alongside the excellent existing work that focuses instead on actual social and historical situations and then reflects on the utility of ideas and practices of international crime and justice.[71] This work offers complementary critiques (to give just a few examples, of the privileging of certain experiences of injustice and modes of redress, and of the distant nature of international justice institutions), but it also provides distinct insights that stem from the particular crimes, institutions, or historical events being discussed.

My concluding chapter calls for a more reflective and long-term approach to pursuing and imagining modes of international interconnection after the formal end of colonialism. It raises the possibility of approaches to internationality, international significance, and international connection that might be more cognizant and respectful of positionality and particularity—approaches that are better able to register the specificity of those communities and people who experience international crime and that foster modes of engagement that acknowledge rather than deny social, cultural, and political location. These would be forms of connection embedded in and aware of the ordinary and everyday, instead of being characterized by their departure from it. My conclusion calls for a greater awareness of the way in which the contemporary valorization of international crime (as exceptionally bad) and international justice (as idealized and transcendent) may exacerbate the tendency of these ideas to become disconnected from everyday life. Problematizing dominant modes of understanding international crime and justice is thus positioned as one step toward reconceptualizing how ethical pledges of human interconnection and solidarity can be framed.

The critical inquiry in this book is one that proceeds from a commitment to the importance of continuing and reflexive consideration of the possibilities (and limits) of ethical modes of engaging with the suffering of others. It is therefore based on a doubled orientation: maintaining hope in the possibilities of global interconnection and remaining aware of the dangers in both past and present approaches to imagining and enacting it. Throughout the discussion to come, I seek to hold together the sense and promise of international interrelation contained in the sentiment that certain crimes may implicate everyone with a postcolonial awareness of the potentially unethi-cal, unfair, and unequal modes of relation that can and have been enabled (and indeed justified) through a discourse of a shared and global humanity. My critical orientation is thus one, to borrow Charles Scott's words, of "self-overcoming and recoil,"[72] based on an initial interest in the possibilities of ethical interconnection enabled by ideas of international crime and justice, as well as a growing awareness of the unjust and discriminatory relational forms they might promote and justify and the need to question them.

In so doing, I recognize that such an inquiry, including the time and resources it takes to engage in it fully, requires a space and freedom that those working hard in the field of international criminal justice and international humanitarianism do not always have. Thus, I intend this critical work to be read as motivated by a hope for the possibilities of ethical global intercon-nection that may also inform the idealism (and indeed realism) of some international criminal justice advocates and practitioners, at the same time as it opens up a conceptual space in which to think seriously and carefully about whether—as some justice advocates argue—strengthening the existing model is the most desirable option. Indeed, I conclude by underscoring the importance of a long-term and collaborative approach to envisaging and enacting ethical modes of intercultural, interpersonal, and intercommunal engagement grounded in an acknowledgement of the broader significance of the injustice experienced by others in the world. I also ultimately ques-tion, as noted earlier, whether notions of crime and justice can ever be the proper terms through which to pursue humanitarian sentiments of com-munity and solidarity.

1

On International Crime, Justice, and Community

There can be no global justice . . . unless the worst of crimes—crimes against humanity—are subject to the law. In this age, more than ever, we recognize that the crime of genocide against one people truly is an assault on us all—a crime against humanity.

—Kofi Annan, "Advocating for an International Criminal Court"

Let the voice and the verdict of this esteemed global court now speak for the awakened conscience of the world.

—Benjamin Ferencz, "Ferencz Closes Lubanga Case for ICC"

INTERNATIONAL CRIME AND INTERNATIONAL JUSTICE are powerful ideas. They are associated with a rich and vivid imagery of heinous atrocities, injured humanity, and an international community seized by the need to act. Distinctly international crime and justice are demarcated from their national counterparts as fundamentally different and somehow more important and humanitarian in nature. International crime and justice are frequently associated with a range of different spaces and subjectivities: the international sphere, global peace and security, humanity, civilization, and the international community as a whole. There is also, arguably, an ethical promise embedded in the ideas of international crime and justice, which are seen to fundamentally embody and reflect a sense of global solidarity. International crimes, as exemplified by the words of Annan and Ferencz above, are conceptualized as "an assault on us all" while international justice is positioned to "speak for the awakened conscience of the world." It is in this way that international criminal justice has always been a representational project as much as a practical endeavor, which has not only entailed the development of international criminal laws and tribunals, but also the imagination of distinctly international forms of crime and justice and an international constituency united, in part, by its opposition to extreme suffering.

In this way, ideas of international crime and justice are central, not secondary, to what international criminal justice fundamentally is, as well as serving to legitimate the emergence and power of international criminal laws and institutions in the world today. In this chapter, I foreground the significance of the ideas (or, more properly stated, ideals) of international crime and justice and their ethical potential to embody and enact a sense of cross-cultural interconnection. I argue that ideas of international crime and justice are vivid and emotive as well as productive, figuring and enacting the spaces and subjectivities of which they speak. These discourses and representations of internationalized crime and justice are thus ethically significant, as they do not simply reflect the consolidation or existence of an already existing global community or common humanity with established norms and values. Rather, it is in and through representations and discourses of international criminal justice that such global subjectivities and modes of global responsibility and interconnection are productively imagined.[1] In particular, it is through representations of crimes against *humanity* and global justice that there emerges a sense of a new sphere of crime, justice, and community. Through ideas of international crime and international justice, the international is demarcated as a new social, legal, and geographical arena in which there exists a concept of crime, a socio-legal order that it contravenes, and a community that is implicated in its occurrence and responsible for its redress. It is thus *through* notions of international crime and justice that the international is constructed as a new "crimino-legal" sphere in which crime can be committed, justice dispensed. and community found.[2]

It is in this sense that ideas of international crime and justice have ethical possibilities, potentially connecting those who suffer (at any given moment in time) with those who do not (at any given moment). The framing of certain offenses as crimes against "us" all, and of certain justice mechanisms as representative of the international community, has the capacity to connect people and communities with the suffering of others and figure justice for such harms as a matter of global responsibility.[3] Yet the ethical possibilities inherent in the enterprise of international criminal justice are a product of the way in which it is conceived of and operates. It is in this vein that Chapters 3 and 4 offer a more detailed interrogation of exactly how these notions are given content. This chapter, though, sets up this analysis by first drawing out the significance of these ideas—that is, by demonstrating their distinctive and productive nature. Furthermore, while later chapters consider the specific attributes associated with notions of international crime and international justice, this chapter also highlights the limited and particular nature of thinking about human community and connection through crime and law. For while ideas of international crime and justice function to productively imagine a common humanity, they do so particularly through the "figure of crime" and the framework of law (evident in Annan's reference at the beginning of this chapter to the importance of "crimes against humanity" being "subject to the law").[4] In addition, as Alison Young has highlighted, constructing community through crime is always problematic,[5] and law is a particular framework through which to understand social issues, apprehend victimization, and envision the possibilities for justice. This discussion foreshadows my final observation in this book that it may be misplaced (at best) or even unethical (at worst) to pursue projects of global solidarity through notions of crime and practices of retributive legal justice.

In this chapter, I first discuss dominant representations of international crime and justice and their productive effects, demonstrating their ethical and relational potential to productively imagine an interconnected social world. Second, I tease out the distinctively criminological, legal, and spatial nature of the international sphere imagined in and through ideas of international crime and justice. Third, I consider how these structural characteristics shape and constrain the relational possibilities of these ideas, and I conclude by emphasizing the vital importance of scholarly and public engagement with the representational, as well as institutional, facets of international criminal justice.

The Distinctiveness of International Crime and Justice: Writing Space and Subjectivity

International crime and justice have their own discursive regime that sets them apart from so-called national forms of crime and justice. In contrast to the portrayal of national criminal justice systems as punitive and potentially flawed—as criminal *in*justice systems—the ideal of international criminal justice is described in glowing and humanitarian terms. It is a "dream" that has been realized, a progressive and humane global enterprise.[6] Meanwhile, through a contrast with national and transnational crime, international crime is depicted as especially heinous and wrong: the "head of the parade of the hideous monstrosities" (explored further in Chapter 3).[7] Moreover, the distinctiveness of international crime and justice is not simply an implied claim. It is one asserted by scholars and practitioners, who contrast international crime and justice with "ordinary" or "common" crime, "national" criminal justice, and "local" justice processes and insist on the uniqueness of the former.[8]

Hannah Arendt, for example, contends that "nothing is more pernicious to an understanding of these new crimes . . . than the common illusion that the crime of murder and the crime of genocide are essentially the same. . . . The point of the latter is that an altogether different order is broken, and an altogether different community is violated."[9] International crimes are portrayed here as contravening a different, distinctly international, social order and affecting a different, internationalized, constituency. International criminal law and criminal justice are often described in similar terms, as a sui generis amalgamation of different national legal principles, jurisdictions, and processes that has evolved into a new form of criminal justice.[10] There is thus a sense that notions of uniquely international crime and international justice belong to a particular self-contained and self-referential socio-legal order that is distinct from national and local ones.[11]

In this way, international crime and justice are both legally situated as properly belonging to a particular international jurisdictional order, as well as being commonly situated in a geographical context different to that of so-called ordinary criminal justice—residing and operating at a different "level".[12] James Ferguson and Akhil Gupta consider how spatial concepts of verticality are key to imagining the state as "above" society, and the "aboveness" of international crime and international justice is also instantiated through their vertical and hierarchical placement vis-à-vis other (national) forms of crime and justice.[13] As a system of criminal justice proper to the international level, international criminal justice is seen to exist and function in an arena constitutively above the nation-state. Thus, international crime is defined in contrast to transnational crime as crime that does not necessarily cross borders but transcends them. Meanwhile, the "aboveness" of international criminal justice is imagined, for example, with reference to its distance from the politics and injustice associated with the national sphere (see Chapter 4). In implicit or explicit opposition to national justice systems, international criminal courts are seen to be "above" national political pressures and considerations and hence able to offer a more impartial and apolitical form of legal justice.[14] As Ruti Teitel explains, "international law is thought to lift justice out of its politicized national context."[15] "Aboveness" is thus equated with superiority in the figuring of international justice as more fair and rigorous than national justice and—in a different way—in the positioning of international crime as the worst form of criminal behavior, the crime of crimes (see Chapter 3).

As well as existing as meaningful concepts in a distinct geographical sphere, international crime and justice are also situated in a different social context to their national counterparts—commonly associated with a specifically global regime of subjectivities whose values and interests they represent. The preamble of the Rome Statute of the International Criminal Court begins with a statement of international community, proclaiming that the statute is based on a recognition, a "consciousness," "that all peoples are united by common bonds, their cultures pieced together in a shared heritage."[16] The crimes contained therein are then described with reference to this global community's values, as acts that "deeply shock the conscience of humanity," constituting "the most serious crimes of concern to the international community as a whole."[17] As noted earlier, international crimes are conceived of as crimes against "humanity," "civilization," and "us" all. And international criminal justice is framed as an endeavor undertaken on behalf, and in the name of, the international community or the world. The concepts of international crime and justice are imagined with reference to the existence of an international community with shared values that are enshrined in an international legal order that speaks in that community's name.[18] Here, international crime—as far as it is conceptualized to represent an affront to shared values—connotes community.

Importantly, however, such ideas and practices of international criminal justice are not simply expressions of already existing global spaces and subjectivities. Rather, they actively constitute the entities, geographies, and social connections that they name. Globalized identities such as the international community or humanity are socially produced,[19] as are the geographical spaces and networks of relations in which they are situated.[20] It is through the performative declaration that certain acts are crimes against humanity and in the framing of the pursuit of accountability for such acts as a "plea of humanity to law"[21] that a global humanity is productively named and imagined, its contours traced, and its content defined.[22] In this way, dominant understandings and practices of international crime and justice are ethically salient as they both visualize and produce international space and subjectivity.[23]

Thus, although international criminal justice presents itself as working beyond national territorial boundaries, as Robert DeChaine illustrates in relation to humanitarian movements, international criminal justice "reterritorializes" space by mapping the international as a new socio-legal domain.[24] That is, although—like humanitarian movements—international criminal justice supposedly constitutes a disavowal of the supremacy of nationally defined borders, territories, and corresponding identifications, it nevertheless constitutes an expression of geopolitical power through its active mapping, or imagination, of a new socio-legal space: the international.

Through the productive imagining of international crime and justice, the international is thus constructed as a new site of crime, justice, and community: a social and legal sphere in which crime can occur and signify; defendants can be prosecuted and punished; and, importantly, community can be found. In part, this development is attributable to the practical and institutional development of an infrastructure of international criminal justice, through the passage of international criminal laws and the establishment of international courts and tribunals. However, it also has a discursive element: it is a product of the rich and vivid imagery associated with international crime and justice. Through both the discourse and practice of international criminal justice, which positions international crime and justice as distinct and names their distinctiveness as a function of their internationality, the international is constituted as a crimino-legal sphere, in which suffering is criminalized and justice is done.

The Constitution of Crimino-Legal Community

The international (figured through ideas of international crime and justice) is a uniquely crimino-legal sphere in the sense that it is criminologically, legally, and spatially structured. First, it is an inherently criminological space in the sense that it is a sphere of relations, laws, and practices stemming from the image and imagination of crime. Young has drawn attention to the resonance of crime as a "potent sign" and the central role of the image and imagining of crime in the constitution of identity and community.[25]

Similarly, in an international context, it is crime that forms the basis for the recognition of global community, and it is crime that is repeatedly cited to legitimate the legal order established in this community's name. It is the occurrence of crimes such as the Holocaust that is used to underscore the existence of and the importance of recognizing "our" shared humanity. Thus, on the United States Holocaust Memorial Museum website in an online exhibition on "Why We Remember the Holocaust," the materiality of humanity is productively affirmed in the framing of this event as "an unthinkable scar on humanity" that compels a global "us" "to remember the humanity that is in all of us."[26] As such, as Teitel observes, humanity is somewhat paradoxically "defined by its breach," "not in aspiration but on its underside, in the practices reflecting the degradation of the human."[27] The international is thus the site of a distinctively criminological community—a social collectivity that is visible and appreciable in the commission of crime and criminality and united through their repudiation and redress. It is a community, as Young has highlighted at the national level, that is based on the criminal, rather than a social, contract: it is grounded in the materiality and imagination of the offense rather than the legal fiction of consent.[28] It is a public body characterized by its rejection and refusal of crime and the criminal and is therefore oppositionally defined in the image of both.[29] As Adeno Addis explains, it is "the notion of enemies of human kind" that "endows the idea of humankind with the depth of solidarity of which it has never been certain."[30]

Moreover, regarding the international legal order, it is the event of international crime that is seen to compel the existence and legitimate the enterprise of international criminal justice. For example, Antonio Cassese narrates the emergence of seminal international justice institutions—such as the Nuremberg and Tokyo Tribunals, and the International Criminal Tribunals for the former Yugoslavia and Rwanda—as legalized expressions of a global "sense of outrage" at the crimes committed during World War II and the conflicts in Rwanda and the former Yugoslavia.[31] Rather than being conceived of as a product of the development of international criminal laws and institutions, international crime is seen to have preceded and authorized their existence.[32] In this vein, as William Schabas notes, the 1948 *Convention on the Prevention and Punishment of the Crime of Genocide* begins with an allusion to the existence of the crime of genocide before the enactment of the convention, through the statement that "genocide has inflicted great losses on humanity" in "all periods of history."[33]

Moreover, in a more abstract way, it is human suffering that is repeat-edly referenced and represented to authorize the practice of international criminal justice. Images of suffering thus feature prominently in promo-tional materials for the International Criminal Court (ICC)—such as in the "Justice Matters" slide show that depicts a male African teenager with bandages on his head, a young African woman who was the victim of rape, an African man with an amputated leg, and a close-up shot of an African woman whose face has been mutilated—as evidence of the need for the court.[34] Meanwhile, Sara Kendall and Sarah Nouwen discuss how the vic-tims of international crimes (and their suffering) are also ritually invoked nonpictorially as the "*raison d'être*" of international criminal justice and, more specifically, the ICC, whose legitimacy is tied to its framing as a mode of global governance undertaken "*in the name of* 'The Victims' *by* the 'in-ternational community.'"[35] As Kendall and Nouwen explain, "the court's first prosecutor once contended, 'My mandate is justice; justice for the victims.' And at a press conference in Côte d'Ivoire, his successor claimed that she had opened an investigation in that country 'for the victims—to give them a voice.' She added, 'The sole *raison d'être* of the ICC's activities in Côte d'Ivoire is the victims and the justice they deserve.'"[36] Furthermore, it is international crime that constitutes the most basic parameters of the ICC's jurisdiction as a judicial body that—first and foremost—has author-ity regarding four core crimes (although its ability to invoke its jurisdiction regarding these crimes is based on the consent of states to do so in their territory or against their citizens).[37] As such, it is once again crime that oc-cupies a fundamental position: it is the basis of international engagement with the harm experienced by others.

Second, the international is also a distinctively legal, as well as crimi-nological, space. Crime, as a foundational concept in and of the interna-tional, is legally coded harm, enabling the positioning of legal justice as an important societal response to such injury. As John Hagan and Ron Levi highlight, the legally structured nature of the international is thus evident in the positioning of law as the proper "solution" to the problem of crimi-nalized suffering.[38] Within discourses of international criminal justice, for example, the problem of international crime is frequently portrayed as a problem of the existence of impunity at the national level for international crimes—that is, as a problem of the absence of law in the face of crime (see Chapter 4).[39] Thus, international criminal justice initiatives are claimed to "contribute to the transformation of a culture of impunity that has hitherto implied the political acceptability of massive human rights abuses."[40] In turn, the pursuit of international legal accountability is seen as an appropriate response to internationalized injustice and injury. As the former president of the ICC explained, "we must be united in our resolve to defeat impunity and the lawlessness . . . that it represents."[41] Ensuring accountability for international crimes—particularly the accountability of those deemed to be most responsible for them—is also seen as a means of achieving other broader goals, such as deterring future potential perpetrators. In this way, law is positioned as a crucial response to injustice, its redress, and its prevention, reflecting what others such as Gerry Simpson have characterized as the juridification of politics.[42]

Finally, but crucially, the international is also a spatial entity in two related senses. On the one hand, as I will continue to discuss throughout this book, the ideas of international crime and justice rely on distinctively geographical imagery—whereby international crime and justice are seen to inherently exist at another, higher level to the national and the everyday. International crime is conceptualized as the worst form of mass harm, and international justice is seen to embody the highest legal standard. On the other hand, the international is spatially configured in the sense that it is a sphere of (and one constituted through) relations, interactions, and engagement. Here, then, space is not a concept limited to physical geography. Rather, space—as cultural geographer Doreen Massey explains—is a social production that is relationally figured and produced. Just as space more generally is constituted "through practices of material engagement,"[43] the international crimino-legal sphere is constituted through the social, legal, and political practices of acknowledging, denouncing, and remembering certain events as crimes against "us" all, and through prosecuting such harms (although sparingly) through international criminal tribunals.

Space is also the locus of interaction, interrelation, and coexistence. Indeed, a key feature of notions of international crime and justice is that they envisage and enable cross-cultural relations, potentially bringing people and communities closer to the suffering of others. By presenting the injustices of others as matters of broader, global concern (affecting and implicating humanity as a whole) and underscoring the importance of justice measures outside the nation-state that can speak on behalf of "us" all, ideas of international crime and justice produce a sense of global interconnection. From this perspective, the portrayal of certain events—such as the Rwandan genocide, the conflict in the former Yugoslavia, and the atrocities in the

Democratic Republic of Congo—as crimes against *humanity* serves to position them as matters of broader concern, inviting people and publics outside these geographical contexts to understand these events as occurrences that implicate and affect them.[44] The use of the language of international crime (to name certain atrocities) and the practices of international criminal justice institutions (to prosecute them) has the potential to map relational space, creating relations of proximity between those who have suffered and those who have not at any given moment in time.

I would argue that the international, as it is currently constituted through dominant understandings of international crime and justice, can be understood as a space of relations—specifically, relations of injury, affect, and responsibility. Notions of international crime and international justice construct, and are embedded in, relations of *injury and victimization.* In the words of one international judge, international crimes are seen to injure more than their direct victims and "cause . . . a tear in the common fabric of humanity."[45] Furthermore, through the discourse and practice of international criminal justice, certain events of harm and suffering can have an *affective life* beyond their specific geographical and historical context. Reflective of broader discourses and practices of humanitarianism throughout time, emotion and sentiment play a primary role in the imagination and instantiation of global relations.[46] It is in this sense that the experience of the Rwandan genocide, as will be discussed in Chapter 2, is understood to have caused "sorrow" to more than its direct victims and be a source of "bitter regret" and "shame" for those who failed to prevent it.[47] The Srebrenica massacre is also framed as a moment of "shame" and "regret" that continues to "haunt" those beyond its direct victims.[48] Such crimes are seen to circulate and signify more broadly, touching and moving those who did not physically endure them. Thus the "mobilization" of feelings of sympathy, empathy, and sadness for the suffering of others is a key component of the envisioning and configuring of relations between those who suffer and those who do not (although, as will be discussed in the next chapter, such emotions can still be self-focused as well as externally engaged).[49]

Representations and practices of international criminal justice also assume and instantiate relations of *global responsibility* for the suffering of others. It is in this vein that successive events of violence—from the Holocaust through to the Rwandan genocide and the violence and suffering in Darfur—are understood to have occurred, at least in part, because of the inaction of individual and communal bystanders and that there is now a contemporary emphasis on the Responsibility to Protect people and communities experiencing severe harm and injury that is not adequately addressed by their own governments and leaders.[50] Within the sphere of relations constituted in and through discourses of internationalized criminal justice, individuals and communities around the world may be moved or injured by the commission of international crime, but they are also asked to do something about its occurrence.

Community Through Crime and Criminalization?

Dominant ideas of international crime and justice therefore have ethical and relational potentialities. Ideas of international crime situate certain harms as globally and historically significant and emphasize their impact upon and implications for "us" all. Notions of international justice are based on the sentiment that accountability for and prevention of such crimes is a shared goal, to be undertaken by external parties on behalf of humanity. Together, these concepts of international crime and justice serve to establish a sense of an external and apolitical relational and jurisdictional space in which devastating harm can be appropriately recognized as criminal and justice institutions might be established to facilitate its redress. Indeed in practice, as I discuss in Chapter 3, labels of *genocide* and *crimes against humanity* are deliberately applied to attract social and political attention to events of harm, while international criminal justice is portrayed as a disinterested global framework devoted solely to the apolitical and best-practice redress of harm (Chapter 4). Conceived of through such humanitarian imagery, international criminal justice is framed as a benevolent enterprise dedicated to preventing suffering throughout the world.

Yet it is a key contention of this book that the ethical and relational potential of ideas of international crime and justice depend on two decisive factors. First, the nature and "quality" of the connections enabled through ideas of international crime and international justice depend on the way in which these ideas are given specific content (as discussed in Chapters 3 and 4).[51] Second, as discussed below, they depend on the structural characteristics of the crimino-legal sphere that they collectively produce. Put simply, it matters that the relational sphere produced through notions of international crime and justice is criminological (premised on the visualization and repudiation of crime), legal (prioritizing law as the key framework of response), and spatial (relying on geographical imagery and produced in and through interactions). These features shape and constrain what suffering can appear in this international sphere and how people's experiences of injury are enabled to circulate and signify within it, as well as moderating the ways in which external parties are invited to understand, interact with, and respond to such injury.[52]

As a distinctly legal sphere of engagement, for example, the international is a regulated space.[53] As many scholars have highlighted, criminal law is selective in its recognition of harm: not all injurious behavior or events of social injustice are criminalized or even legally recognized.[54] Thus, in a practical sense, for example, international criminal law names, problematizes, and promotes global engagement with harms occasioned by acts deemed as *war crimes*, but not those resulting from armed conflict per se. In addition, it is only relatively recently that sexual assault and rape in war have been officially recognized as internationally legally justiciable harms.[55] Moreover, the individualistic framework of liberal legal systems, such as international criminal justice, ensures that structural harm is constitutively excluded from view (and redress) through an emphasis on individual accountability. Structural socioeconomic, institutional, and historical injustices, for example, are not the focus of international criminal laws, nor are they adequately addressed through the practice of international criminal courts.[56] Thus, for example, the International Criminal Tribunal for Rwanda tried individual Rwandans for their alleged involvement in the genocide, but it did not and could not address how the legacy of Belgian colonialism and French neocolonialism; the policy and practice of external development aid programs; and the supply of arms to Rwanda before and during the genocide by private companies and countries such as China, South Africa, Egypt, and Zaire also contributed to the conditions in which the massacres occurred (this is discussed further in Chapter 2).[57] And although the ICC has the potential to prosecute corporate executives for their involvement in international crime, the harmful behavior of collective actors, such as corporations and international institutions as a whole, remains largely outside its jurisdiction.[58]

Furthermore, as a sphere defined and delimited through law, the international is also shaped more specifically by the jurisdictional limits imposed by the governing statutes of existing international criminal tribunals—particularly that of the permanent ICC. In relation to this court, Kendall and Nouwen highlight the restrictive effects of what they term "juridified victimhood": a limited legal status of recognized victimization that is available to only a select number of people experiencing harm and injury whose suffering fits into predetermined legal classifications and who successfully navigate the necessary bureaucratic legal processes.[59] That is, although international criminal justice seeks to operate in the name of victims, in practice it does not recognize all victims of a conflict. Rather, only those victims directly associated with the particular charges against the accused are legally recognized as eligible victim participants in cases before the ICC; and problematically, their victim status can be revoked if the charges against the defendant are altered.[60] Their victim status is legally defined and thus can be legally denied. It is in this sense that the ICC, for example, forecloses a broader, nonlegal definition of victimhood through its definition of victim status, stating that "victims are those who have suffered harm as a result of the commission of any crime within the jurisdiction of the Court."[61] While the lived experience of victimization clearly exceeds this definition, such unqualified legal statements produce a crimino-legal sphere in which only certain harms, committed during certain time periods and in certain geographical spaces by certain actors, can be fully "seen, felt, and known."[62]

On a more practical level, law is also a physically regulated and exclusive site. Although courts are public institutions, not everyone can gain substantive access to them. There have thus been critiques of the prohibitive cost for people from countries affected by international crime to travel to international justice institutions at external sites.[63] The ICC also has a range of procedural rules that arguably stymie universal access to it and condition people's behavior within it. Although the previous process of applying for information visits to the court has been removed, valid and acceptable photographic identification are still required. The courtroom is also officially closed to certain individuals, such as those younger than sixteen—who are not permitted to enter the courtroom alone in the interests of public order.[64] The "ICC Rules of Decorum" stipulate that visitors must "observe appropriate standards of conduct" or risk being "immediately expelled from the premises of the Court and thereafter denied access." The "appropriate conduct" includes refraining from talking in the gallery even when the court retreats to private session and making sure not to "point or gesture at anyone seated in the Courtroom."[65] This particular court thus discriminates on the basis of age, despite (as noted below) its specific interest in protecting the rights of child victims of international crime.[66]

It places limits on how people may engage with each other and the court proceedings and is also tethered to structures—like identification cards—of primarily state regulation and recognition, despite the implication of the state in much international crime.

Meanwhile, the *criminal* (or crimino-legal) nature of the international shapes not only what appears in the international sphere but also how it appears. Those who have experienced crime appear primarily as suffering bodies: their visibility in the international sphere is confined to their status as suffering victims.[67] A more holistic appreciation of their individual and social life circumstances is subservient to their signification as evidence of international crime's occurrence and impact. For example, in a video exhibition in the court's foyer in 2017, there was looping footage of victims explaining what harms they had experienced, but their stories were limited to that and visitors to the court were not given the opportunity to understand them as more complex individuals with particular life histories. Visitors were enabled to hear the testimony of a "victim of rape" rather than a person with a proper name. In this way, these victims became not "subjects of human rights concern but . . . symbols of human wrongs inflicted on other populations."[68] Moreover, any recognition of their agency, politics, and particular concerns is obscured, along with their status "as a political person—with interests, relationships, and strategies" and "a political narrative of the past and a vision for the future."[69] Yet suffering is also an experience, rather than a subject position; hence my choice in this book to refer to those who suffer and those who respond *at any given moment in time*. Such a temporal qualification is designed to acknowledge the temporal specificity of suffering as an important way of resisting discourses that fix suffering to certain places and people and conflate people with their experiences of suffering. Furthermore, as Judith Butler, Zeynep Gambetti, and Leticia Sabsay have argued, one's vulnerability—which may be attributable to one's particular social, historical, and political situation—does not preclude one's agency, strength, and resilience nor inevitably require paternalistic responses.[70]

Moreover, when suffering is recognized as a *crime*, people's experiences of such injustice become visible as examples or manifestations of more generalized categories of prohibited behavior. Victims appear as the representative victims of broader crimes against "us" all, as in Arendt's framing of the Holocaust as "a crime against humanity, perpetrated upon the body of the Jewish people."[71] Simpson discusses this dynamic as a tension between the universal and the particular, observing how the Nuremberg trials "universalized the *victims* of crimes against humanity" and thereby "elided the unique circumstances of particular classes of victim."[72] The specificity of people's experiences is further lost through the reading of the harms they have endured as particular instances of more generalized categories of injurious behavior, as crimes against a broader legal order that purportedly reflects the values and interests of a wider community.[73]

Furthermore, despite the current association of notions of international crime and justice with humanitarianism and progress, the crimino-legal nature of this sphere should serve as a reminder of its punitive orientation and connection with the expansion of global governance.[74] In early International Law Commission debates on a specifically international criminal jurisdiction, it is thus described as a "criminal repressive jurisdiction" that serves to legally inaugurate "individuals as objects of measures of repression,"[75] while the Regulations of the Registry of the ICC provide guidelines for the "Discipline and Control" of its detainees and the Court's landscape is described as being "ingeniously used for security" (figure 1).[76]

International criminal justice is first and foremost focused on the arrest, prosecution, and punishment of individuals—all acts that may be considered justifiable and important following the commission of an international crime but that are also inherently punitive. They are also, perhaps, ones to monitor given the continued constitutive exclusion of states, international organizations, and other influential sociopolitical institutions from the purview of international criminal law. This is especially the case because the way the ideal of international criminal justice is operationalized in practice functions to shore up the power of certain states and institutions (see Chapter 4).

The criminological character of the international also shapes the nature of the communal relations found in this sphere.[77] As discussed earlier, the international is the site of a criminological community grounded in the image of international crime and its disavowal. As such, it is a field of communal relations grounded and relying on events of extreme suffering.[78] This is a sphere of shallow social relations, the site of a community that rallies together only in the most terrible of circumstances, in which membership is most certain in the face or experience of extreme injury.[79] Moreover, this international community is defined in relation to, and hence dependent on, the specter and event of suffering. It is a means of imagining a community of humanity, defined in opposition to inhumanity and its recognition, repudiation, and redress.[80] Defined and performed in this way,

FIGURE 1. Security considerations are evident as one approaches the International Criminal Court and proceeds into the security screening area. Photo taken by author.

this community is dependent on suffering and inhumanity to visualize its contours and affirm its existence. This is not to say that it is a collectivity that desires suffering. However, it is a community of humanity defined, at least in part, through the event of inhumanity and thus constitutively requires the image, if not the occurrence, of inhumanity to reaffirm its sense of self. As Young observes at the national level, "crime is a sign, speaking of that which is most reverenced (as essential for the founding of the community and its criminal contract)."[81] My point here is that to conceptualize global community with reference to its reaction and response to extreme human degradation has relational consequences.

Finally, as a spatial arena, the international is not simply a site of relations but one of power relations.[82] As Massey explains, "global space, as space more generally, is a product of material practices of power."[83] The relations that constitute and characterize the international are relations of power with powerful effects. As such, the nature of these power relations in turn informs the shape and content of the international and the global interconnections to which this crimino-legal sphere gives rise. As a spatial arena, the international therefore has the potential to be both a sphere of ethical engagement, as well as a sphere of relations of inequality and injustice.[84]

In this respect, critiques of the cultural bias of the permanent ICC—which to date has largely focused on prosecuting African defendants and African crimes—are relevant.[85] For, although it is possible that the court will not always operate in such a culturally particular way, and although there are justifications offered for its conduct to date, the fact of the culturally particular nature of its operations has effects. In a practical sense, as it is constituted through the work of the ICC, the international is a site of culturally structured power relations in which African bodies are figured as victims and defendants requiring the intervention of those representing the international community. Through the practice of international criminal justice, the international is currently the site of culturally discriminatory relations in which African defendants and leaders are prosecuted "in the name of humanity."[86] This is made visually evident, for example, in the maps often used to depict the work of the ICC that plot its (clustered and largely African-focused) operations on a map of the world, or in the head shots of African people facing prosecution on its website.[87] Understood through such visual representation alone, the court indeed appears to be a culturally targeted institution. Echoing broader and more long-standing critiques of the culturally discriminatory logic of contemporary practices of humanitarianism and humanitarian intervention,[88] international criminal justice also inaugurates a sphere of culturally and racially hierarchical global relations. More broadly, it is a space in which the suffering of some—women, children, and African people and communities, to name a few—is drawn upon as a means of and motivation for imagining an international community and an international crimino-legal sphere.[89]

However, as a spatial arena, defined and constituted by interaction and interrelation, the international is also a dynamic, rather than a fixed, site of global engagement. As Massey explains, space is "always under construction . . . it is always in the process of being made. It is never finished; never closed."[90] As a domain of interaction, the international can be constituted differently, in particular moments and interrelations, and its structural conditions can change. Meanwhile, dominant understandings and practices of international crime and justice sit alongside alternative or more contextual conceptualizations of, engagements with, and performances of these ideas—which in turn produce different interactional spaces and modes of engagement. It is these possibilities that are also important to remember in analyzing the ethical limits and potentials of the ideas of international crime and justice, and which I return to throughout this book.

A Discursive Project

At a 2014 guided tour at the ICC in The Hague, one of the employees of the court gestured to the significance of the very idea of the court and the broader endeavor of international criminal justice. She told a story about the beginnings of the court's official operations—of an initial press conference held by the few people actually working at the court, who answered questions about its operation as though it was fully operational, after which they walked up the stairs behind them into the building where the court was to then operate. But as the tour spokesperson explained, they walked into an empty building: at that early stage, the ICC was still just an idea.[91] It was an idea in which much hope and energy had been invested, one that was positioned as an important progressive and humanitarian step toward ending injustice through the pursuit of accountability, but one that nonetheless was still to be institutionally and practically realized.

To inquire into the discursive configuration of international crime and justice and to describe the international relational sphere produced through them as imagined is not to downplay the materiality and import of both. Rather, doing so is to recognize the centrality and significance of representation and of imagination to the very notion of international crime and justice—to acknowledge, as Young has done at the national level, that crime is "always already *textual*."[92] The contemporary constitution of the international as a sphere in which there exists a concept of crime, a practice of criminal justice, and a sense of global community requires significant and ongoing discursive labor. It involves the scripting of certain offenses as worldly in nature, as crimes against humanity as a whole; the imagining of certain justice processes as uniquely international in character and configuration; and the productive conceptualization of an international community that is injured and affected by such crimes and implicated in their redress. It is in and through this representational work that the international is constituted as a site of crime, justice, and community.

It is in this sense that such socio-legal conceptualizations of international crime and justice have ethical and relational possibilities: instantiating international crime as implicating and affecting a broader community, positioning international criminal justice as a mode of response that represents "us" all, and producing a new site within which injustice is perpetrated but justice is also done. However, it is also crucial not to stop with an acknowledgment of the productivity and ethical potential of ideas of crime and justice. Rather, it is important to enquire further and deeply into exactly how these concepts are given meaning and, in turn, what relational and ethical effects this has. In the wake of colonialism particularly, it is not possible to claim that purportedly humanitarian intentions and rhetoric speak for themselves. Nor is it possible to assume that external engagement with the suffering of others (through representation or specific acts) is innately ethical, given the significant critiques that have been offered of discourses and practices of humanitarianism to date (as mentioned in the Introduction). Thus, Chapter 2 turns to the now globalized event of the Rwandan genocide to demonstrate the ethical centrality of the grounds on which a crime, event of harm, or form of justice becomes configured as inherently international, as well as to caution that internationalization cannot be regarded as an intrinsically humanitarian and positive move.

2

"Rwanda"

The Production of a Global Event

There must be no more Rwandas.
—Gareth Evans and Mohamed Sahnoun,
"The Responsibility to Protect"

THE 1994 RWANDAN GENOCIDE NOW OCCUPIES a special place in global and historical memory. It is widely known as the genocide that could have been prevented, the genocide that was ignored. "Rwanda," as this event has become known in shorthand, is understood as an experience of international failure, a moment in which nation-states and international institutions around the world failed to respond to the genocide of the Tutsi. In its wake, the experience of "Rwanda" is called upon to inspire a sense of global solidarity and to ensure a more robust commitment to cosmopolitan interventionism. Commentators caution that a situation must not become the "next Rwanda," in a context where—as articulated by Gareth Evans and Mohamed Sahnoun above—there is a sentiment that "there must be no more Rwandas."[1] "Rwanda," as an event of international failure and an argument for global interconnectedness, transcends both the borders of the Rwandan nation and the history of its people. Instead, it circulates, exists, and signifies in the narrating and making of international social, legal, and political history.

Thus, in contrast to the external disinterest in the Rwandan genocide when it was occurring, "Rwanda" is now firmly constructed as an international event that has meaning and significance for non-Rwandans. Indeed,

"Rwanda" is a somewhat seminal event in the field of international criminal justice. It has inspired the establishment of one of the key international justice institutions to date, the International Criminal Tribunal for Rwanda; it has been acknowledged by the United Nations (UN) as an unforgettable moment of failure in that institution's life; and it has contributed to the development of the global norm of a Responsibility to Protect in future situations of mass harm in which national governments are unwilling or unable to act.[2] Furthermore, the post hoc internationalization (or making international) of the Rwandan genocide generally appears as an ethical move: a belated, yet justified, acknowledgment of its "rightful place in international memory."[3] In the face of the previous failure of external parties to adequately engage with the genocide, the contemporary global prominence afforded to it can appear as innately moral and just.

Yet in this chapter, I argue that the post hoc internationalization of the Rwandan genocide is also a social, legal, and political act that has ethical limits and possibilities. On the one hand, it arguably facilitates a sense of proximity between non-Rwandans and Rwandans and their experiences of harm, as the Rwandan genocide is taken up as a moment in all of "our" shared history.[4] On the other hand, I argue that current frameworks for understanding this event are culturally structured and tether its significance to its non-Rwandan elements and implications. They frame the Rwandan genocide as a moment of distinctly Western failure to prevent harm in Africa and focus on the Western victims, heroes, and experience of this event. "Rwanda" is understood primarily as a Western event: a moment of Western indifference and inaction that is drawn on to underscore the importance of Western intervention in African conflicts in a time of postcoloniality. It offers a way for non-Rwandans to connect with the Rwandan genocide, but one that systematically loses the Rwandan victims, survivors, and people. As with understandings of international crime more broadly (to be discussed in Chapter 3), the global status of this event is instantiated through an emphasis on its implications for others elsewhere.

In the context of this book's broader consideration of social and legal understandings of international crime and justice, the internationalization of the Rwandan genocide underscores the centrality of the *way* in which specific harms experienced by particular people become constructed as global and of significance to "us" all. It shows how being labeled or recognized as international is not an inherently positive and humanitarian move. Rather, the Rwandan case demonstrates the significance of *how* and *on what grounds* categories of crime and forms of justice are constructed as international or important on the global stage (or conversely not afforded this privileged status).

To make this argument, I begin with a sketch of the legal, social, political, and cultural interest in the Rwandan genocide in its aftermath, leading to its construction as a globally significant event. I then tease out dominant discourses on how and why this event now matters before highlighting their limited and culturally particular nature. Finally, I reflect on the tension between the potential for grounded and contextual engagements with the specific people and communities who have experienced harm and mainstream approaches to configuring events as global and important.

The Cultural Aftermath of the Rwandan Genocide

It is now well established that during the 1994 genocide in Rwanda, national and international actors failed to intervene effectively to stop the violence. Despite increasingly dire information about what was happening in Rwanda, both before and during the genocide, and the presence of a UN peacekeeping force in Rwanda at the time, nation-states and international bodies remained reluctant to respond militarily, legally, or diplomatically. The French government did send a French-dominated, so-called multilateral force to Rwanda near the end of the genocide called Opération Turquoise. However, it is generally accepted that this was not primarily designed to end the genocide and that although it managed to protect some Tutsi, it also provided protection to some of the perpetrators of the violence. Ultimately, the genocidal killings in Rwanda were only officially halted in mid-July, when the Rwandan Patriotic Front, an army of Tutsi refugees, managed to militarily defeat the genocidal authorities and subsequently assert political control over the Rwandan nation.

In striking contrast to the international disinterest in the Rwandan genocide when it was occurring, since 1994 the genocide and the international failure to halt it have become popular subjects of discussion and objects of inquiry. In its aftermath, the genocide and the response that it received have been depicted, discussed, and denounced across public, academic, popular cultural, and political spheres. In the public arena, a plethora of nonfiction texts—nongovernment reports, newspaper articles, pieces of investigative journalism, and documentary films—have sought to document the genocide and expose the "truth" behind governmental and institutional inaction regarding it.[5] Purporting to tell "the full story of perhaps the darkest and most brutal tragedy of our time,"[6] these texts endeavor to reveal what they regard as "one of the greatest scandals of the twentieth century."[7] Collectively, they provide a vivid picture of the extent of governmental and institutional knowledge of the genocide during 1994, which is damningly contrasted with the minimal international efforts to halt it. Their central revelation is thus that certain countries (predominantly the United States, the United Kingdom, France, and Belgium) and international institutions (the UN) knew about the genocide while it was occurring yet failed to intervene to protect the Rwandan Tutsis. As Samantha Power argues, "the real reason the United States did not do what it could and should have done to stop genocide was not a lack of knowledge or influence but a lack of will. Simply put, American leaders did not act because they did not want to."[8]

In the academic sphere, the genocide and international failure have become the focus of a significant body of literature. While previous academic works on Rwanda were primarily authored by Rwandan or African specialists, following the genocide, scholars from a variety of disciplinary and geographical locations turned their attention to the country.[9] There is now a substantial field of academic work that focuses, first, on the genocide, its history, and dynamics; second, on the international response that it received (in fact, it is now rare to find a piece of academic research on the Rwandan genocide that does not include at least a section on the international failure to stop it); and third, on the postgenocide context in Rwanda. In this scholarship, the international failure to halt the genocide has been framed as a problem to be explained and understood. The failure has been problematized as an unjustifiably "indifferent" and "passive" reaction to the crime of genocide,[10] and academics have sought to understand "why the early warnings of an emerging genocide were not translated into early preventative action."[11] In line with the public texts discussed above, international inaction and indifference are attributed to a lack of political will, given the supposed strategic, political, and economic unimportance of the Rwandan nation and people on the global stage. As Michael Barnett explains, "Rwanda did not magically become important" when the genocide began; rather, it remained a country of little strategic, economic, and political significance to "world powers."[12]

Such understandings of the international failure are also taken up in a range of popular cultural texts that have also emerged since 2004. These films,[13] novels,[14] and first-person accounts[15] provide a more personal perspective on the lived experience of the genocide and the international response to it. Unlike other representations, they account for the "sounds, smells, depredations, the scenes of inhuman acts" that constituted these events.[16] Symptomatic of the role of narrative and representation in humanitarianism throughout time,[17] they are oriented toward a more affective mode of engagement, providing an opportunity for their viewers and readers to not only know about, but also feel about and hence feel connected to, these historical events. Initially authored primarily by non-Rwandans exposed to the genocide, but increasingly written by Rwandans themselves,[18] these texts bear witness to the genocide and enable their consumers to do the same.[19] Importantly, complementing the public and academic works, many of these popular cultural texts—particularly those written by non-Rwandans—also bear witness to the Rwandan genocide as a moment of international indifference and inaction. Many of the feature films, for example, contain scenes depicting the evacuations of expatriates from Rwanda in the first few days of the genocide, which have become symbolic of the international abandonment of the Rwandan people.[20] International indifference is also referred to more directly at times, as in the Hollywood blockbuster *Hotel Rwanda*. In one of the best known scenes of the film, a Western reporter, Jack Daglish, explains to the Rwandan protagonist, Paul Rusesabagina, and the film's audience that the footage of the killings he has filmed will not spark any substantial reaction from Western viewers: "they'll say, 'Oh my God, that's horrible,' and then go on eating their dinners."[21]

Meanwhile, in the political sphere, there has been a global outpouring of remorse and regret regarding the international response to the genocide. Since 1994, governmental and institutional officials have visited Rwanda, touring the various memorial sites in the country and offering their apologies and condolences for the genocide and the international failure to intervene. The former American president Bill Clinton has repeatedly confessed that "Rwanda" constitutes one of his "greatest regrets," and in 1998 he traveled to Rwanda and admitted that the international community should have done more to stop the killings.[22] The former UN secretary-general Kofi Annan has echoed these sentiments, asserting that "the international community failed Rwanda, and that must leave us always with a sense of bitter regret and abiding sorrow."[23] In offering such statements, both leaders have also framed the international failure as a more personalized error or sin, which has informed their subsequent global actions.[24] Similar personalized expressions of remorse have also been offered by other political leaders, such as former president of the World Bank Paul Wolfowitz, former prime minister of Belgium Guy Verhofstadt, and former president of South Africa Thabo Mbeki (to name just a prominent few).[25] France remains the only country that Rwanda has called upon to apologize that has not done so.[26]

Various governments and institutions have also undertaken commissions of inquiry into their response to the 1994 genocide. In 1997, the Belgian Senate initiated the first national inquiry, followed by the French National Assembly in 1998.[27] Two institutional commissions of inquiry were also subsequently conducted by independent panels charged with the responsibility of examining the respective responses of the UN and the then Organization of African Unity to the 1994 killings.[28] Designed to determine "what went wrong" in 1994, these reports have focused on identifying and articulating the range of "errors," "deficiencies," and "failures" that allegedly culminated in the international failure to act.[29] In doing so, they present the international failure as a discrete mistake that can now be understood and hence avoided in the future. Conducted in the wake of growing public criticism of the international response, these inquiries therefore offered a way for national governments and international institutions to acknowledge and regain control of societal debates regarding the genocide and to provide their own authoritative account of "what really happened."[30] To that end, the 1998 French inquiry, in particular, has been regarded in some quarters as a "whitewash"—more focused on deflecting criticism from the French state than on examining the nature and impact of its interventions.[31] Accordingly, partially to contest the veracity of the findings of the French government's inquiry, the Rwandan government launched its own inquiry into the role of France in Rwanda before, during, and after the genocide. This inquiry found that the French government was complicit with those who committed genocide, both before during its occurrence.[32]

In recent times, both the genocide and the international failure to halt it have also increasingly been remembered through various memorials and commemorative practices at the national and international levels.[33] Since 1995, the anniversary of the genocide has been commemorated in Rwanda, usually on April 7 each year—a date that marks the beginning of a national week of mourning. On the tenth anniversary of the genocide, in 2004, the Kigali Genocide Memorial Centre was opened in Rwanda's capital city, and it is now accompanied by memorials in each district of Rwanda and by exhibitions about the genocide around the world.[34] In 2004, commemorations of the genocide also assumed a distinctly international character. The

Canadian-based volunteer organization Remembering Rwanda expended
time and resources on drawing attention to the tenth anniversary of the
killings, underscoring the importance of commemorating a genocide that
it claimed was already (or still) being forgotten by the rest of the world.[35]
That same year, the UN named April 7, 2004, the International Day of
Reflection on the 1994 Genocide in Rwanda, and around the world both
the genocide and the international failure to prevent it were remembered.[36]
This level of international involvement in the commemoration of the genocide continued with the launch of the UN's Outreach Programme on the
Rwanda Genocide and the United Nations, which focuses on preventing
genocide through the remembrance of the Rwandan genocide.[37] In such
forums, the international failure to halt the Rwandan genocide is again
foregrounded as a central feature of this historical event, which is said to
have "underscored the international community's failure to make the prevention of genocide a reality."[38]

Thus, somewhat paradoxically, although the Rwandan genocide was
treated as unimportant as it was occurring, both the genocide and the
international failure to stop it are currently understood to be extremely
important—or, as Rhoda Howard-Hassmann claims, they have "induced
much Western soul-searching."[39] Through this plethora of cultural, political,
social, and legal responses to the Rwandan genocide, it has thus emerged
as a globally significant event, implicating and affecting non-Rwandans.
In their very existence and multiplicity, these representations testify to the
global significance of the genocide, its "rightful place" in international social, legal and political history. They figure the genocide as significant to
Western publics and the broader global community (who need to know
its full details); an event deserving scholarly attention beyond Rwanda; an
experience non-Rwandan publics should both know and care about, as well
as bear witness to; a harm that external nonintervening parties bear some
responsibility for; a sign of governmental and institutional failure in non-
Rwandan contexts; and a matter of global as well as local commemoration.

Remembering "Rwanda": The Rwandan Genocide
on the Global Stage

Produced in and through these post hoc representations, the Rwandan
genocide has assumed a distinct identity in its aftermath. Echoing a dynamic
similar to that of the belated construction of the Holocaust as a globally and

historically significant event, the idea of "Rwanda" has emerged as a discrete cultural complex characterized by a dominant discourse about its meaning and global significance.[40] More specifically, as is succinctly captured in the title of the Organization of African Unity report, the 1994 Rwandan genocide is now commonly known as the "preventable genocide."[41] "Rwanda" is now known not just as the site of the extermination of the Rwandan Tutsis but also as a moment of international failure.[42] According to this mode of thinking, the Rwandan genocide did not just occur: it was permitted to occur. The international failure to stop the genocide is conceived of as its condition of possibility, a necessary precondition to its occurrence. The Rwandan genocide is conceptualized as a product of a failure—not just of the Rwandan people, but also of those non-Rwandan countries, institutions, and individuals that did not stop or prevent it.

Since 1994, the international failure to halt the genocide has been coded as distinctly shameful, and "Rwanda" has gradually consolidated as a matter of Western and international shame. "Rwanda" is shameful in the sense that it is understood to constitute a failure of Western countries and international institutions to live up to national and societal expectations of their global role.[43] Rather than acting as the human rights defenders that they had claimed or were expected to be, actors such as the United States, the United Kingdom, Belgium, and the UN failed to militarily intervene in the genocide, despite their ability to do so. This understanding of "Rwanda" can be seen in various public texts—such as documentary films and investigative journalism works—that juxtapose the failures of certain countries and institutions with their national or institutional constituency's expectations of them. For example, in her widely read work, the investigative journalist Linda Melvern explains that "there was a time when the sight of a single blue helmet at a checkpoint flying the UN flag was a symbol of peace. . . . The peacekeeper's weapon was not the rifle slung over the shoulder but his credibility," but "after Rwanda that symbol may have been irreparably tarnished."[44] In turn, in its inquiry into the genocide, the UN has affirmed such sentiments, describing its own inaction in the presence of the genocide as "terrible and humiliating."[45] Thus, there are important similarities between critiques of the international failure from civil society and academia and governmental and institutional responses to it: both frame the international failure as a regrettable occurrence and assert that there should have been a more interventionist response. In the aftermath of the genocide, Clinton has publicly stated that there should have been an American military action in

1994, as that would have saved many lives.[46] And Annan has affirmed that "if the international community had acted promptly and with determination, it could have stopped most of the killing."[47]

This framing of the Rwandan genocide has also been endorsed to some extent in official and mainstream Rwandan discourse. In his speeches at the annual national commemoration ceremonies, President Paul Kagame frequently refers to the international failure to halt the genocide (for more details, see the discussion below),[48] reflecting broader understandings of the centrality of the international failure to the event of the genocide. Meanwhile, the lack of international intervention is also cited at prominent memorial sites in Rwanda, such as the exhibition at the Kigali Genocide Memorial Centre, where a section on the "International Response" depicts how "the world withdrew . . . and watched as a million people were slaughtered."[49] Rwandan civil society has also been receptive to the conceptualization of the Rwandan genocide as the "preventable genocide", calling for those external national and international actors implicated in the genocide and the international failure to provide reparations and compensation to survivors.[50]

Notably, the Rwandan government has also drawn upon such conceptualizations of the genocide to pursue its own political goals.[51] Understandings of the Rwandan genocide as a moment of Western inaction have lent legitimacy to the existing government, which includes many former Rwandan Patriotic Front soldiers—the force that ultimately ended the genocide.[52] Meanwhile, the status of the event as the "preventable genocide" has also been invoked by Rwandan political actors in their international relations. For example, in response to external criticism of legal restrictions on freedom of speech in postgenocide Rwanda, the Rwandan government has asserted that it cannot adopt the same stance as international actors did during the genocide.[53] The government was referring specifically to the international failure in 1994 to disable the RTLM (Radio Télévision Libre des Mille Collines) radio station (which was broadcasting hate speech and instructions regarding the genocide) and to the American justification for not doing so (which was that it would have contravened American commitments to free speech). Meanwhile, a cynical view has been expressed in academic and political commentary that not only is international aid for postgenocide Rwanda shaped by Western guilt,[54] but that this guilt has been skillfully exploited by the Rwandan government in the postgenocide era.[55]

Across public, political, and academic spheres, there is therefore now a dominant discourse about the Rwandan genocide and its global significance. The genocide is now understood as an event that should have been prevented, while the international response to it has been problematized as a regrettable and shameful lack of action regarding a crime that required a more interventionist response. "Rwanda" is no longer a term that just refers to the Rwandan nation, its culture, and its people. Rather, it is now a shorthand term for current global understandings of the Rwandan genocide and, particularly, the international failure to halt it. Hence the call from Evans and Sahnoun at the start of this chapter that "there must be no more Rwandas."

Media commentators too, for example, warn that contemporary atrocities must not become the "the next" or "another Rwanda."[56] Thus, in its use as a frame through which to conceptualize the international implications of subsequent events of suffering throughout the world, "Rwanda" has also—as Andreas Huyssen argues of the Holocaust—become a "metaphor for other traumatic histories."[57] It has been reported that it was the memory of "Rwanda" that motivated certain leaders to support an international intervention in Libya in early 2011.[58] In the American context, former president Barack Obama's support for the intervention has been attributed to the fact that he "doesn't want another Rwanda on his watch."[59] This account of the Libyan intervention references both former president Bill Clinton's inaction regarding the Rwandan genocide and former president George W. Bush's reaction to it and the subsequent Darfur conflict. It is now well known that in 2001, when Bush received a summary of one of Power's influential investigative journalism articles on the international failure to halt the Rwandan genocide, he wrote on the document: "NOT ON MY WATCH."[60] The repetitive use of this phrase shows that just as Bush's approach to Darfur was shaped by the experience of "Rwanda," so was Obama's subsequent reaction to the Libyan atrocities and civil war.

Indeed, as many commentators have noted, it is perhaps in relation to the violence in Darfur that the invocation of the memory of "Rwanda" has been most pronounced.[61] For example, Mahmood Mamdani notes that the American-based, yet globally oriented, "Save Darfur" movement developed from the commemorations of the tenth anniversary of the 1994 Rwandan genocide and involved the popular portrayal of the Darfur violence as the "next Rwanda."[62] In turn, using "Rwanda" as a frame to relate to the conflict in Darfur has shaped and influenced how external parties conceptualized this suffering and conceived of responding to it.[63] Thus, in light of the Clinton administration's reluctance to officially recognize the 1994 Rwandan killings as a genocide at the time that they occurred, with respect to Darfur, much political and public emphasis was placed on recognizing the genocidal nature of the violence occurring in Darfur (although this designation of the violence in Darfur itself attracted controversy and did not necessarily lead to a more effective international response).[64]

Conditions of Possibility: The Limits and Potentials of Existing Frames

There are clearly ethical potentials in the post hoc internationalization of the Rwandan genocide. The belated global interest in the genocide has served to situate this event as one connected to the world around it and related to the actions and inactions of many. It testifies to the broader significance of the genocide beyond the Rwandan nation, figuring it as an important focus of representation and a necessary event to witness and remember. The multiple forms of social, legal, political, and cultural engagement with the genocide also provide numerous opportunities for non-Rwandans to learn about, connect with, and understand their relation to the violence, as well as to remember and mourn it in the future.

When the genocide is understood as a moment of Western and international failure, for Western audiences, "Rwanda" is transformed from a potentially geographically and culturally remote event to one that directly implicates them and their leaders.[65] It becomes more proximate, related to their lives and their experience of the world. Moreover, the more recent use of "Rwanda" as a framework to conceptualize subsequent events of suffering on the African continent provides a means for non-Africans to understand such future violence as their concern, enabling "new lines of sight" and facilitating new possibilities for global engagement with suffering across the world.[66]

Moreover, the contemporary frame of "Rwanda" invites not just cognitive connections but also affective ones.[67] For non-Rwandans, "Rwanda" has become the name for an event that is not just now *known*, but also for an interpersonal experience that has been belatedly *seen, felt*, and *appreciated*.[68] It is a site of mourning, prompting sorrow and solemn remembrance; a means of redemption, enabling catharsis through the confession of remorse and regret about the past; and a source of inspiration, motivating commitments to international responsibility for African suffering. In practice, the memory of "Rwanda" is deployed and said to move people—it is used to get officials to act in the face of future atrocities and to get broader publics to feel or care about other events.[69]

However, the ethical potentials of the contemporary internationalization of "Rwanda" are nevertheless constrained by the particular grounds upon which it has been constructed as a global, and globally significant, event. The terms of existing discourses on "Rwanda" shape and direct how non-Rwandans relate to this event and subsequent events of atrocity throughout the world that are presented as similar to it.[70] Just as Jeffrey Alexander has critiqued mainstream understandings of the Holocaust because they serve to occlude the diversity of stories and experiences connected with that event, so too do dominant understandings of the Rwandan genocide emphasize certain aspects, while making others difficult to appreciate.[71] It is in this sense that the construction of "Rwanda" demonstrates the power of humanitarian narratives to connect people with the suffering of others, to inspire emotive and affective connections. But it also acts as a reminder of the social and political dynamics of representations of suffering that each come with their own contexts, interests, and biases and that can disenfranchise the very people whose suffering is at issue as well as inspire global engagement with their situation.[72]

First, although the international response to the Rwandan genocide is deserving of analysis and attention, the current conceptualization of the international failure as a key condition of possibility of the genocide can have undesirable implications. A focus on the centrality of the international response to the genocide can create the illusion that the genocide itself was somehow inevitable. It is transformed from a planned, deliberate, and potentially preventable occurrence into a predetermined one. Against a backdrop of historical and contemporary depictions of Africa as a site of war, violence, and anarchy,[73] the genocide itself is seen as simply one more instance of violence on the continent and symptomatic of a continued trajectory of disorder in Africa.

In turn, the capacity of external countries and international institutions to prevent or stop the genocide is figured as the only tenable way of ensuring that the genocide of the Tutsis did not occur. As Barnett explains in relation to academic texts on the international failure, many studies are directed toward imagining "a counterfactual world in which a possible action is logically connected to a chain of events that would have caused the perpetrators to abandon their crusade."[74] The purpose of such hypothetical endeavors is to show "that this genocide could have been prevented,"[75] but only—and always already—by the external Western spectator. The agency of the Rwandan people (perpetrators and victims) is downplayed through such a focus on the power of the bystander to genocide.[76] The stories of Rwandan resistance to the genocide at Bisesero, Bugasera, and Murambi and the emphasis on the responsibility of Rwandan perpetrators found at the Rwandan national level have no significant place in this dominant global remembering of the genocide and the international failure to respond to it.[77] This globalized memory instead repeats broader neocolonial discourses that figure the West as agent and hero in the face of African victimization and barbarity.[78]

Second, while current understandings of "Rwanda" appropriately highlight the implication of external parties in the 1994 violence, they do so in a highly selective and particular manner. Conceptualized as the "preventable genocide," "Rwanda" is understood as a site of failure and omission, a moment in which certain nation-states and international institutions across the world failed to act to halt the genocide of the Tutsis. Thus, in the wake of the genocide, the focus has been on the failures and omissions of countries and institutions: the failure of countries such as the United States to officially name the killings a genocide (preferring instead the phrase "acts of genocide"); the withdrawal of the Belgian contingent from Rwanda in the early days of the genocide, after ten of its peacekeepers were killed; the reluctance of national and international parties to exert pressure on the Rwandan authorities to stop the violence; and perhaps most of all, the failure of the UN and its members to authorize a wider mandate and reinforcements for the peacekeeping force already in Rwanda.[79]

Occluded from view in this account of "Rwanda" are the actions of non-Rwandans before and during the genocide, which arguably contributed to its occurrence. In terms of active involvement during the genocide, as discussed below, the Rwandan government has consistently sought to draw attention to the potentially criminal nature of the French intervention. Meanwhile, in his book on the role of France in this event, Andrew Wallis argues that "the point gets overlooked that genocide often occurs because of too much, not too little, Western interference."[80] With respect to external involvement in Rwanda before the genocide, departing from mainstream academic discourse, scholars and public commentators such as Peter Uvin—as well as David Newbury, Mamdani, Melvern, and Anne Orford—have emphasized that it was the very involvement of outside countries and international institutions in Rwanda that contributed to the social, economic, and political conditions in which the genocide occurred.[81] Uvin, for example, emphasizes the impact of the policy and practice of development aid on Rwandan society.[82] Furthermore, academic literature on the genocide has drawn attention to the ongoing legacy of colonialism in Rwandan society.[83] From this perspective, the problem of "Rwanda" becomes not one of inaction but one of historical and contemporary action. The role of countries and international institutions is no longer one of externality, as such actors were already "present" in Rwanda in certain ways.[84] The failure to acknowledge these types of structural and historical responsibility for the Rwandan genocide represents a missed opportunity to think in more complex ways about the nature of global interconnection and the diverse ways in which external parties might be implicated in the suffering of others (see also Chapter 3). It demonstrates a preference for decontextualized images of humanitarian heroes and victims in need, which does not do justice to the diverse historical and political cross-national relations that actually exist in the world.

For its part, the Rwandan government has taken a more nuanced approach to the question of international responsibility for the genocide. At the fifteenth commemoration of the genocide, Kagame stated that external parties bore two types of guilt, or two types of responsibility: the first relating to colonial and neocolonial interventions in Rwanda over time, and the second relating to the nonintervention of non-Rwandans while the genocide was occurring.[85] With regard to the first type of guilt, the Rwandan government—like some academic commentators—has emphasized the ongoing impact of colonial and neocolonial Western involvement in Rwanda, describing it as "a history going back many decades" that created the necessary conditions for genocide to occur.[86] It is in this sense that Belgium's exacerbation of Rwandan societal divisions through its style of colonial rule and introduction of identity cards demarcating Hutus and Tutsis is emphasized.[87] And with regard to the second type, official government materials and speeches (as noted earlier) also highlight the responsibility of non-Rwandan actors for their failures regarding the genocide, proclaiming that the world "watched as a million people were slaughtered."[88] The Rwandan government has also drawn attention to a third type of external responsibility, specifically in relation to the French state: French complicity and participation in the genocide. This was clearly a focus of the Rwandan government's commission of inquiry into the role of France before, during, and after the genocide, as well as of the thirteenth commemoration of the genocide that was deliberately held at a site where French troops were stationed during the killings.[89] The dominant Rwandan approach thus accounts for both the inactions and actions of non-Rwandan parties with respect to the 1994 violence, as well as placing such responsibility in a longer historical trajectory leading to different forms of culpability. Such forms of interconnection are messier and more complicated but might better acknowledge the ways in which different peoples and communities are historically and currently related and might give rise to new conceptualizations of international responsibility.

Third and finally, in terms of its limits and biases, "Rwanda" in many ways constitutes a self-focused and racially structured Western construct. At a basic level, it largely concerns the actions and inactions of certain Western countries (the United States, France, the United Kingdom, and Belgium), and it is constructed in and through visual, written, and verbal texts primarily produced in Western contexts by Western academics, speakers, journalists, and filmmakers (although in the decades following the genocide this has changed, with more Rwandan voices being heard in memoirs, documentaries, commissions of inquiry, and academic research).[90] More substantively, though, "Rwanda" names a mode of thinking in which the West occupies the position of the subject—the West's actions and inactions are condemned, its shame and remorse is confessed, and its lessons are learned. Conceptualized as a moment of Western and international failure, "Rwanda" constitutes a mode of coming to terms with the genocide that foregrounds the actions, experience, and emotions of the Western and international bystander. Thus, many of the representations that constitute it focus, for example, on the experiences of those Western people who tried to stop the genocide, traveled to Rwanda to bear witness to it, or "shamefully" failed to respond to it appropriately.

In one respect, the Western nature of global memories of "Rwanda" could be explained as a simple function of the cultural dynamics of global knowledge production: a sign of the ongoing hegemony of the West in the international sphere.[91] Yet it is also reflective of the current role of the figure of "Rwanda" on the global stage—namely, as has been argued by James Dawes, Mamdani, and others, as a site for the West to imagine and visualize itself as the moral, global savior it failed to be. For Dawes, this is why the international failure has "become a more potent and vivid story in the West than the genocide itself ever could be. We are culpable, and it feels good to be culpable. It assures us that we are good people, because we are the kind of people who feel bad about these sorts of things."[92] Meanwhile, Mamdani extends Dawes's insight to the contemporary invocation of "Rwanda" as a frame for relating to subsequent events of suffering. Mamdani demonstrates how—through the lens of "Rwanda"—Darfur became a geopolitical location at which Western publics and governments could perform themselves as "good" and "moral" global subjects in the aftermath of the 1994 genocide and the second Iraq War.[93] As it is applied to both the 1994 genocide in Rwanda and the more recent conflict in Sudan, "Rwanda" constitutes a self-focused Western mode of understanding, concerned with how the West responds to events of suffering throughout the world. It is in this vein, that in relation to Darfur the actor George Clooney warns contemporary international leaders: "How you deal with it will be your legacy, your Rwanda."[94]

"Rwanda" is also a racially structured discursive construct. The specter of "Rwanda" is not necessarily invoked indiscriminately. Rather, it appears that "Rwanda" has been predominantly drawn upon as a means of understanding the significance and implications of violence on the African continent. "Rwanda" is overwhelmingly conjured up as a conceptual framework to relate to human rights abuses in countries such as Sudan, Libya, the Central African Republic, Zimbabwe, and Cameroon (although there are exceptions, such as its invocation regarding injustice in Myanmar).[95] Thus, although the memory of the Holocaust is characterized by its "generalizability" (the "generalization" of its "victims," "perpetrators," and "significance"),[96] the construct of "Rwanda" is less widely applicable—or, at least, it is generalizable in a different way. Concerned with the problem of Western noninterventionism and predominantly invoked as a frame to understand the global import of African conflicts, "Rwanda" is a discourse premised on the relationship between the West as a potential global hero and Africa as a potential population in need of assistance.

Reflective of a more generalized historical tendency for dominant (read: Western) productions of Africa to function as a way for the West to trace its own contours and justify its own actions,[97] "Rwanda" thus represents the appropriation of the experience of the 1994 genocide to affirm a distinct Western subjectivity and Western military interventionism in a postcolonial world.[98] Once again, as highlighted by Achille Mbembe, "narrative about

Africa is always a pretext for a comment about something else, some other place, some other people."[99] The story of "Rwanda" is one that concerns the renewed importance of Western emotional engagement and practical intervention in African contexts in the postcolonial era. "Rwanda" is invoked in contemporary times to remind Westerners that, unlike in 1994, they should care about and actively respond to suffering and violence on the African continent—regardless of any gaps in their knowledge or understanding of the conflict or the best way to resolve it.[100]

The Grounds of Global Engagement

It is ethically complicated to critique the post hoc global interest in the Rwandan genocide and its production as a globally significant event. And the aim of this chapter is not to suggest that the Rwandan genocide should not be regarded as internationally important, nor is it to discourage external engagement with the experiences and desires of the Rwandan nation and people. On the contrary, my critique is motivated by a concern that it is such specific engagement with the Rwandan people, as those most directly affected by the genocide, that is constitutively downplayed through its dominant construction as an event of Western failure. The suffering of the Rwandan Tutsis remains the missing referent in global discourses about "Rwanda," which focus predominantly on the actions, experiences, and emotions of the Western bystander to genocide. Current ways of understanding "Rwanda" offer a limited, self-focused, and culturally structured mode through which non-Rwandans can relate to the genocide and subsequent events of violence through their own past indifference, present remorse, and determination to react more forcefully to future suffering. The genocide is made international—of broader global significance—through an emphasis on its implications for others, elsewhere.

Moreover, produced in and through internationally prominent texts and discourses, "Rwanda" comes to circulate and signify well beyond the Rwandan context from which it borrows its name.[101] "Rwanda" is no longer just an event related to the experiences of the Rwandan people; instead, it becomes a frame for thinking about (and advocating for) global responsibility for future occurrences of conflict. In this sense it also becomes a somewhat independent memory or idea that can be used to serve broader social and political roles.[102] Although the memory of the Holocaust is understood to have been mobilized in the name of establishing a system of international human rights, "Rwanda" is also said to have inspired much political and legal progress in the international arena, leading to the establishment of the International Criminal Tribunal for Rwanda and the development of the Responsibility to Protect doctrine.[103] According to the authors of this doctrine, past events such as the Rwandan genocide—alongside the atrocities in Bosnia and Kosovo—underscore the importance of international intervention when a state neglects to protect its citizens from harm.[104] Jennifer Welsh thus writes of the "Rwanda effect" that, she argues, enabled the re-articulation of state sovereignty as compatible with human rights, which is the central tenet of the doctrine.[105]

Like other global events such as the Holocaust, "Rwanda" thus becomes narrated as an event with a life that exceeds Rwandan history. Instead, it is an experience inserted into more general narratives—for example, of international history and progress—a distinctly international event.[106] As moments in international legal history in particular, "Rwanda" and "Auschwitz" become "the darkest chapters of recent human history [that] have motivated the world to move toward ending impunity for unspeakable crimes."[107] As with other globalized events of mass harm, "Rwanda" is transformed into a crucial moment, a lesson learned, in a broader "progressive narrative" toward a more just world, free of suffering.[108] As globally oriented discursive constructs—which primarily concern the broader significance of certain events for external audiences—such globalized harms can also be defined by the fact that, in practice, they are drawn upon and utilized to achieve global social, legal, and political goals. In this way, the production of these events as distinctively international ones can appear as a positive and ethical trend, fostering an enhanced sense of global interconnectedness. It is in this vein that Daniel Levy and Natan Sznaider (among others) praise the humanitarian legacy of the memory of the Holocaust, which is understood to have provided the grounds and impetus for human rights doctrine and its global acceptance and ascendancy.[109] From this view, such globalized events bring "us" together as well as demonstrating "our" interrelation.

All these aspects of the post hoc construction of "Rwanda" as a global event demonstrate that it is important to remain aware of the *grounds* upon which an event, form of crime, or mode of justice is figured as distinctly important or international (and the effects of such internationalization). The case study of "Rwanda" demonstrates that the internationalization of an event of harm or crime is a socially, historically, legally, and politically situated process that has a range of ethical and relational implications. The production of a specific experience as a distinctly global one cannot be assumed to be an innately humanitarian move leading to deeper and contextualized connections between those who have suffered and those who have not (at any given point in time). With respect to the Rwandan genocide, internationalization has entailed an appropriative dynamic whereby the Rwandan genocide has become globally important through an emphasis on its implications for non-Rwandans.[110] In addition, the experience of the genocide and even the proper name of the country have been redefined as moments in a more generalized sociopolitical global history, in which both are made to signify in relation to a range of diverse ends. It is thus crucial to consider the specific grounds upon which events of suffering are made to matter to those not directly affected, and the ethical implications of how they are made to do so.

This argument is one that aligns with the work of various scholars who have considered the social, legal, and political constructions of a range of different experiences of harm. In his work on the Bosnian genocide, for example, Gearóid Tuathail demonstrates the ethical salience of the varied frames used to understand it.[111] When understood by Western publics as the next Vietnam War, the Bosnian violence became a potential "quagmire" for intervening countries and thus associated with a stance of nonintervention, while its alternative portrayal as the next Holocaust established its relational proximity to Western outsiders and compelled a more engaged response. His work clarifies how geopolitical and affective relations to suffering elsewhere are socially constructed and negotiated: the way in which an event is conceptualized and represented actively determines the sense of "proximity" or "distance" that external spectators may feel toward it. Meanwhile, Charlotte Mertens charts the problematic effects of conceiving of the Democratic Republic of Congo (DRC) through an exceptionalizing and spectacularizing lens of sexual violence. She demonstrates how the recent internationalization of the DRC as the "rape-capital of the world" repeats colonial discourses of the DRC as "the heart of darkness" and significantly compromises how varied experiences of harm in the DRC are understood and the response that they receive.[112] When the focus is on responding to sexual violence as a recent and discrete harm, international interventions in the DRC fail to align with local realities or be attentive to the continuities between sexual violence and other injustices. They also downplay the structural violence that informs the broader conflict and establish an unhelpful hierarchy of victims in which those who have been subject to sexual violence are the main recipients of humanitarian aid (and also of the objectifying humanitarian gaze). Finally, I have noted throughout this chapter that Mamdani has also critiqued the terms of global engagement with the conflict in Darfur, arguing that the strategic invocation of "Rwanda" and an emphasis on the genocidal nature of the violence has enabled the promotion of a simplistic narrative about the wrongness of the harm and the need for Western interventionism that downplays the specificities of what occurred in Darfur.[113] The work by these various authors and others, in its detailed attention to different case studies of internationalization, also serves to underscore the need to investigate and interrogate both what forms and events of harm are internationalized and the ways in which that is done.[114]

In this case of "Rwanda," the internationalization of the Rwandan genocide sits in tension with a respect for the specificities of this historical experience and the particular lives and people that it touched most directly (a violence that is then repeated when it is used as a frame for other events, whose unique characteristics are also downplayed).[115] The Rwandan genocide becomes international due to its implications for non-Rwandans. The next chapter argues that a similar dynamic marks the International Law Commission's conceptualization of "international crime," a phenomenon that is also defined in a way that loses specificity and links the international character of such harm to its effect on others: humanity, the international community, international peace and security.

3

International Crime as Spectacle

Scale, Subjectivity, Ethics

What is the justification for the special place that they occupy?
—Doudou Thiam, "Third Report on the Draft Code
of Offences Against the Peace and Security of Mankind"

IN RECENT DECADES, social, political, and academic commentators have devoted significant amounts of time and energy to establishing that certain events constitute a genocide or a crime against humanity. "This is a genocide," Azeem Ibrahim wrote in 2017 in relation to the Rohingya persecution, "and we, in the international community, must recognize it as such."[1] While Amnesty International has emphasized that such persecution may also constitute a crime against humanity, which it underscores as significant because "crimes against humanity are exactly what the term suggests—crimes so serious that they are the concern not only of their victims, survivors or the state in question, but of humanity as a whole."[2] These declarations accompany civil society campaigns, legal actions, academic work, and governmental inquiries that have sought to formally and publicly acknowledge the distinctively genocidal character of a range of devastating harms, including (to name a few) the destruction of the Armenian people, the violence in Darfur, the suffering in Palestine, and the enduring and more recent colonial injustices experienced by Indigenous peoples in settler-colonial states such as Canada and Australia.[3] In turn, many invocations of the labels of *genocide* and *crimes against humanity* themselves attract considerable legal and academic attention, with lawyers assessing whether they accord with the legal meaning, and political and social commentators sometimes delegitimizing the use of these terms.[4] As with many claims of settler-colonial genocide, the categorization of the Canadian government policy over time as genocide in the 2019 report of the Canadian Government's National Inquiry into Missing and Murdered Indigenous Women and Girls, for example, sparked notable debate, being initially discounted by some as "propagandist."[5]

Both the campaigns to use the labels of *genocide* and *crimes against humanity* and the resistance to their application speak to their social capital and perceived importance. So too does the ever-growing body of academic literature across a range of different disciplines that seeks to elucidate what constitutes a distinctly international crime or a *crime against humanity*. This literature focuses on articulating the key characteristics of these categories of harm, usually by analyzing existing dominant understandings of the categories and seeking to advance normative theory of what an ideal definition might be.[6] These inquiries range from strict legal and doctrinal discussions to philosophical and normative debates about the proper content of these categories, and they reveal a sense that there is much at stake in how the labels of *genocide, crimes against humanity*, and *international crime* are defined and applied. The acknowledgment of the genocidal status of a particular event is seen to be a powerful act, one that establishes the global significance of particular violence and can mobilize external parties to care and act in relation to it. As Michael Barnett argues in relation to the Rwandan genocide, "it was only after the killing in Rwanda was labeled a 'genocide' that it received international attention and there were demands that something be done."[7] More recently, Eleanor Ross reports that at least sixty members of the British Parliament are lobbying for the crimes of ISIS against minority groups in Iraq to be recognized as a genocide, because of the consequences that would have—triggering obligations to prevent and punish under the 1948 *Convention on the Prevention and Punishment of the Crime of Genocide* and potentially leading to post hoc prosecution.[8] Of course, in practice, there is often a disjuncture between public recognition of an injustice as a genocide or crime against humanity and the ultimate external response to it.[9] It is in this sense that Caroline Fournet argues that a contradiction marks the crime of genocide: it is valorized as the worst possible crime, but actual events of genocide often fail to receive the necessary attention and global response.[10] Yet it can still be said that as ideas, notions of international crime, genocide, and crimes against humanity are understood to name a distinctive as well as a privileged type of harm. Hence, genocide is often described as the "crime of crimes," with crimes against humanity understood to be characterized by their "particular infamy and horror."[11] Alongside war crimes and the crime of aggression, these crimes are understood to be the core international crimes, deemed by the International Criminal Court (ICC) to be the "most serious crimes of concern to the international community as a whole."[12]

This chapter focuses on this privileged category of core international crime and its socio-legal conceptualization. In contrast to much work on this topic, this book is not concerned with proposing a further normative definition of international crime or focusing on the academic debates and their merits. My focus is on tracing how this category of crime is conceptualized in the reports of the International Law Commission (ILC) in its attempt to formulate a general international criminal code. In the wake of World War II, the newly formed commission was tasked by the UN with developing a draft international criminal code, designated (in notably gendered language) as a "Draft Code of Crimes Against the Peace and Security of Mankind" (the Code).[13] The Code was meant to codify and prohibit a select number of harms deemed to be particularly significant and worthy of international condemnation. That is, the commission understood its role to be to draft an international criminal code that encompassed not all international crimes, but only those deemed to be the most serious international harms requiring global condemnation and, potentially, prosecution. The Code was not necessarily connected to a specific mode of enforcement (such as an international criminal court) and was ultimately never enacted as an international treaty. Yet the commission's work on the Code informed the later mandate of the ICC (discussed in Chapter 4). More importantly, in the drafting of the Code, the commission actively engaged with the questions of how to conceptualize and ultimately define the notion of international crime and how to articulate its distinctive character. And it remains the only official attempt to formulate such a comprehensive international criminal code to date.

The commission began its operation and its work on the Code in 1949, and its work was divided between two main time periods (or parts)—spanning 1949–54 and 1982–96, respectively.[14] The two parts to the commission's deliberations differed in their outcomes, with part I producing a Code that specified thirteen crimes and part II producing a Code that enumerated only five crimes. My analysis here focuses on the commission and special rapporteur reports for the second session of the commission's work on the draft code, as these discussions are more related to my focus in this book. Through my analysis of the commission debates, I demonstrate how international crimes are often defined with reference to their seriousness, large-scale or systematic nature, effect on the international community or international peace and security, and (less frequently) relation to state power. I argue that such approaches to international crime have an integrally scalar character, actively configuring internationality as a matter of scale. For example, international crimes are portrayed as higher and more important harms than other forms of injury (that is, they are *the most* serious harms); they occur on a mass or large scale; and they affect generalized states and constituencies (being said to threaten international peace and security as well as humanity and its values). I argue that such scalar conceptualizations of internationality may be premised on an ethics (being grounded in a commitment to underscoring the particularly atrocious nature of such harm), but in fact have a series of problematic relational effects. Overall, they function to create affective and relational distance between those who have experienced internationalized and other serious harms and those who have not (at any given moment in time). That is, I argue that it is the very emphasis in commission debates on the extreme horror and broader implications of international crime that makes it hard to see and relate to the people and communities such crime most directly affects.

My analysis is informed by the work of Judith Butler on the "frames" through which violence and injury throughout the world are represented.[15] She underscores the significance of the discursive frames through which the suffering of others is perceived, which condition the affective and practical response it receives. Such frames, she argues, are affectively and politically important, determining which and whose experiences of suffering and injury are deemed to matter and what social, political, and legal response they are seen to demand.[16] In her words, frames thus constitute "cultural modes of regulating affective and ethical dispositions through a selective and differential framing of violence."[17] Her work therefore underscores the argument advanced in Chapter 2: that it matters exactly *how* international crime (as globally significant harm) is represented, for different framings of harm have different ethical and relational consequences.

I begin by introducing the idea of distinctly internationalized crime, highlighting its social, legal, and political "resonance."[18] I then discuss the commission's understandings of the key defining characteristics of such harm and demonstrate their inherently scalar nature. The rest of the chapter focuses on three intersecting and problematic effects of such scalar understandings of international crime. First, their framing of international crime as particularly extreme or exceptional serves to spectacularize internationalized harm, making it difficult to connect with it as an experience that is lived.[19] Second, their ranking of violence in terms of importance downplays the significance of some harms in relation to others. Third, they focus attention on a more generalized international community and state of global peace and security, losing the specificity of the individuals and communities directly affected by international crime. In light of these problems with the commission's approaches, I conclude by questioning whether the social, legal, and political valorization of international crime—as particularly bad, a crime against *humanity*—serves to stymie rather than promote affective and ethical connections between people and communities around the world. Although insisting on the global significance of the harms that are mentioned, I nevertheless raise the possibility of understandings of international crime (and, more broadly, suffering around the world) that bring external parties closer to, rather than farther from, its specificities and nature as a lived phenomenon.

The Hold of International Crime: A Contested Incontestable

The notion of distinctly international crime is socially, culturally, and politically resonant and rich.[20] International crime is understood to be a distinctive, as well as a privileged, type of harm. As discussed in Chapter 1, uniquely international crime is contrasted with so-called ordinary or common crime. It is referred to in the commission debates as being defined by "its special character, its tone, its consistency, and its unusual dimensions."[21] As such, it might seem strange that there is no sole or authoritative approach to what constitutes an international crime. As M. Cherif Bassiouni explains, there is no "agreed-upon definition of what constitutes an international crime, the criteria for international criminalization, and how international crimes are distinguished."[22] Indeed, there is not even a consensus on how to refer to this privileged and unique form of harm, which is referred to by a variety of nomenclatures including "crimes against humanity," "international" or "universal" crime, crimes against "civilization," "crimes against the peace and security of mankind," crimes that have an "international element," and crimes that "are international by their very nature."[23] These terms are sometimes used interchangeably within a single text or statement. They are sometimes invoked as general, all-encompassing terms (for example, as including a range of more specific, legislatively defined harms such as genocide, war crimes, and so on), and at other times they are used to refer to specific articles of prohibition in particular statutes or treaties.

More substantive debate, then, focuses on how to articulate the defining characteristics of this category and what harm and historical events may accord with the preferred approach. Even the commission struggled with the task of formulating an overall definition of what it referred to as "crimes against the peace and security of mankind," stating that "members of the Commission wondered to what extent the concept of an offence against the peace and security of mankind was a homogeneous one."[24] In its first session on the Code, it opted instead for the approach of listing the harms it felt could be classified in this way, without determining whether they reflected or embodied a shared character.[25] In its second session, it again considered the difficulty of formulating a global definition of such crimes, choosing for a second time to focus on behaviors to be criminalized rather than on formulating a general definition that would then guide the identification of concrete expressions of it.[26] It also addressed such questions as whether crimes against the *peace* of humankind could be said to be of a similar nature to crimes against the *security* of humankind,[27] and it appears as though, throughout the commission's debates, different behaviors have been criminalized at different times on different bases. For example, different international crimes are distinguished on the basis of whether they affect international peace and security, the right to self-determination, or the safety of the human being.[28] Thus, despite the notion of a distinct category of special and international crime that characterizes both the commission's debates and academic work in this area, there is an acknowledgment of the potential lack of coherency of this legal category.[29] Moreover, in practice, as Bassiouni observes, there is also an enduring ambiguity about its definition: different legal textbooks take divergent approaches, with some including three or four acts, and others expanding their list to twenty-seven.[30]

In general, however, there are understood to be three or four so-called core international crimes: genocide, war crimes, crimes against humanity, and aggression. These crimes are recognized as international crimes in most legal textbooks and many statutes governing international criminal tribunals. Notably, they are also the sole focus of the jurisdiction of the ICC.

Moreover, despite many suggestions that further harms should be included in this privileged category, there is a general consensus that these included crimes are core international crimes, or crimes of the greatest importance. Torture and terrorism are regarded by some as also included in this category of exceptional harms and are anticipated—along with drug trafficking—to be formally included in it in the future.[31] Meanwhile, piracy is often described as the first international crime, at the same time as it is distinguished in nature from the current core crimes.[32] Other respected legal academics would characterize a much broader range of harms as international crimes, such as slavery, apartheid, and mercenarism.[33] And although the final draft code proposed by the commission was limited to the core crimes mentioned above (with one addition),[34] throughout both its first and second sessions a much wider field of harmful behavior was seriously discussed, including (to name just a few) the crime of colonial domination, harms against the environment, mercenarism, apartheid, economic aggression, and drug and people trafficking. Some of these were deemed at the time to be crimes that easily fell within the definition of crimes against the peace and security of mankind—particularly colonialism, apartheid, damage to the environment, crimes against diplomatic agents, and mercenarism.[35]

It is also notable that despite the frequent narrowing of the official legal category to the crimes of genocide, crimes against humanity, war crimes, and aggression, the prosecutor of the ICC regularly receives communications from outside parties regarding a more expanded list of harms (including ones from the commission's earlier discussions).[36] This may indicate the existence or endurance of a more liberal social understanding of what constitutes—in the terms of the ICC's Rome Statute—"the most serious crimes of concern to the international community as a whole." Both legal and other academics and activists also continue to lobby for both the criminalization of other serious harms and their recognition as international crimes, crimes against humanity, or forms of genocide. For example, Thomas Pogge has argued strongly for the recognition of poverty as a crime against humanity;[37] there are ongoing debates about the proper scope of the definition of genocide and whether it should protect political groups and include cultural genocide;[38] there are proposals for more sustained acknowledgment of the seriousness and criminality of harms to the environment or the mistreatment of animals;[39] and there are consistent calls from criminologists to refocus social and legal attention on state, institutional, and corporate crime.[40]

The very idea of international crime is therefore one premised on an inherent tension. On the one hand, it is understood to name something solid and incontestable. Not only is the wrongness of internationalized crime seen to be beyond debate, but there is also a presumed essence to this category. In one of the special rapporteur's reports for the commission, international crimes are described as harms "whose gravity is such that everyone must be aware of their incompatibility with the basic tenets of human society."[41] Moreover, the commission and academic texts also refer to such harms existing outside the law as moral wrongs.[42] On the other hand, the legal and socio-legal ambiguity regarding definitions of international crime and their application demonstrates that this category of crime is contextual, political, and constructed. It is *contextual* in the sense that authoritative definitions of international crime are openly acknowledged to be the outcome of social and political dynamics.[43] The very work of the commission in its two sessions—between which the potential crimes to be included varied significantly—testifies to the socially located nature of definitions of international crime, which change over time.[44] The category of international crime is also *political*: in its deliberations, the commission was guided by a commitment to articulating a feasible Code—namely, one that would be accepted by states. Its consideration of the broad question of "what constitutes an offence against the peace and security of mankind" was always already narrowed to that of "what was today generally acceptable to States?"[45] In the first session, there is a reference to striving for the "narrowest interpretation" of crimes against the peace and security of mankind for practicality's sake; and later it is observed that "the Commission was a codifier of the political will of States."[46] This approach arguably informs the desire of some commission members not to criminalize the manufacture of illegal arms, forms of retaliation to an invasion, the use of nuclear weapons, or the crime of colonial domination (although a more flexible approach was taken in the commission's first session).[47]

Thus, it can also be said that the category of international crime is ultimately *constructed*: it is the product of human decision making at particular times in particular places. This is recognized by the commission, whose reports demonstrate an acknowledgment of the arbitrariness of different approaches to defining international crime. The reports note that "even among jurists there were wide divergencies [*sic*] of view with regard to the definition of offences against the peace and security of mankind."[48]

Commission members emphasized the subjective and constructive nature of their task, observing that they were faced with a "choice among several solutions" and even that the "whole question was a matter of taste."[49] These observations, along with the social and political dynamics that shape what is criminalized and when, also therefore demonstrate the potential contestability of what the idea of international crime actually means.

However, while this may seem straightforward to acknowledge, what may remain more difficult and controversial is the recognition that the special global position of international crime is itself a social, political, historical, and cultural construction. Yet as will become clearer, a key thread in my analysis of how international crime (and international criminal justice, discussed in Chapter 4) is configured is to critique the social and political valorization of this category of harm, which the commission notes is often approached with a sense of "romanticism; a lyrical style."[50] That is, what is deemed to be significant here is not just the question of what harms should be included, but also the nature of the category and how it functions. The next section analyzes more closely what the commission considered to be the defining characteristics of this category of harm.

Writing Global Significance as Scale

The Approach of the Commission

How is this "special" and "unusual" type of criminalized harm constitutively imagined through the commission's work? Despite the diversity of approaches taken to defining international crime and the enduring debates about its essence, three common themes ran throughout the commission's deliberations. First, internationalized crimes are understood to be particularly serious. In fact, in its second session, the commission ultimately held "extreme seriousness" to be the defining characteristic of international crime.[51] International crime is distinguished by its "degree of extreme seriousness," "degree of horror and barbarity," "especial seriousness," and "particularly odious character."[52] That is, despite the commission's difficulty in articulating an all-encompassing definition of international crime, the particular seriousness of international crime is ultimately determined to be the characteristic that united the range of harms included in this category. This also seems to accord with subsequent operationalizations of the idea of international crime, such as the focus of the ICC's jurisdiction on the "*most serious* crimes of international concern" and cases of "sufficient gravity."[53]

Second, international crime is also seen to be defined by its "mass" or "large-scale" nature.[54] For commission members, a reference to mass was not necessarily related to the number of victims of certain crimes.[55] Instead, scale was predominantly conceptualized as related to the "mass nature of the crime."[56] International crimes are not merely isolated acts of extreme cruelty; rather, they are generally acts whose true character is appreciated by seeing them as one component of a broader criminal endeavor. This characteristic was often mentioned in relation to crimes against humanity in particular, which were described as "repeated acts" that are part of some "pattern," characterized by their "system, plan and repetitiveness" and constituting a "link in a chain."[57] International crime involves different criminal acts (such as rape, murder, and persecution) that are systematically perpetrated according to a common plan or joint criminal enterprise.[58] Thus, in the commission reports it is noted that "serious systematic or repeated violations" were what characterized this form of harm.[59] These discussions of the large-scale character of international crimes also intersect with an emphasis on the way in which crimes against humanity specifically target groups. They are systematic campaigns of violence directed at particular social, cultural, political, or religious groups.[60] This emphasis on systematicity also led some commission members to emphasize that international crimes "in many cases, could only be committed by States," integrally involving an "abuse of sovereignty or misuse of power"—given the resources and exercise of authority such crimes entailed.[61] Ultimately though, in its final draft of the Code, the commission still pursued a form of individual criminality responsibility popularized through the Nuremberg and Tokyo trials.[62] However, a more substantive recognition of the state-based nature of this distinctive and internationalized harm could have led to a wholly different conceptualization of this sphere of crime and justice—as one defined by its focus on accountability for state and structural harm (as it is often conceived of by human rights advocates), rather than by its concern with large-scale phenomena or the purportedly higher status of certain forms of crime and justice (see Chapter 4). This alternative conceptualization would, in turn, give rise to different relational possibilities and forms of transnational connection.

Finally, international crime is deemed to be characterized by its implications for and effects on a more generalized class of subjectivity and geography. Put simply, international crime is harm that has impacts on a broader human community and a broader state of international peace and security.[63] Such assertions start by assuming the existence of a broader, global community, which is referred to as the international community, "humanity," the "entire human race," "civilized nations," "mankind," "human society," and even "the human" or "universal conscience."[64] International crime is then defined as an offense against this community and its interests and values. International crimes are described as "crimes that assail sacred values or principles of civilization" and threaten "a fundamental interest of the international community."[65] The broad community of humanity is thus seen to be cohesive and organized, with identifiable foundations and principles. This is interesting, given that in its decision to adopt those definitions of international crime that are least contested and to avoid areas of controversy (see the discussion above), the commission also implicitly acknowledges the lack of cohesiveness of the international community and its values.

Importantly, as foreshadowed in Chapter 1, international crimes are also seen to affectively move and injure an international community. They are said to evoke "horror" in the "universal conscience" and "affect the human race wherever they are committed," as well as actually causing harm to it.[66] One special rapporteur report submitted to the commission explains that the "international dimension" of these crimes "simply means that the offences have greater repercussions in that they affect peoples, races, nations, cultures, civilizations and mankind."[67] International crimes are framed as crimes that are "directed against all the peoples of the world," with their "physical result" being "the destruction of human life in all countries."[68] As such, they are commonly described as crimes against humanity or the international community *as a whole.*

In a related way, international crimes are also conceptualized as acts that integrally affect not just a broader community, but also a wider, global state of affairs. In discussions of international crime, references are made to "international public order," "international peace and security," a "sphere of civilized nations," and "the international level."[69] Indeed, the name of the proposed draft Code itself reflects the commission's understanding of international crimes as offenses *against the peace and security of mankind* that compromise a notion of an international or universal order.[70] Thus the effect of these crimes is generalized, with the observation that they may be "directed against the lives and security of individuals or peoples but threaten or violate international peace and security."[71] This notion of international crime is particularly evident in the commission's debates about the crime of aggression, which—it was argued—was important to criminalize because of its impact on a broader sense of international peace.[72]

Scalar Imaginings

Despite their diverse emphases, these four approaches to defining international crime are arguably united by a shared iconography of internationality. The approaches have a spatial character and are spatializing—producing international crime and the international as distinctly spatial concepts. More specifically, these understandings of international crime construct it—and the quality of internationality more generally—as an inherently scalar phenomenon. Scale concerns the intersection between the perspective from which a given phenomenon is seen and how it is conceptualized in spatial terms. Scale is related to size (whether something is seen as small or large, or part of a larger whole) and height or level (whether something is seen as higher and lower).[73] Indeed, the very idea of the international or global is often presented in inherently scalar terms—as a distinct sphere or place, residing at a level that is different from or higher than the national and local (see Chapter 1).[74] But scale also affects how a given object or event is perceived.[75] For example, the use of a large scale—that is, seeing matters up close—is conventionally understood to provide a more specific view as opposed to the perspective afforded by zooming out on an issue.[76]

There are at least three ways in which the above commission understandings of international crime imply a scalar approach. First, internationality is equated with height. That is, what is apparent in commission framings of the seriousness of international crime is their comparative and hierarchical nature.[77] As mentioned in Chapter 1, international crime is often understood in contrast to other so-called ordinary crimes, as well as somehow worse, more serious, or more important than them. The existence of a hierarchy of crimes is explicitly acknowledged in the commission's debates and is central to its representation of international crime. Commission reports note that there is "a kind of hierarchy of these international crimes. Offences against the peace and security of mankind are at the top of the hierarchy. They are in a sense *the most serious of the most serious offences.*"[78] In this way, the distinctiveness of international crime, in contrast to both national crime and transnational crime, is produced as a function of scale—namely, its higher placement in an imagined hierarchy of criminalized harms.[79] Indeed, elsewhere in the commission's archives, international crimes are described as the highest form of criminal behavior, residing at the "top of the scale" or being the "most serious crimes in the scale of criminal offences."[80]

Second, in scalar terms, international crime is conceptualized as a large-scale phenomenon, in the sense of being characterized by its breadth (or its widespread nature), systematicity, and mass. By definition, international crimes are not isolated acts, and it is not possible to apprehend international crime in its specificity—as a sole act, committed at a particular time, against a particular person. The focus of definitions of international crime is on groups and populations that are targeted, and thus individual victims are apprehended as representatives of a broader collectivity.[81] Thus, in one special rapporteur's report to the commission, human rights abuses and international crimes are distinguished on the basis that "human rights violations" affect individuals. In contrast, international crime "relates to different concepts: race, nationality, and political or religious entities. It is directed against groups. . . . If such a crime affects the individual, it does so indirectly; the crime is directed against him not as an individual."[82] Thus, to properly see international crime requires a zooming out of perspective. It necessitates a way of seeing that can appreciate the fact that individual acts of violation are actually part of a broader whole. And it is this broader whole—in its entirety—that is understood as the proper object of international criminal law. Only defendants or perpetrators of international crime are consistently visualized in their individuality.

Third, international crimes are mapped subjectively and geographically onto a broader, global scale. International crimes are defined by their impact on the international community *as a whole* or a broader state of international peace and security. Notions of an international community as a whole or global peace and security writ large are inherently abstracted or generalized. They too involve a zooming out of perspective so that—for example—the international community becomes visualized as a distinct subject affected by and implicated in international crime, and the focus is on the impact of such harms on international peace or security. Again, this is a function of scale, indicating the placement and conceptualization of international crime as a phenomenon existing at a more generalized scalar level.

Scale is therefore intimately implicated in the commission's approach to internationality: it becomes one of the "general conditions on the basis of which recognition" of international crime "can and does take place."[83] It is a sense that an event is of a larger scale—the most important, widespread, and systematic, and properly located at an abstracted global level—that qualifies it as a distinctively international crime. As a norm of recognition, the frame of scale also has a regulatory effect, shaping both what can and cannot be seen and felt as an international crime, and how such harm is encountered and understood.[84] In other words, representations of scale are not natural but socially, legally, and politically constructed.[85] Moreover, they are consequential: scale may be a construct, but it has demonstrable and affective implications.[86] It is thus important to be aware of the ethical and relational implications of the construction of international crime through scale, which is what I consider next. I argue that scalar conceptions of international crime are implicated in the spectacularizing, hierarchization, and generalization of international crime, and they serve to create relational distance between people and communities who experience harm and others.

Scalar Framings and Ethical Effects: Spectacle, Occlusion, and Appropriation

International Crime as a "Spectacle of Excess"

First, apprehending international crime through the notion of scale constructs international crimes as a "spectacle of excess." This term, taken from the work of Roland Barthes on the game of wrestling, is used by him and others to refer to modes of exaggerated and dramatic signification.[87] Barthes writes of the "rhetorical amplification" and "excessive portrayal of Suffering" that characterize the wrestling match, while Njabulo Ndebele uses Barthes's work to describe "a highly dramatic, highly demonstrative form" of representation.[88] I noted in the first section of this chapter the rich symbolism associated with international crime and the commission's own recognition of the "romantic" and "lyrical" character of discussions of it. Indeed, the idea of international crime is associated with a vivid and emotive representational regime (see Chapter 1). International crimes are more generally conceptualized as crimes against *humanity*, perpetrators of international crime are labeled *hostis humani generis* (or "enemies of mankind"), and international crimes are described in the commission debates as "the most odious and most monstrous of offences," the "head of the parade of the hideous monstrosities."[89] Indeed, this understanding of international crime circulates more broadly. As David Luban notes, "the "big idea" seems to be that these are crimes whose sheer ugliness places them beyond the pale of ordinary criminality."[90] On this view, harms become international crimes once "they exceed a certain degree of seriousness" or "cruelty."[91]

In this way, scalar approaches to international crime, specifically, are implicated in its production as a spectacle of excess. It is through the commission's portrayal of international crime as "especially horrible, cruel, savage and barbarous," "the most abominable," the worst of the worst, and the apex in a hierarchy of inhumanity that international crime is spectacularized.[92] This is an exaggerated regime of representation: not in the sense that international crimes are not as atrocious or horrible as they are depicted, or in the sense that they are not difficult to represent and a challenge to traditional Western legal approaches to crime.[93] It is exaggerated in its emphasis on international crimes as exceptional, "extraordinary," and extreme—somehow beyond and excepted from everyday life, contrasted with ordinary and common crime.[94]

As a mode of signification, however, the spectacle of excess has problematic implications. For example, it simplifies and reduces at the same time as it dramatizes. Rhetorical flourish is substituted for detailed explication; complexity and nuance are sacrificed for intelligibility and understanding.[95] Thus, Barthes explains that—in the depiction of the "spectacle of excess"— "each sign . . . is therefore endowed with an absolute clarity . . . the public is overwhelmed with the obviousness" of what is being depicted.[96] Notions of international crime are characterized by a similar absoluteness. This assumption of the "obviousness" of the meaning of international crime accords with the commission's implication that it was possible to somehow intuit what harms fit in this category, despite the commission's inability to finally define it. More broadly, international crimes are depicted as inherently wrong, committed by evil masterminds and affecting innocent victims. Terms such as *genocide* can function in social and political spheres as much as forms of social and political denunciation than as explanatory terms. They are less a technical legal term and more a "symbol, with instant meaning."[97] As Alex de Waal notes, once the label of genocide is affixed to a certain event, "a single, powerful script" can be conjured up—one of unjustifiable atrocities, clear aggressors, and innocent victims.[98]

In making these observations, my point is not that it is possible to somehow justify international crimes and excuse their perpetration. Regardless of the social, political, and historical context in which they occur, such harm and injury are never justifiable. Rather, my concern is to draw on the insights of Barthes and Ndebele regarding the spectacle to demonstrate how scalar and spectacularizing forms of understanding international crime can direct attention away from more complex and multifaceted conceptualizations of it. Within the terms of the "spectacle of excess," "causality is a matter of making simple connections in order to produce the most startling and shocking results. There is very little attempt to delve into intricacies of motive or social process. People and situations are either very good or very bad."[99] And it is a similarly critical and reflective sentiment that can be traced, for example, in the work of scholars who have increasingly tried to highlight the artificiality of dominant binaries between an evil perpetrator and an innocent victim that characterize international criminal justice.[100] Their point is not that victims are somehow to blame for their suffering, but that perpetrators and victims may be the same people in different situations and that the perpetration of international crime is a more complex phenomenon than individual pathology (as demonstrated, for example, by the fact that many people involved in international crime do not continue to commit crimes following the cessation of conflict). Cases such as the ICC's prosecution of Dominic Ongwen, who had been abducted and forced to be a child soldier before being implicated in subjecting other children to this experience, are widely seen to demonstrate the fluidity between experiences of victimization and perpetration in conflict settings.[101] It is this complexity and messiness that may not be captured in simple and dramatized narratives of international crime as supreme evil, involving evil perpetrators and innocent victims. Yet it is such complexity that some survivors must live and grapple with in their everyday lives—not only the overlap between experiences of victimization and perpetration in the past, but also the presence of former perpetrators and victims within the same families and communities.[102]

Such exceptionalizing regimes of understanding international crime are also incapable of being translated into coherent sentencing regimes. Although these ideas of international crime would seem to necessitate the application of extreme sentences, in practice international criminals can receive sentences much lower than those accused of so-called common crimes and enjoy early release from their sentences.[103] These ideas also hinder a full appreciation of the continuities (as well as the differences) between international crime and national crime. This has been a key contribution of feminist international legal scholars who have demonstrated both the continuities between sexual violence inside and outside war and the continuance (and sometimes intensification) of sexual violence and gender-based crimes in nominally postconflict periods.[104] They link sexual violence in all of these instances to shared structural causes, particularly continued gender inequality.

Dramatic understandings of international crime may thus be emotively resonant without assisting broader comprehension of the nature of internationalized harms and the most just, effective, and ethical response to them.[105] The value of the "spectacle of excess" is its capacity to offer respite from the "constitutive ambiguity of everyday situations."[106] In the face of the unjust and terrible nature of events of international crime, spectacular understandings offer an intelligible framework. Moreover, ideas of perpetrators as *hostis humani generis* may nicely align with the preference of international criminal tribunals and internationalized justice processes to pursue a form of individualized retributive justice: holding accountable evil perpetrators, particularly those leaders and masterminds deemed to be the worst of the worst.[107]

Yet such processes and understandings may direct attention away from a more complex understanding of the etiology of internationalized harms and the best way to redress them.[108] Crimes such as genocide and crimes against humanity are acknowledged in the academic literature to be inherently collective crimes, defined by widespread participation and engagement.[109] For example, Alette Smeulers and Lotte Hoex show how the perpetration of international crime is a multifaceted function of personal circumstances, group dynamics, and a broader communal context.[110] They also clarify the differential involvement of various actors, from leaders who plan and orchestrate such harm and those who willingly participate in violence to those who feel compelled to do so. As a category, international crimes are unique because many perpetrators seek to abide by prevailing social norms, rather than act in ways that could be classed as deviant.[111] Thus, as Mark Drumbl has demonstrated in his analysis of justice in postconflict Rwanda, individualized forms of retributive justice may not be the best response to such experiences of both victimization and perpetration.[112]

Yet it is the lived and embodied experience of international crime that becomes difficult to connect with through its scalar and spectacular framing as the "head of the parade of the hideous monstrosities." In this way, spectacular modes of representation—which may be motivated by a desire to condemn the perpetration of international crime and underscore the seriousness of victims' suffering—may do so in a way that fosters affective and ethical distance rather than proximity.[113] Wendy Hesford draws attention to the relational significance of the "normative assumptions about the conditions of social and legal recognition" that characterize dominant approaches to visualizing and depicting human rights abuses.[114] Here, too, it can be said that using the frame of scale as a norm of recognition offers a particular way of apprehending those who have experienced internationalized harm. That is, when international crime is figured as "the most odious and most monstrous of offences," those affected by it are seen as people and communities that have been touched by or undergone something extreme. Thus, on one hand, the victim of international crime is currently a romanticized subject position (see Chapter 1). On the other hand, when appraised through the discourse of spectacle, the victim is also the one who has endured the unimaginable, the worst of the worst—the most atrocious, heinous, and hideous crimes. As such, through spectacular discourse, the victim of international crime can almost come to figure as an abject (or at least objectified) body, whereby the "unfathomability of such atrocity renders the perpetrators and the victims inaccessible and incomprehensible."[115]

This mode of recognition gives rise to limited and potentially problematic relational forms between those who are most affected by international crime (at a given point in time) and those who are not. When international crime is conceptualized in scalar and spectacular terms, victims and perpetrators are potentially placed in "uninhabitable" subject positions. They are "uninhabitable," in Butler's terms, because they are forms of existence that cannot be easily understood or related to as livable lives.[116] The subject positions of victim and perpetrator—as conceived of through a language of spectacle—are conflated with experiences so extreme that it becomes difficult, if not impossible, to understand them as recognizable and intelligible lives that are capable of being practically lived and, importantly, survived.[117] Instead, victims and perpetrators are positioned as being defined by their relation to the incomprehensible, inhumane, and heinous.[118] There is a chasm drawn between those who have not been exposed to international crime (living notionally normal lives and only being spectators of international crime) and those who have endured or even perpetrated "the most abominable" offenses. The experiences of victims are removed from the rhythms of ordinary life and, in this sense, othered. It is in this way, as Ndebele demonstrates, that spectacular modes of understanding shift attention from the ordinary and everyday toward a spectacle of the extreme.

This focus on international crime as exceptional and extreme is also socially and politically located and has political effects. "Deployments of spectacular rhetoric" explains Hesford, "advance political, cultural, and moral agendas."[119] An alternative to viewing international crime as the exceptional acts of evil individuals would be to focus on the broader social, political, cultural, and historical structural inequalities that inform such violence. It is in this vein that the spectacle of violence can "both contain and expand public engagement with human rights issues."[120] Scalar understandings of international crime might contain external engagement to a restricted focus on individual etiology. Meanwhile, a more expansive approach could emphasize the potential vulnerability of all people to state harm and organized violence. In this sense, Butler underscores the precariousness of all life, in the sense that all life relies on social, political, institutional, and environmental assistance to survive.[121] In so doing, she underscores how people's direct experiences of precarity—such as being a victim of international crime—are a function of social, political, economic, and historical inequities, or what she terms a "differential allocation of precarity."[122]

A more expansive, non-scalar, approach to international crime offers a fundamentally different understanding of the nature of suffering, one that importantly leads to different ethical and relational possibilities. It can foster a sense of proximity between those who suffer and those who do not by emphasizing the "radical substitutability" of both because both are at the mercy of the supports needed to live a safe and secure life.[123] In so doing, it may reduce the relational distance between external parties and those who have experienced international crime, placing spectators in the frame as people who too may suffer. Suffering is transformed from a subject position into a transient and contextualized experience located in time, place, politics, and history. Moreover, such an approach also invites a greater recognition of the role of external parties—from nation-states and international organizations to individual and communal bystanders—in shaping the local social, economic, and political conditions in which experiences of injustice occur. As a result, a whole range of different levels of human action and inaction come into view. This may lead to either a greater sense of the implication of external parties in notionally distant suffering or their similar subjection to unjust processes of neoliberal globalization and international social, political, and economic intervention.[124] It may also enable different conceptualizations of international crime, as a form of harm fundamentally implicating the state and related institutions of power. Or it may facilitate discussions about the responsibility of the community in which such state-perpetrated harm is allowed to occur.[125] Such reframing may, in turn, lead to fundamentally different questions regarding justice and injustice—questions of what constitutes injustice, who is responsible for it, and why?

Affective Hierarchies

Scalar understandings of international crime can also serve to discount the broader global significance of other forms of suffering. Through the imagination of a hierarchy of crime, the commission's approaches to international crime implicitly devalue other harm and its broader implications.[126] Such devaluing is evident in the commission's debates, in which injuries—such as grievous bodily harm—are described as "merely correctional" or "trifling" offenses.[127] There is also a reference to the Code being "weakened," and an observation that the "essential considerations" would be lost if the category of international crime was too inclusive.[128] The valorization of international crime therefore works by way of subjugation, its power dependent on its exclusive and exclusionary character.

This creates a paradox whereby the occurrence of certain crimes becomes a source of inspiration for a sense of global responsibility and interconnectedness, but an emphasis on their exceptional nature (vis-à-vis other harm) can serve to stymie engagement with other forms of violence and suffering.[129] As Mahmood Mamdani notes in relation to genocide specifically, "more and more, universal condemnation is reserved for only one form of mass violence—genocide—as the ultimate crime, so much so that counterinsurgency and war appear to be normal developments."[130] In relation to the Rwandan genocide, for example, it has been claimed that the focus on the genocidal character of the violence (which is now known as the genocide against the Tutsi) has served to downplay the suffering and loss occasioned by the contemporaneous civil war, and particularly the harms experienced by Rwandan Hutus as part of that war or due to their resistance to the genocide.[131]

Yet to place different experiences of violence in hierarchical relation to each other is clearly disrespectful and artificial. Indeed, genocide and other forms of violence, such as civil war, are qualitatively different (just as every separate event of international crime is a unique phenomenon).[132] Yet there is no necessity for one to be placed above the other or considered as more important. By applying Michael Rothberg's argument regarding memory in another context, it is possible to argue that there is not a finite amount of violence that can be acknowledged and responded to globally.[133] It is not inevitable that a recognition of certain harms necessitates the implicit devaluation of others. On the contrary, the capacity for international crimes to inspire a sense of communal responsibility and outrage is evidence of the possibilities that exist for thinking about the broader significance of suffering in the world.[134]

Ultimately, international crimes have a restrictive legal definition—the term *genocide*, for example, refers solely to certain specified acts committed against certain groups with the requisite intent. Not all crimes deserving of international attention and condemnation will necessarily fit this definition. But the potential inherent in the way that the labels of "genocide" or "crimes against humanity" can inspire a sense of global connectedness should be seized upon and enhanced, rather than unduly restricted.[135] The affective force of these terms could act as a springboard for the development of further emotive and material relations between those who have experienced suffering and those who have not. When international crimes are defined in a comparative and hierarchical way, this expansive approach is shut out because it threatens the exclusiveness and related power of the international crime frame. The existence of a hierarchy of crimes also gestures again to the ethical quandaries associated with the valorization of certain harm as especially important, despite the apparent ethics of such a claim.

Zooming Out: Mass Harm and Appropriation

Finally, configuring internationality as inherently scalar has important implications for how international crime is viewed and, relatedly, where and to whom it is seen to belong. Scale integrally shapes how a matter is both understood and perceived.[136] For example, Boaventura De Sousa Santos explains that a "close-up" perspective "is rich in details and features; describes behaviour and attitudes vividly; contextualises them in their immediate surroundings; is sensitive to distinctions (and complex relations)."[137] This means, according to him, that a choice of scale fundamentally affects *what* is even apprehended as being seen. He explains that "different forms of law create different legal objects upon eventually the same social objects. They use different criteria to determine the meaningful details and the relevant features. . . . In sum, they create different legal realities."[138] The point is therefore not just that zooming in provides a detailed view, and zooming out provides a generalized, abstract view of the same phenomenon (indeed, there could be just as intricate a picture sketched of high-scale issues and dynamics).[139] Rather, De Sousa Santos shows how the nature of the subject or object that is perceived is constituted (in part) by the scale at which it is viewed. Conceiving of international crime through a logic of scale shapes what international crime is apprehended to be, entail, and affect.

As discussed earlier, international crime is defined as inherently large-scale or mass harm that implicates and affects an international community and a global state of peace and security. In this way, the concept of international crime is dependent on a sort of zooming out, whereby discrete acts against specific individuals can be conceptualized as component parts of a broader pattern of international criminality. This frame shapes how the specific individuals and communities affected by international crime are apprehended by others. In a way that is reflective of broader humanitarian discourse and spectatorship (adopting what Christine Schwöbel-Patel deems to be a "fundraising image of victimhood"), through a scalar conception of international crime, the people injured by such crime are primarily conceived of as part of a mass or wider victimized population.[140] They are visualized (to borrow Liisa Malkki's words now) as part of a "singular category of humanity," and it becomes difficult to discern their individuality.[141] Thus, as well as being conceived of as apolitical and nonagentic subjects (as discussed in Chapter 1), victims of international crime are also stripped of the "very particulars that make of people something other than anonymous bodies, merely human beings."[142] This has important relational implications, stymieing an appreciation by outsiders of the individuality and specificity of victims of international crime. This in turn shapes what forms of interpersonal, intercultural, and intercommunal engagement are made possible, arguably compromising the potential for substantive, contextualized, and particularized engagement between those who have experienced internationalized harm and those who have not.

In addition to shaping how victims of international crime can be perceived, configurations of scale also determine what and who international crime is understood to affect and involve. Conceived of as a high-scale matter, international crime becomes associated with other generalized and high-scale notions: "universal values," a broader state of "international peace and security", an "international level," the "*entire* human race," and "human kind."[143] Geographically, international crimes are seen to reside or occur in an imagined international sphere, and subjectively, attention is focused on their effect on and implications for a common humanity. Thus, although zooming out makes it difficult to appreciate individuality and specificity, it makes it possible to see the world as a whole, conceive of the diverse peoples in the world as forming a common humanity, and understand this common humanity as having a stake in specific events of international crime.[144] It is by zooming out that subjectivities become inherently generalized and international crimes are understood as harms that "affect peoples, races, nations, cultures, civilizations and mankind."[145] It is also by zooming out that diverse events of international crime—from the Rwandan genocide to the Cambodian genocide, ethnic cleansing in the former Yugoslavia, and crimes against humanity and war crimes in East Timor and Sierra Leone—become comparable as similar manifestations of a broader, abstracted category of international criminality.[146] Configurations of scale, therefore, situate, contextualize, and orient.[147]

Hence, a shift in scale entails a movement, a transformation: "in order to get from one to another, a change must take place, a work must be done."[148] As such, when internationality is equated with scale, the internationalization of an event or category of harm (its construction as international) involves its *re*situation and *re*contextualization. It has to be placed in an international order and associated with a different regime of subjectivities. For example, in the distinction of the special rapporteur between human rights abuses and international crime (mentioned earlier in this chapter), the subjective affiliation of the harm shifts: "in the case of the former, it is the individual whose fundamental rights are infringed, whereas in the case of the latter, the offences concern all of mankind."[149] The special rapporteur thus observes, as noted above, that "if such a crime affects the individual, it does so indirectly; the crime is directed against him not as an individual." Hannah Arendt makes a similar claim regarding the Holocaust—that "the physical extermination of the Jewish people, was a crime against humanity," although one "perpetrated upon the body of the Jewish people."[150] This understanding of the Holocaust underpins the argument that the trial of Adolf Eichmann should have occurred in an international forum because the "crime against the Jewish people was *first of all* a crime against mankind."[151] Hence the observation of the International Panel of Eminent Personalities in its inquiry regarding the Rwandan genocide that "genocide, almost by definition, becomes the world's property."[152]

In this way, internationalization, as scale, becomes an appropriative move. To establish an event or crime as international or global it must be understood to exist outside its specific social, historical, political, and cultural context. To be international is to become situated elsewhere, to affect others, to concern broader states and subjectivities.[153] This mode of thinking about internationality significantly compromises the relational forms that emerge from claims of the international character of a certain event or form of harm. From this perspective, the international implications of an event are not embedded in its material and lived occurrence, but rather in its effects on other states and subjectivities elsewhere. Arguably, this encourages external parties not so much to relate directly to particular communities and their unique experiences as to appreciate that a seemingly particular event is actually more generally situated and important (or, more narcissistically, has implications for them). Claims that certain suffering properly belongs to certain global orders establish the global and the local as competing rather than coexisting spheres. Moreover, such claims of ownership can serve to construct experiences of injustice as a form of property, at the same time as the victims are denied their "proprietary" rights. In turn, a potential conflict can arise between those who were directly affected and those who speak in humanity's name—because, as Luban notes, "humanity's interest may differ from the interests of the victims."[154]

However, it should be acknowledged that the appropriative character of this approach to internationality is a function of a contestable understanding of both scale and internationality. First, scale is understood as a fixed and hierarchical relation of levels: an independent and separate global, national, and local.[155] Yet, as mentioned earlier, conceptions of scale are socially constructed, and global and local scales can be conceptualized as coexistent, rather than competing.[156] Second, international significance and import need not be tied to the effect of a certain act and injury on others elsewhere, or on a more generalized humanity or global peace. Although scale is an enduring characteristic of the iconography of international law more generally (through which internationality has historically been associated with scope and size),[157] the international need not be configured as a particular place associated with particular subjectivities. International significance could instead be found in the specificity of the lives of those most affected by international crime—a form of connection that often spontaneously happens when people are exposed to the stories and experiences of others.

Taken as a whole, scalar understandings of international crime seem to imply the imagination of a particular seeing subject, as well as being premised on a duality of subjectivities.[158] International crime is conceptualized in ways that other and objectify victims and perpetrators, who are defined by their association with the atrocious, hideous, and extreme. It appears as most accurately apprehended from a distance (by zooming out) as a phenomenon affecting others than its direct victims. As Hesford argues in relation to human rights, such approaches to international crime are thus premised on an implied distinction between those who experience international crime and those who apprehend it, giving preference to the perspective of the latter in defining the phenomenon. This is a form of acknowledging suffering that therefore professes a global interconnectedness—that crimes against certain people are crimes against "us" all—while also offering (in Hesford's words) a form of hierarchical relation "wherein the spectator is configured as the holder of rights and as their distributor to those who are unable to claim them independently."[159] However, this is an observation about the perspective and subjectivities implied by the commission's representations of international crime, not a claim about whether those who experience such harm might perceive it as affecting humanity, particularly horrible, or as part of a broader plan.

International Crime as Life That Is Lived

> The ordinary day-to-day lives of people should be the direct focus of political interest because they constitute the *very content* of the struggle, for the struggle involves people not abstractions.
> —Njabulo Ndebele, "The Rediscovery of the Ordinary"

In his work on the spectacle, Ndebele calls for a "rediscovery of the ordinary," "the forcing of attention on necessary detail," and complexity.[160] He and Barthes problematize the tendency within spectacular modes of representation to simplify and reduce through a substitution of interiority for exteriority.[161] This mode of representation, Ndebele argues, "calls for emotion rather than conviction; it establishes a vast sense of presence without offering intimate knowledge; it confirms without necessarily offering a challenge."[162] In this way, the commission's approaches to international crime as a whole adopt a spectacular orientation, and so arguably do many other forms of social, legal, and political representation of international crime (including academic ones). They offer their audiences a clear and unambiguous image of abhorrent and intentional mass harm and a global community seized to address it (see Chapter 1). They invite an understanding of international crime as involving unjustified injury, innocent victims, and evil perpetrators. Furthermore, they foreclose more complicated, contextual, and complex engagements with international crime as a distinctive form of harm and the wide range of people it affects and implicates.[163] As such, through scalar understandings of international crime, the specific lives of individuals and communities injured by international crime are lost; the complexity, context, and causes of international crime are lost; and the capacity for external parties to connect with other, different forms of violence in the world is lost.[164]

I have shown how an emphasis on the special and unique nature of internationalized harm—an emphasis that could be understood as an ethical and humanitarian claim—can serve to reduce the capacity of those who have not suffered (at any given moment in time) to meaningfully connect with those who have. However, because of their apparent claim to ethics, it is difficult to challenge conceptions of international crime as a privileged and special category of criminal behavior. As with other situations of spectacular representation, these conceptions are now "conventional."[165] To question the spectacular and extraordinary frame through which international crimes are viewed could thus itself be labeled as a potentially unethical enterprise, an amoral and unhelpful critique of the rightful acknowledgment of the place and significance of such harms in the world. In this sense, though, it also becomes possible to appreciate the normative hold and political power of the idea of international crime.[166] And given the problematic relational consequences of existing understandings, it remains important to ask (in Butler's words) "what new norms are possible, and how are they wrought? What might be done to produce a more egalitarian set of conditions for recognizability" for internationalized harm?[167] Part of this inquiry involves questioning whether the societal and legal privileging and valorization of international crime is indeed implicated in the problematic ethical and relational consequences of the extant modes of defining it.

From this perspective, there may be potential in the continued uncertainty of how to define international crimes and debates about what harms "deserve" to be placed in this category. Perhaps these ongoing discussions signify an opening—a possibility of continuing to think about the place and work of this idea and alternative approaches. For current approaches to international crime are not natural or inevitable; international crime is conceptualized in other ways, and scalar conceptions can be contested.[168] Indeed, the possibility of different definitions of and approaches to international crime is evident in the more expansive social applications of terms such as *genocide* and *crimes against humanity*. While they can be discounted in the public sphere on the basis that some of them do not accord with the real or actual legal definitions, this may also misrecognize the nature and power of such claims. Social and political activists who invoke the label of *genocide* to describe certain harms may themselves not be referring to the legal definition found in the *Convention on the Prevention and Punishment of the Crime of Genocide*. They may instead be using the term in a way that refers to social conceptions of it and may seek to capitalize on its sociopolitical power. That is, they may be deliberately using the term exactly as their critics suggest: untethered from its legal meaning, but to emphasize the global importance or salient characteristics of a particular occurrence.

Thus, in the Australian settler-colonial context, Eualeyai/Kamillaroi woman Larissa Behrendt writes about the "distance between law and life," highlighting how the failure of Anglo-Australian legal and political systems to officially recognize genocide in that country do not account for "the feeling Indigenous people have that this is the word that adequately describes our experience as colonised peoples."[169] She describes genocide in Australia as an "event" that has unfolded over several generations, through intersecting and complex governmental policies and acts, and involving many people. Pertinently, she argues: "For Indigenous plaintiffs, it doesn't matter whether the crime of genocide was committed as it was defined by international law. . . . What seems to be more important from the Indigenous perspectives are the *effects* of the actions of the government. . . . This moves the discussion outside of the words of the statute to the side-effects and legacies of those sanctioned actions."[170] Meanwhile, in his work focusing on settler-colonial genocide in Canada, Andrew Woolford also makes it clear that "as a sociologist" he is "not interested in adjudicating this case according to an official legal definition of genocide," because "rigid legal concepts can interfere with understanding the social nature of group destruction. It can flatten the analysis of group relations. It can serve as a hammer to pound a complicated history into a singular event."[171]

Butler suggests that for frames to be dominant and authoritative, they must be widely invoked and applied. As such, in their application in different situations and circumstances, they "break" with the original context of their formulation. It is in such a breaking that Butler identifies the possibility for both questioning and destabilizing the inevitability and power of dominant representational modes, enabling "a new trajectory of affect."[172] In this way, alternative social uses of international crime terminology may underscore the inadequacy of existing legal definitions that fail to fully capture a broader societal sense of what events of harm demand external attention, sanction, and response. Or they may spark a willingness to recognize how the act of valorizing certain harms can delegitimize others and encourage an exploration of how the sense of global solidarity associated with crimes such as genocide could be used as inspiration to further ethical and affective engagement with other forms of harm. Or they may prompt a reconsideration of whether the global interconnection imagined through the image of international crime is one that needs to be exclusive to be made meaningful. The imperative in considering such alternatives lies in the cultural, gender, and other biases that in practice shape what comes to be seen as sufficiently serious, and hence recognizable as an international crime.[173] The next chapter too considers the possibility of alternative approaches to expressing and enacting cross-cultural connection, following my critique of representations of international justice as also fundamentally disconnected from ordinary life.

4

The Ideal of International Criminal Justice

Transcendence, Otherness, Myth

> Law operates in a social world yet exists separate from and dominant over it. Law can relate integrally to that world without being existentially exhausted in the relation. It provides a principle and point of transcendent order and unity for the diversity of social relations.
>
> . . . Thus modern law emerges, in a negative exaltation, as universal in opposition to the particular, as unified in opposition to the diverse, as omnicompetent in contrast to the incompetent, and as controlling of what has to be controlled.
>
> —Peter Fitzpatrick, *The Mythology of Modern Law*

THE INTERNATIONAL COURT OF JUSTICE in The Hague is a grand institution. It is housed in the Peace Palace, a building that lives up to its palatial name. The Peace Palace has the look and feel of a royal residence: it is a stately brick edifice in a neo-Renaissance style, foregrounded by a lawn dotted with trees. Inside the building, high ceilings, stained glass windows, chandeliers, and walls adorned by huge oil paintings provide a sense of formality and ceremony. It feels like a special place, and it feels momentous to be here, at this international court of justice.

I attended the Court's hearings in the *Application of the Convention on the Prevention and Punishment of the Crime of Genocide (Croatia v. Serbia)*. During a break in the hearings, I approached a security guard. As I was unable to stay for all of the next session, and given the importance of this place and the harms being discussed, I asked him about the correct protocol for leaving mid-session. Based on the convention in Australia, I asked him whether I should stand and bow toward the judges, before leaving quietly.[1] He laughed in response and said that it was not necessary to bow, as "this is not Japan." His statement struck me in the way that it literally brought the ideal of international justice down to ground. Indeed, we were not in Japan, we were somewhere else. And we were not nowhere—somehow groundless, placeless, outside culture and history, as international justice is often implicitly imagined to be. We were in The Hague in the Netherlands, as was affirmed by my visit to the neighboring International Criminal Court at which court materials were translated into Dutch—a local language, but not an official language of the court. The security guard's statement that "this is not Japan" was one that was emplaced in and referred to a specific time and place. In grounding international criminal justice as a legal practice unfolding in a particular time, geographical space, and cultural context, the guard did something that was refreshingly different from many of the dominant representations and understandings of international criminal justice.

In this chapter, I interrogate mainstream understandings of distinctly international criminal justice, which is frequently portrayed as transcending and separate from the social, political, cultural, and historical contexts in which it works. My discussion is based on an analysis of a range of official representations of the International Criminal Court (ICC) in particular—the public materials on the ICC's website, the opening statements of delegates at the Rome Conference at which its founding statute was finalized and adopted, and the *Rome Statute of the International Criminal Court* (hereafter, Rome Statute) itself.[2] The ICC occupies a special place in the imaginary of international criminal justice, often being described as both a "truly international" institution and the ultimate realization of the international criminal justice project (despite being an embodiment of particular social, cultural, historical, and political dynamics).[3]

In contrast to international crime, I found it hard to locate one site (or set of texts) at which the notion of international criminal justice is debated and defined. Indeed, I started my analysis by interviewing people working in and with the ICC and international criminal justice more broadly. However, my interviewees often responded to my questions about the internationality of international criminal justice with as much curiosity as I had—explaining that it was interesting to have the opportunity to reflect upon these questions and offering a range of different answers (some consistent, some distinct from each other) that often seemed exploratory rather than definitive. In academic and practitioner texts, the concept of international criminal justice is also often (somewhat problematically) assumed to be a shared "constant" or starting point (with discussions focusing instead on evaluating its performance, goals, and utility).[4] Similarly, I found that the key public materials of the ICC do not often address this question explicitly or in much depth. Thus, they are supplemented here with my analyses of the opening statements of delegates to the Rome Conference and the court's statute. My argument also draws out this relative lack of debate on the definition of international criminal justice and theorizes that silence (or lack) as central to how international criminal justice—as an idea and practice—has been given meaning.

In this chapter, I demonstrate how the special character of international criminal justice is tied to its constitutive otherness and externality to everyday life in the world. That is, the identity of international criminal justice is clarified not through direct definition, but through its contrast with the national and the local. In its contrast with national politics and impunity and with local harm and devastation, international criminal justice finds its identity as other. Indeed, I argue that the idea of international criminal justice is somewhat exhausted through this contrast—as a concept, international criminal justice is defined most substantively by what it is not, rather than by a sense of its positive attributes. To recall Peter Fitzpatrick's description of modern law above, international criminal justice also "emerges" primarily "in a negative exaltation, as universal in opposition to the particular." It is only through comparison with a particularized national and the local, the specific, and the lived that the idea of international criminal justice gains its unique identity as: geographically, politically, and culturally transcendent; above culture, politics, and territory; and operating "in a social world" yet existing "separate from and dominant over it."

Again, my concern in this book is with the ethical and relational implications of such definitions of internationality and international criminal justice. I show here how, as with international crime, international criminal justice is valorized and idealized, frequently presented as a humanitarian and progressive global enterprise. Moreover, I explain how, as with international crime, the special identity of international criminal justice is dependent on its constitutive distinction from the everyday. By definition and most substantively, international criminal justice is other to and disconnected from life as it unfolds in the world: its distinctiveness *is* its transcendence of geography, culture, and politics. Thus, I continue here my critique of modes of imagining internationality and international crime and justice that serve to create distance between international criminal justice and life as it is lived and, particularly, the lives and contexts of those most directly affected by international crime.

Yet I am also especially concerned in this chapter with demonstrating the mythical quality of the ideal of international criminal justice. As Fitzpatrick has argued about modern law, the ideal of international criminal justice is mythological. It is at once a "constant" (a socio-legal construct understood in similar ways by both critics and advocates) and a concept characterized by a series of tensions and contradictions.[5] For even as international criminal justice is defined in contrast to the national, it is acknowledged to be a creature of nation-states; even as it is conceptualized as other to the local, it is also recognized as having a material existence, unfolding in particular times and spaces. As such, in this chapter, I draw out these contradictions not simply to demonstrate the social and cultural distinctiveness of international criminal justice or call for more localized responses to international crime. Rather, inspired by the work of Fitzpatrick (although using it to my own ends), I seek to make visible the operation of myth in current approaches to international criminal justice, which are as engaging and important as they are unfulfilled and problematic. There is no actually existing form of authorless, transcendent justice that embodies best practice and operates beyond reproach. Nor, I would submit, is such justice desirable or achievable. Yet this concept of international criminal justice is currently powerful, one used to authorize and legitimate new forms of global power (the building of new institutions, the establishment of new professions, and the development of legal frameworks). However, it is an ideal that should be unsettled because of its artificiality and undesirability. Such an unsettling would provide the space to think about new ontologies of international engagement with the suffering of others, including those "actually existing" forms of solidarity and interconnection that are grounded in particularity and the relation of specific groups to other specific groups.[6]

I start my discussion by outlining the contemporary idealization of international criminal justice, before discussing how this ideal is given content. I then offer two key critiques of current understandings of international criminal justice: first, that they separate international criminal justice from ordinary life and, second, that they are as problematic as they are inspiring. Together, both tendencies demonstrate the need to be aware of the power effects of the idea of international criminal justice and the need to interrogate, rather than unquestioningly accept, it. In making these arguments, as in Chapter 3, my focus is on both the content of the concept of international criminal justice and its contemporary valorization.

"The Cause of All Humanity": An Ambiguous Ideal

Marking the official establishment of the ICC in 1998, then secretary-general of the United Nations Kofi Annan famously declared that the court was "a gift of hope to future generations," and in 2003 he stated that it embodied the "cause of all humanity."[7] His sentiment is striking less for its rhetorical flourish than for its consistency with dominant portrayals of international criminal justice. At the opening session of the Rome Conference, delegates spoke about their divergent priorities regarding the negotiation of the court's statute, but they agreed on the significance and importance of international justice itself. They described the potential establishment of a permanent international criminal court as an "aspiration of the international community," one that would mark a "monumental step in the name of human rights and the rule of law" and "would make the world a more just, safer and more peaceful place."[8] More broadly, the court is lauded as a progressive and humanitarian institution, a "humanitarian ideal of justice" whose establishment would represent "a great step forward."[9] It describes itself as a "milestone in humankind's efforts towards a more just world."[10] Through such rhetoric, international justice appears as both a "dream" realized and a "bastion of hope" for the future.[11] It is framed as a distinctive and humanitarian global enterprise that uniquely addresses an "urgent need" for justice and law that exists but has not—until this point—been met.[12]

Indeed, international criminal justice institutions have been tasked with achieving a range of ambitious and important goals. International courts are portrayed as able to end impunity for international crimes through holding individuals accountable; achieve general and specific deterrence, thereby preventing further crimes; establish the international rule of law necessary for global peace and security; recognize and serve the needs of victims; create a historical record; and, more so in the past, enable societal reconciliation.[13] There is now more cautiousness in the academic literature about the ability of international criminal courts to fulfill these expectations,[14] but they are nevertheless the ones associated with the courts' operation. Indeed, even when pared back to the more selective goals of ending impunity for international crimes and thereby contributing to their prevention, the ICC sets impressive targets for itself.[15]

In practice, however, the possible breadth of activities and institutions to which the term *international criminal justice* might refer is delimited by a series of successive synecdoches, in which the part comes to stand for the whole. First, the term *international criminal justice* is primarily used to describe the development and work of international criminal courts and tribunals that have been established to prosecute individuals for their involvement with certain crimes. For example, Christine Chung, a former ICC attorney, claimed that "the Rome Statute, in short, creates both a court and an international criminal justice system."[16] A more expansive conception of international criminal justice as, for instance, a project encompassing a variety of mechanisms and activities focused on both the prevention and punishment of criminalized harm—underpinned by key philosophies, theories, and goals—is not at issue. This is in comparison to the more comprehensive notion of criminal justice at the national level, where criminal justice systems are understood to include policing, judicial, and imprisonment arms as well as (increasingly in Western countries such as Australia) innovative and perhaps more substantive justice processes, such as neighborhood justice centers, where a defendant will appear in a court but also have access to a range of social services located at the same court.[17] It is also possible to think of globally located justice as relating more broadly to "social struggles against poverty and for access to basic services."[18] Instead, even if it is associated with broader and more comprehensive transitional justice processes, the notion of international criminal justice is mainly associated with the establishment of international judicial bodies that prosecute and judge individual defendants for their responsibility for international crimes. In this way, as Kamari M. Clarke and others have demonstrated, international criminal justice has come to stand for an approach to both criminality and justice that locates responsibility for mass harm with individual political and societal leaders through a punitive system of prosecution and accountability that is undertaken in the name of the victim.[19]

Second, the remit of international criminal justice is then further delimited through its equation with the establishment of certain historically and socially particular international criminal courts. Mainstream narrations of the field of international criminal justice begin with the Nuremberg and Tokyo trials in the aftermath of World War II, which introduced the principle of individual accountability for mass harm and adjudicated some of the core types of international crime that are still prosecuted today.[20] There is considered then to be an interval in the development of international criminal justice, which began again in the early 1990s—after the Cold War—with the establishment of the ad hoc International Criminal Tribunal for the former Yugoslavia and the International Criminal Tribunal for Rwanda.[21] These tribunals were followed by a variety of different international or internationalized criminal justice institutions—the so-called hybrid international/national courts in East Timor, Sierra Leone, Cambodia, Lebanon, and Kosovo—and the development of the first permanent ICC in 1998.[22] These courts are both the institutions of international criminal justice and, in practice, the main form in which it has been realized. It is in this sense, for example, that the more generic World Day for International Justice (July 17) takes place on the anniversary of the adoption of the Rome Statute.

Of course, from a broader perspective of postconflict justice, such international criminal courts can be (and are often in practice) appraised as simply one initiative among many designed to help societies deal with their experiences of systematic, state, and mass harm.[23] International criminal trials are only one component of broader transitional justice models, which are more likely to be located in the countries in which the conflicts occurred and involve a series of interconnected justice-based responses (including national trials, truth commissions, reparations and apologies, memorialization, vetting, and other rule of law reforms).[24] Accountability for international crimes can be (and is) also pursued through domestic prosecutions in the affected country or in other countries through the invocation of universal jurisdiction.[25] Yet although international criminal justice can be helpfully contextualized in this way, and thereby de-seated as the only and preeminent way of dealing with international crime, the valorized notion of international criminal justice still retains a distinct personality and meaning tethered to the institutions, goals, and aspirations mentioned above.

However, despite the significance accorded to the project of international criminal justice, there has historically been a relative dearth of engagement with the question of what makes international criminal justice institutions distinctly international or distinctive per se (although such work is starting to emerge).[26] Indeed, Gideon Boas observes that "what is understood by the phrase 'international criminal justice' is surprisingly difficult to articulate comprehensively."[27] Meanwhile, key descriptions of institutions such as the ICC refer, for example, to its jurisdiction (it "tries individuals charged with the gravest crimes"), its aims ("in a global fight to end impunity . . . to hold those responsible"), and its key features as a court (independence, permanence, emphasis on due process, and victim participation).[28] In contrast to the extensive debates about what constitutes an international crime or a crime against humanity (see Chapter 3), there has been a comparatively limited discussion regarding what makes a court a distinctively *international* one, representative of humanity and its causes.

To be sure, distinctions are drawn between national, local, and international courts (as will be discussed below), and hybrid courts are described as having national and international elements (relating mainly to their funding, legal framework, location, and staff, but also to their high standards), attaching the quality of internationality to specific tribunal characteristics.[29] And there is a critique of the particular way in which international criminal justice has developed—for example, as privileging an individualistic, retributive form of justice.[30] The Rome Conference also included many discussions about the design of one particular justice institution (namely, the ICC), which considered issues such as the scope of the prosecutor's independent powers, the relationship of the court to the United Nations (UN) Security Council, how the court should be funded, what crimes it should focus on, and whether it should have universal jurisdiction.[31] Throughout these discussions, however, the already existing ideal of a distinctive form of international criminal justice was often taken as a shared starting point. Thus, it was observed at the Rome Conference that "no State had contested the need for an international criminal court. The issue was what kind of court it should be."[32] As Fitzpatrick argues in relation to modern law, the idea of an international criminal justice—or a distinctively international criminal court—appears as a stable and coherent object, and the focus is on its particular configuration and remit.[33]

This could be attributable to the tautological definition of international criminal justice as justice administered by institutions created through international law. On this account, international criminal justice might simply refer to institutions established through international legal instruments and bodies such as the UN that are already deemed to be "international".[34] This fits with the implicit suggestion made in some of the literature that international crimes, laws, and institutions belong to and emerge from a shared, self-contained international legal order (see Chapter 1). Thus, delegates at the Rome Conference observed that "a permanent international court would make an important contribution to public international order."[35] The notion of a somewhat independent international or global sphere is taken as the context, and an international criminal court is framed as a necessary complementary institution—"the missing link in the world legal order," the "missing element" that would "fill a gap."[36] In other contexts, international criminal justice institutions are often framed as a necessary response to international crimes. One special rapporteur of the International Law Commission states that "after the experiences of mankind during two world wars of this century there undoubtedly is an urgent desire for such jurisdiction."[37] Hannah Arendt similarly contends in relation to the Holocaust that "the very monstrousness of the events is 'minimized' before a tribunal that represents one nation only."[38] International crime and international justice are seen to match in their extreme and privileged nature; the ICC "soars with the loftiest of ideals as it grapples with the basest of human acts."[39] While international crime is seen as the most atrocious harm, international justice is viewed as a "gold-standard" response. Again, such a definition is somewhat tautological, in the sense that one must be able to define what is distinctive about international law and international crimes to then understand why international criminal courts constitute the most "fitting" response.[40]

The lack of debate about the internationality of international criminal justice perhaps reflects the dominance of international legal perspectives in this field.[41] From an international legal perspective, as evinced in the early International Law Commission's debates about the establishment of an international criminal jurisdiction, the innovation is more centered on whether it was "desirable to establish a judicial organ for the trial of international crimes," to introduce "penal justice" to the already existing international law terrain.[42] In contrast, it is from a criminological perspective that the internationality of international criminal justice might be seen as its distinguishing feature.[43] For criminologists who have traditionally focused on crime and criminal justice within national jurisdictions, what might be more striking about this new field is the development of distinctly international versions of crime and criminal justice. On this view, the relative absence of discussion about the internationality of the international criminal justice project may reflect the continued dominance of legal practitioners and scholars in the field of international criminal justice.

However, simply to define international criminal justice as a legal institution belonging to a particular international legal order misses something important. As is evidenced by the discursive privileging of international criminal justice, the notion of international criminal justice is clearly understood to symbolize something more than simply a judicial enforcement body created through an international treaty or Security Council resolution.[44] Although this definition of international criminal justice is clearly accurate, the powerful idea of international criminal justice connotes something more. As with the idea of international crime, there is much invested in the notion of international criminal justice. Moreover, there is a sense of global interconnection and ethics associated with it. The ICC is understood to speak in the name of, and to represent, humanity, and international justice is valorized as a best-practice response to international crimes.[45] For example, the Coalition for the International Criminal Court explains that through maintaining "the very highest standards," "the ICC can set the bar for justice standards around the world."[46] According to this view, international criminal courts can maintain the most robust and defensible fair trial standards and be staffed by experts in the fields of international, criminal, and humanitarian law and human rights. All these elements of international criminal courts are emphasized in the ICC's materials—which explicitly state that the court "observes the highest standards of fairness and due process," demonstrated by the fact that "the Prosecution is independent," "defendants' rights are upheld," and Court staff members, from the Registry to the Judiciary divisions, are people with "high" qualifications and of "high moral character" working to the "highest standards of efficiency, competency and integrity."[47] Even the ICC detention facilities are demarcated as embodying "the highest international human rights standards for the treatment of detainees."[48] The notion of scalar height is firmly embedded in the imaginary of international criminal justice, with delegates to the Rome Conference referring to the "high standards of international criminal law and justice" and the potential for the ICC to serve as a "model of excellence."[49] Again, as with international crime, international criminal justice is figured as residing at the top of a hierarchy of justice forms.

Thus, if international crime can be framed (as I did in Chapter 3) as a contested incontestable (a debated but also natural concept), international criminal justice emerges as an ambiguous incontestable (an undefined but powerful concept). In the next section of this chapter, I substantiate this claim by demonstrating the transcendental character of the privileged notion of international criminal justice, which is predominantly defined through its contrast with a pathologized and particularized national and local other.

Making Justice International:
Otherness and Transcendence

In its valorized state as a "bastion of hope in a troubled world,"[50] international criminal justice is most clearly defined by what it is not. Like modern law, the ideal of international criminal justice is produced in "negative exaltation."[51] The dominant image of a distinctively international form of justice is constituted through its contrast with a much more detailed and specific image of national justice and local harm. It is through a series of oppositions between national justice, national crime, local communities, and local injustice, on the one hand, and international justice, on the other hand, that the notion of a unique form of international justice is produced. This way of conceptualizing international criminal justice has two key features: first, distinctively international criminal justice is defined not so much by what it is as by what it is not; and second, international criminal justice emerges as most definitively other. That is, through this contrast, international justice is constructed as that which is constitutively external and other to life as it is lived on the ground, and the internationality of international criminal justice becomes equated with its uniquely nonlocal and nonnational nature.

International Justice as Other Than

First, international criminal justice—and the ICC—are figured in contrast to the national.[52] At a basic level, the very need for the ICC's existence is established through an image of national lack and failure. That is, international criminal justice is designed to end impunity for those who commit international crimes, "to ensure that persons guilty of the most heinous crimes did not go unpunished."[53] This impunity is found at the national level, where a different historical trajectory to international justice is charted—not one of redress and accountability, but one of a continued failure of nation-states to prosecute people (particularly leaders) for their involvement in crimes such as genocide and crimes against humanity. As one delegate to the Rome Conference explained, "it was precisely because that [national justice] was not always effective that an international court was needed."[54] And the ICC materials affirm that it operates "when the national authorities have failed."[55] From this perspective, the focus is on the deficiencies of national courts to justify the need for different, international ones. This can be seen more recently in the call from investigators contracted by the UN for a "'truly international'" tribunal for the Central African Republic because they "do not believe that national judges have that type of independence."[56] Sometimes the failure of national criminal justice is traced to a lack of capacity in war-torn countries, where capacity is understood to refer to available financial resources, legal staff, and infrastructure (rather than the ability of a community to decide what justice measures are in its best interests).[57] At other times, national failure is framed as a political decision designed to preserve existing power structures.[58] Yet it is through this image of national impunity and incapacity that the ICC gains its identity as "an institution that would be able to act when national courts do not do so or were seen as being ineffective."[59] Its very mandate, based on the principle of complementarity, is to act only when "national authorities have failed."

The current system of complementarity at the ICC—whereby it is empowered to act only when a nation-state is unwilling or unable to do so themselves—is a defining feature of the court, which has been emphasized by advocates over time.[60] The opening statements of delegates at the Rome Conference are striking in their consistent emphasis that "the principle of complementarity was central to the basic notion of the international criminal justice system."[61] They emphasize that "a balance had therefore to be struck" and that the ICC is a "court of last resort."[62] And although at first glance an emphasis on the court's complementarity can be conceived of as a challenge to its internationality, it can also be appreciated as another way that the identity of the international is consistently figured through its productive contrast with the national. For complementarity at its basis and the consistent emphasis on it assume and affirm that there are separate and independent systems of justice—a national system and an international one—that can be brought into relation.[63]

Furthermore, international criminal justice is also figured as separate or divorced from the politics of the national sphere (a portrayal that is increasingly contested by critical legal scholars).[64] I discussed in Chapter 1 the dominant framing of international criminal justice as existing somehow above the politics of the nation-state and hence more independent and impartial than its national counterpart.[65] Thus, one Rome Conference delegate explained that "as an international judicial body, it [the ICC] must not be influenced by political, financial or other considerations."[66] In this way, the ICC asserts its credentials as "independent" and "impartial" in a context where national justice is claimed to lack the characteristics of "legitimacy," impartiality, and independence.[67] Furthermore, international crimes by their very nature are figured as crimes of states and political leaders: "All too often, such crimes were part of a systematic State policy and the worst criminals might be found at the pinnacle of State power."[68] International crime is produced as a "state" problem, and international criminal justice is figured as the necessary supranational remedy (not, pertinently, through addressing state structures and institutions, but instead through holding individuals accountable and leaving unjust state frameworks for national reform).[69] It is through these representations that international criminal justice is given its form as somehow other to, or outside of, the nation-state, its politics, and its people.

The distinction between the national and the international is further demonstrated through seemingly positive attempts to bring the two closer together. For example, the idea of hybrid courts—which seek to blend key elements of national and international courts to create an ideal type of institution that capitalizes on the strengths of each while overcoming their weaknesses—is based on the assumption that national and international justice are constitutively different, each with distinctive attributes.[70] Importantly, as Aaron Fichtelberg explains, "unlike a purely international court . . . a domestic court can aspire to a form of legitimacy that foreign courts cannot provide."[71] Matters such as personnel, location, funding, and law are coded as either national or international, largely based on their externality to the country where the crimes occurred (the more external, the more likely they are to be international).

International criminal justice is also defined as constitutively other to the local. The way in which the ICC frames its witness and outreach programs, for example, relies on an assumption of separateness from where it resides and where the communities most affected by international crimes come from and live. Information on the witness program makes a distinction for witnesses between their "place of residence" and the "seat of the Court," implicitly foreclosing the possibility that they could be the same place.[72] When discussing its outreach program, for example, the ICC refers to the importance of "bringing the Court closer" to those it is meant to serve, stating that "no matter how far victims might be from the Court, the ICC endeavors to reach out and engage with them and their communities."[73] To do so, it sends "missions" to concerned countries; engages with "affected communities," "local" actors, intermediaries, and "local media"; and aims to be aware of "local languages" and sociopolitical contexts.[74] Moreover, ICC offices in these "local" spaces are not standing regional offices. Rather, they are its ad hoc "field offices," as opposed to its permanent headquarters in The Hague, where most of its work takes place.[75]

As such, if the national is the site of potentially flawed retributive justice processes, the local is the site of harm and victimization.[76] The local is comprised of "situation-related" countries, or those places in which the situations considered by the court occurred.[77] It is where victims reside, while international justice is where prosecutions are undertaken elsewhere in their name.[78] Importantly for the contrasting image of international justice that is produced (discussed below), the local is also territorially situated and culturally particular, located in a particular place and society in the world. A video on the court's website explains that "the process of victim's participation starts on the ground, in the situated-related countries, in affected communities, in the towns and villages where the victims reside," thereby grounding the idea of the local.[79] And geographical maps are frequently used in the court's informational and promotional materials to plot the site of the atrocities with which its cases are concerned, further locating the local. The situations that come to the court are social, political, cultural, and historical events, but they are visually represented by the territory in which they occurred. An informational video on the court's work in Georgia, for example, starts with a spinning globe and then geographically locates the country, before providing some basic geopolitical facts and information on the conflict there.[80] In a demonstration of a tendency critiqued by postcolonial theorists, certain events and communities thereby become inextricably associated, or even conflated, with context, while the court (representing the international) is seen to resist such specific attributes.[81]

That is, in such dominant depictions by the court and its commentators of a national and a local from which international criminal justice is separate, the court's internationality becomes tethered to its nonnational and nonlocal character. The very idea of international criminal justice is dependent on its national and local counterpoint; it is not possible to speak of what international criminal justice is outside this contrast.[82] Thus, in one of the few statements in which the ICC explicitly addresses its internationality, it describes itself as "an international rather than national or local court" that "may function differently from that in your national jurisdiction."[83] It positions itself as constitutively external to those who experience international crime when it explains that "as an international . . . court, the

ICC is not on the doorstep of those most affected by the cases it hears."[84] Indeed, it almost situates itself as constitutively external to all communities when it explains that "since the ICC is international and not a local Court, it is often impossible for *most people* to attend hearings in person."[85] A key focus of the court's outreach is thus to "reach out" and "bridge the distance" between it and the rest of the world.[86] It is through these contrasts that an image of international justice begins to emerge—as always separate from the local and the national, as always other.

What is crucial to highlight here, however, is the way in which the identity of a distinctive international criminal justice relies on its contrast to the national and the local. It is not just that international criminal justice is placed in a binary relation to the national and the local—echoing a broader opposition between the global and the local, in which each is associated with opposite attributes. Rather, it is that the ultimate definition of international criminal justice is that it is different from the national and the local: it is international *because* it is not national, not local. It is thus through such contrasts that international criminal justice comes to gain its ambiguous yet broader identity—as unlocated, apolitical, acultural, and nonnational. It escapes the dictates of its own particular social, historical, political, and cultural location and becomes constructed as somehow constitutively broader, transcendent, and beyond, and desirable because it is so.[87]

International Justice as a Transcendent Universal

In his analysis of the construction of modern law as a unified and sensical notion, Fitzpatrick observes how it "emerges . . . as universal in opposition to the particular, as unified in opposition to the diverse, as omnicompetent in contrast to the incompetent, and as controlling of what has to be controlled."[88] Antony Anghie charts a similar dynamic in relation to international law specifically, whose universality is instantiated through the imagination of particularized and localized others.[89] This is reflective of a broader colonial enterprise that was premised on the framing of Western values and ways of living as transcendent and acultural (and preferable), in opposition to a geographically and culturally specific non-Western other.[90] Similarly too, through its figuring of a particular, located, and flawed national and local, international criminal justice becomes constructed—by contrast— as a nonparticular project and, importantly, an idealized one. Through a contrast with what is geographically located, culturally particular, political, specific, and supposedly potentially flawed (the national and the local), international criminal justice gains its distinct identity as geographically and culturally transcendent, apolitical, independent, and best practice—as distinctively *international.*

First, international criminal justice is often framed as geographically transcendent—by definition, it is not located in the locations where it operates. Although affected countries exist "on the ground," the ICC is found elsewhere.[91] It is in line with such understandings that the ICC, which physically exists in The Hague, is figured as legally distinct from this context. Instead, once you pass through the doors of the ICC, you leave the jurisdiction of the Netherlands and enter the international jurisdiction of the court.[92] The ICC occupies and commands authority over its own jurisdictional space, which representatives of the Netherlands need permission to enter (except in case of emergency).[93] The court has its own security; its communications with the outside world (the Netherlands and beyond) are confidential and protected; and its staff members are given the status of diplomatic agents in the Netherlands regarding certain issues.[94] It even has its own flag: a traditional blue-and-white image of the scales of justice nestled within the logo of the UN's wreaths.

Thus, the court is described as having its "seat" in The Hague, but the Netherlands is simply described as a "host State" to which it is "particularly close."[95] The court is emphatically not seen to be a Dutch institution; it is an international institution, located in the International Zone of The Hague, and it has the notional capacity to travel and hear cases in other countries.[96] But neither is the ICC defined by its location "in the field"; it simply refers to such places in a vague way as "where we operate."[97] Even those detained by the court in prisons around the world (ICC sentences are enforced in the prisons of member states) are not automatically released into the country in which they served their sentence. Rather, they are international detainees, and following their sentence, they must be transferred to the state required to accept them.[98] It is in these ways that the court is figured as geographically transcendent, not defined or limited by where it actually resides and works.

Second, like other institutions of international criminal justice, the ICC is portrayed as being separated from all politics, national and international. As discussed earlier, the court is defined as constitutively distinct from national politics. It is also repeatedly emphasized in court materials and by court staff that the ICC is separate from both the UN structure and the sociopolitical context in which it works—"independent," "impartial," and "not subject to political control."[99] In the opening statements of the Rome Conference, delegates too emphasized that any international criminal court must be "independent," "impartial and free from political interference."[100] This is a common framework for understanding the role of judicial institutions vis-à-vis their political counterparts in Western democratic systems, and it is based on the separation of the ICC from any national or international governing body (such as the UN). With international justice, however, there is also a sense that it stands outside both politics and all sense of time and place. The uniqueness of international justice is related to its representing "the first time in history that an international Prosecutor has been given the mandate . . . to independently and impartiality [sic] select situations for investigation."[101] In its separateness from spaces and places denoted as political, the ICC is marked as other.

Third, the ICC is presented as standing outside and beyond existing identity categories, such as culture, nationality, and gender. Court materials instead emphasize its nationally and culturally diverse and representative nature, underscoring that it is not affiliated with any one nation-state but rather is a new, nonnational entity.[102] In an information sheet, for example, a list of indicators of the court's diversity is presented first: the court employs "900 staff members: From approximately 100 States," operates in six languages (with French and English as its working languages), and has seven field offices in addition to its headquarters.[103] At the time of writing, it had 122 member states, who are grouped (in ICC materials) both regionally and geopolitically.[104] Marc Dubuisson, director of court support services, explicitly links such diversity to the court's internationality, stating that "we are trying to make the institution as international as possible" and explaining further that "the prison director is Irish, and he has assistants of Italian, Congolese and Tanzanian nationality."[105] Moreover, even the prison cuisine is not culturally specific—inmates are not served Dutch cuisine but are instead ideally provided with "food that matches their respective local diets."[106] The multicultural and representative nature of the court's staff was also referred to in my conversations with people working in and on the court as a key part of its internationality.[107]

In practice, specific forms of diversity are enshrined in the Rome Statute—namely, national, gender, and legal diversity and sometimes also regional diversity. For example, the appointment of judges and prosecutorial and registry staff members should "take into account the need, within the membership of the Court" for adequate representation of men and women, different geographical locations and the world's principal legal systems.[108] In addition, the court's website often identifies staff members by their nationality and name.[109] Meanwhile, at a more specific level, there are provisions that the prosecutor and deputy prosecutor, as well as the judges composing the Presidency, will be from different countries—ensuring diversity even within the leadership positions in the prosecutorial and judicial organs of the court.[110] Even imprisonment should follow "principles of equitable distribution," although the offender's views and citizenship can be taken into account.[111]

Meanwhile, in addition to the official and working languages of the court—English and French—an important component of the court's operations is that defendants and witnesses will be able to give and receive information in a language that they understand.[112] The court website explains that the "defendant has the right to information in a language he or she fully understands, thus the ICC proceedings are conducted in multiple languages, with teams of interpreters and translators".[113] Indeed, even those members of the public who (like me) come to witness the court's operations are able to follow the proceedings through live translation relayed via headphones. The court also aims to be accessible to a broader global public, through its webcasting of its hearings[114] and using its Twitter account, which constitute "part of the Court's efforts to guarantee more accessible information in a diverse and transparent way."[115] It also links these initiatives to its status as an international court, stating that "due to the international nature of the Court's work, the ICC takes extra measures to ensure clear and effective communication with those who wish to follow its proceedings."[116]

In this way, the court is portrayed as not defined by any one culture, nationality, gender, or language. Rather, it is infinitely adaptable, able to accommodate yet also transcend any particularities it encounters. Through the figuring of different cultures and peoples that constitute but do not define the court, it comes to transcend them: there is nationality, and then there is the court—which is distinctively nonnational or other (*international*). The staff regulations explain that "staff members of the Court are international civil servants. Their responsibilities as staff members of the Court are not national but exclusively international."[117] In this sense, despite an emphasis on its diversity, the court is not a multicultural or inter-national institution, representing the meeting point of various nations and cultures. Rather, it is an entity that exists beyond the cultures, peoples, nations, and languages that are brought to it. That is, in emphasizing the diverse nationalities of its staff members, the implicit claim is not so much that they each act as national representatives (protecting and advocating for their nation's best interests) as that in their diversity they come to represent the international (as a place and peoples). Otherwise, the court's emphasis on their diverse nationalities would conflict with its insistence on its impartiality and independence (see below). Instead, the court describes itself as belonging to the world (it is "the world's first permanent international criminal court"), and even representative of it (with informational videos on the court explaining that "the world is taking action").[118] It is also globally situated through its use of a global map to depict the world as a whole as its arena of operation, as well as references in the opening statements at the Rome Conference to the establishment of the court as a goal for, and something desired by, "the international community" (see above).

In its irreducibility to any one culture or people, the ICC emerges as its own independent subject. Hence, ICC materials refer to the "we" of the ICC, stating "we are" "passionate . . . about global justice and lasting world peace."[119] ICC staff (primarily in the Registry) assume the responsibility of managing the ICC's external relations with the outside world of states and the broader public. The "we" of the ICC does not refer here to the various changing countries and communities subject to its operations but instead is used to describe its employees such as prosecutors, registrars, judges, and other personnel. Thus, when the ICC invites external parties to "explore *our* stories," it is referring to the stories of its staff members.[120] These staff members—from the information and evidence officer to the outreach field officer—are the "we" of international criminal justice who interact with the more culturally and politically located world around it. In contrast, readers of the court's materials are interpellated as outside the court structure and are told that "the Court wants to connect with you."[121]

Thus, as Fitzpatrick argues of modern law, international criminal justice is presented as a project that "operates in a social world yet exists separate from and dominant over it."[122] It cannot be defined by its location, interests, and priorities; the culture and nationality of those who work there; or the languages in which it operates. As Kjersti Lohne argues, the ICC's "claims to universality imply a type of 'spaceless' justice, as if speaking to and from nowhere in particular."[123] Thus, like international crime, international justice is defined as separate and distant from ordinary life as it is lived around the world. In this way, its very distinctiveness—as unlocated, apolitical, and beyond culture—relies on its contrast with what is lived, particular, and grounded. An inherent distance is built into the idea of international criminal justice, which can never be both proximate and international, showcasing best practices and grounded. Rather, when conceived of through this somewhat discriminatory frame, being international and having the praised attributes associated with international justice (high standards and a humanitarian impulse to respond to suffering, despite countervailing political imperatives) involve being not local and not belonging to a particular culture.

Moreover, it is not just that the idea of international criminal justice is defined as transcendent, it is also valorized because it is so. That is, the contrasts of the international with the local, the national, the cultural, and the political are all binary *and* hierarchical. The implication of all these contrasts is that the latter are somehow problematic. The national is the site of impunity and flawed justice, and the local is where crime occurs—thus, it is better to be apolitical, and culture can be overcome. As Phil Clark notes, there is a "sustained critique of embedded [local] justice that is inherent in distanced justice."[124] International justice is special and distinctive because it is external to the foibles of life on the ground. And it is valorized and privileged because it is other, because it promises (albeit erroneously) to transcend and maintain an existence separate from the located, political, partial, and culturally defined processes that practically exist elsewhere.

In his complementary analysis of the ICC as embodying and prioritizing a form of "distant justice," Clark provides a highly concerning picture of how this plays out in practice. In his long-term examination of the court's operation and impact in the African countries in which it has intervened, particularly Uganda and the Democratic Republic of Congo, Clark also argues that the ICC (and the international criminal justice enterprise more broadly) is conceptualized as philosophically, politically, culturally, and geographically distant from those most affected by the atrocities it seeks to redress, and as superior because it is so.[125] However, he also shows how this has translated into practice—for example, with court staff members spending only short amounts of time in "affected countries," as well as the court having insufficient outreach practices and predominantly non-African staff members.[126] Due to its prioritization of distance as a defining attribute, the court has operated with a sparse understanding of the communities in whose members' lives it intervenes, and it has therefore been open to political manipulation by local governments and has been inadequately responsive to local priorities regarding redress and conflict resolution—which has thus

ultimately compromised the pursuit of both peace and justice in these particular contexts.[127] Crucial to its practice of distancing, Clark argues, has
also been the court's promotion of its own aims and approach to justice
above local conceptions of it.[128] Thus, the dominant understanding of international criminal justice as fundamentally separate from the world around
it has serious practical implications, as well as—I would argue—being an
intrinsically problematic idea.

The Emperor's New Clothes: The Intersection of Myth and Power

However, this prevailing ideal of international criminal justice in its
importance and privilege is mythological. For Fitzpatrick, it is possible to
trace the work of myth in the continued perception of modern law as a
"coherent" and "unified" whole in the face of the numerous tensions and
paradoxes embedded in this very notion.[129] Similarly, although the idea of
distinctively international criminal justice exists (at least to some extent)
as a shared concept, there is nothing stable or coherent about it. Despite
its construction otherwise, international criminal justice is in fact located,
cultured, political, and particular. All those attributes that supposedly define
it as distinctive can also be revealed—like the emperor's new clothes—as il-
lusory. It is possible, that is, to "ground" international criminal justice in the
same way that postcolonial scholars have sought to "provincialize Europe"
or make visible the cultural and geographical specificity of what is European and thus resist the Eurocentrist construction of European knowledge
as universal knowledge and European law as international law.[130]

Central to the ideal of international criminal justice, for instance, is
its constitutive separation from any geographical, political, and cultural
context. Yet the ICC is clearly physically located: at Oude Waalsdorperweg
10 in The Hague, accessible by the number 23 and 22 buses and by car (figures 2 and 3). It is in an architecturally designed building that has housed
it since December 2015, when it moved from its temporary premises to its
permanent ones. The temporary premises were an office building previously
occupied by a Dutch telecom provider, KPN, and the court's low-ceilinged
reception area was supposedly located in the old carpark.[131] In contrast, the
new building was built specifically for the court and purportedly represents
the seven "values" of the ICC: "justice, human dignity, openness, credibility,
safety, global and icon."[132] Consisting of a series of modern-looking towers

FIGURE 2. Grounding the International Criminal Court: the Court in context in The Hague. Photo taken by author.

of different sizes (with the courtrooms in a higher building in the middle), the new building is meant to resemble the up-and-down rolling form of the North Sea dunes behind it.[133] Nor is the ICC exempt from politics. Its politics may differ from the national and local politics of some of the situations it deals with, but it is embedded in other political relationships—with states, the UN, and the Assembly of States Parties.[134] Its decisions have political consequences, and the very notion of an externalized international justice is political. International criminal justice, like life itself, is political.

The court is also culturally located: court materials have appeared in Dutch even though this is not an official court language, and the court takes a holiday on King's Day, the national Dutch public holiday. In this way, it is clearly "local" to some. Meanwhile, even though the court's blend of common and civil law elements makes it different from every other legal system in the world,[135] it is still particular in that respect. And despite its ambitions of universal jurisdiction (which I discuss in the Conclusion), the court only deals with certain crimes in certain countries, and it currently does so in a very culturally particular way.[136] Indeed, as noted in Chapter 1,

FIGURE 3. Grounding the International Criminal Court: bicycles flank the Court, reflecting the cycling culture in the Netherlands. Photo taken by author.

one of the most distinctive characteristics of the court right now is the lack of diversity in its caseload: it has focused almost exclusively on crimes committed in African countries and on the prosecution of African defendants. Moreover, the court itself acknowledges "the chronic nature of the imbalance [*sic*] representation in the Court," particularly regarding Asia-Pacific, Latin American, and Caribbean countries (although it notably still maintains its sense of internationality despite this acknowledgment).[137]

Despite the centrality of the contrast between the national and the international in giving content to the latter, it is impossible to draw any strict distinctions between national and international criminal justice. Like national criminal justice, international criminal justice has been accused of shortcomings, such as bias (as noted above) and a compromise of due process, and has been critiqued for being too expensive and slow.[138] Meanwhile, as was recognized by the International Law Commission in its deliberations regarding the possibility of an international criminal jurisdiction, international judicial models are largely based on national jurisdictional ones.[139] In this sense, international criminal justice appears similar to nationally located justice processes in terms of its architecture, process, and key goals. Importantly, both national and international criminal justice institutions are organizations that wield significant punitive power—to accuse, try, and sentence people for legally prohibited acts.

International criminal justice is also acknowledged as both an invention of states and an intrinsically inter-national system.[140] In practice, it is nation-states that define the authority and jurisdiction of international courts: they fund the courts, and they can also compromise the courts' ability to work and shape which aspects of international justice are prioritized.[141] Although the ICC enjoys "international legal personality," it is also premised on state consent, complementarity, and the continued maintenance of the state as the key political unit.[142] It is in line with such sentiments that the Rome Statute begins by reiterating the continuance of state sovereignty through its reference to the principle of nonintervention in the UN's charter and the importance of pursuing criminal justice at the "national level."[143] The ICC website openly acknowledges all the ways in which it is dependent on its national members. To cite a few examples, it notes that "the ICC does not have its own police force or enforcement body; thus, it relies on cooperation with countries worldwide" to arrest, transfer and imprison defendants, and that it is designed to "complement, not replace, national criminal justice systems."[144] States are explicitly included within the ICC structure in court materials that delineate two sides to this institution: "In establishing the ICC, the States set up a system based on two pillars. The Court itself is the judicial pillar. The operational pillar belongs to states."[145]

The significance of pointing out these contradictions is that they are obvious. They are not revelatory as much as commonsensical. Yet these are attributes of international criminal justice that somehow must be overlooked or suspended if it is also to be seen as intrinsically (and uniquely) separate from geography, culture, politics, and the national and local. This is the story of the emperor's new clothes repeated, in which an ability to make out the idealized notion of an international criminal justice relies on a commitment to overlooking what is clearly visible: that international criminal justice, like all justice, is of this world. It is culturally, politically, and legally particular;[146] it is sociopolitically grounded; and the ability of the idea of international criminal justice to survive and maintain its power despite these inherent contradictions demonstrates its mythical quality. The ideal of international criminal justice is thus unrealized, unrealizable, and—I would submit—fundamentally undesirable. Put simply, it is both impossible and undesirable to have a form of justice that is fundamentally and irreducibly separate from life, context, and history.

Power Effects

Yet to argue that the ideal of international criminal justice is mythic is not to claim it is an empty signifier. Rather, in part due to their mythical quality, the idea and ideal of international criminal justice are powerful. The belief in the importance of international criminal justice has led to the establishment of influential international institutions (such as the ICC) and fostered the development of a community of international justice professionals who represent it.[147] International criminal justice is the subject of books, educational curricula, societal debates, and nongovernmental organizations. At the same time as international criminal justice is understood to connote that which is groundless, with no specific culture, and apolitical, it is also an ideal that justifies the establishment of particular expensive institutions, such as the International Criminal Tribunal for the former Yugoslavia, the International Criminal Tribunal for Rwanda, and the ICC. The ICC alone has an annual operating budget of 148 million euros.[148] In her analysis of hybrid tribunals, Sarah Nouwen notes that these internationalized courts frequently have a budget for their work that exceeds "most states' entire justice systems."[149]

Meanwhile, in 2017, ICC Prosecutor Fatou Bensouda made *Time* magazine's short list of the world's hundred most influential people, for the second time.[150] People considered to be the "we" of the ICC enjoy a protected legal status. For example, key staff are afforded diplomatic immunity wherever they operate as long as they are staff members, placing them beyond normal legal principles in their day-to-day work.[151] The ICC operates as an independent international institution alongside other powerful political institutions such as states and other international bodies. It is part of multiple networks of international institutional power, as shown by the way it retweets the tweets of the UN, nation-states, and other international organizations such as the International Center for Transitional Justice.[152] Although supporters of the ICC refer to it as a "young" institution that represents a push to take "a stand against those who, in the past, would have had no one to answer to" and a "justice start-up,"[153] these diminutive descriptors downplay the social and political power of the court and its spokespeople to denounce alleged criminals, sentence and punish perpetrators, compel witnesses to testify, and participate as a key international legal and political actor. They also downplay, from a legal and criminological point of view, the significance of a body of international actors and institutions that are subject to few external accountability mechanisms and whose power remains largely unregulated in any substantive sense.[154] This also means that, parallel to the way structural inequalities often remain outside the purview of definitions of international crime, structural injustices embedded in the operation of so-called international institutions and frameworks may be able to persist unaddressed by international criminal law.

More broadly, through the establishment of successive international institutions and their interpretation as constituent parts of a more general international criminal justice project, international criminal justice has also become constituted as its own subject, with its own aims, milestones, staff, and—ultimately—subjectivity. Through its framing by practitioners and academics as a progressively unfolding global enterprise, international criminal justice has become more than a diverse collection of ad hoc internationally mandated courts created in varying social, political, and historical circumstances with different goals and different staff. It also has become more than a contextual and tailored response by external parties to the devastation experienced by a certain country and peoples. Instead, it has evolved into an independent and cohesive global project with its own interests and trajectory. This potentially lends an appropriative dynamic to the project of international criminal justice, which has been accused in practice of putting its own priorities above those of the communities and people most directly affected by international crime. Hence Frédéric Mégret's claim that "international criminal justice can be faulted for its propensity to sacrifice not only individuals (who are potentially 'scapegoated' for collective or systemic crimes), but also societies (whose complex transitional deliberations are side-stepped) . . . on the altar of a grand cosmopolitan design."[155] Critical questions can therefore be raised about who does and can speak in the name of international criminal justice, or whose interests are represented by it. As Immi Tallgren demonstrates, the "we-talk" of international criminal justice can be exclusionary and exclusive, with some spokespeople more able to speak in the name of a universalized "we," while others (such as the victims, perpetrators, and communities involved with international crime) remain unheard.[156]

And it is of great significance that this new project of international criminal justice has the power to speak in the name of the universal or the international community, and that it can deny its geographical emplacement, sociocultural foundations, and political character. Colonial global practices that preceded this new project have vividly demonstrated that the ability (or at least the will) to appear and speak as the objective and the unmarked is a function of power and dominance.[157] The capacity to deny one's own place, heritage, and interests is indicative of the power one holds in a given social and political situation. Remnants of colonial ontologies of global relations are also arguably reflected in the construction of such a universal character and voice in and through an image of a particularized and pathologized other.[158] These colonial resonances will be discussed further in the Conclusion.

However, in highlighting the power dynamics of the myth of international criminal justice here, my purpose is not to impugn the daily activities of those working for international criminal justice institutions with the motivation of acknowledging and redressing mass harm. Nor is it to claim that international criminal courts, such as the ICC, have no valuable role, particularly for the individuals, communities, and countries that choose to engage with them. Rather, my focus is on demonstrating the problematic character of the *ideal* of international criminal justice, which describes a form of justice that is both impossible and undesirable to achieve; a form of purportedly international justice that is constitutively divorced from local realities, peoples, and concerns. My hope is that such a critical intervention might work toward unsettling the power and authority of existing frameworks for conceptualizing international criminal justice—which serve to hinder a more wide-ranging discussion of alternative ways of thinking about human interconnection and the responsibility of each of us to respond to the suffering of others.

For example, an ethic of international engagement with the justice issues created by mass harm could still entail the involvement of external actors, but in a way that did not privilege them or disconnect them from the world in which they operate. That is, other transnational solidarities that emerge out of experiences of events of mass harm could be based on more contextualized forms of engagement, grounded in the specificity of those experiencing harm and those able in that current moment to respond.[159] Current modalities of international criminal justice differ, for example, from the way in which women's groups protesting against war and mother's groups (collectives of mothers who have been affected by war and state crime) in diverse locations have connected with each other regarding their localized struggles for justice and accountability. An example is the now widespread Women in Black movement. The first Women in Black group emerged in Israel, opposing that country's occupation of Palestine through the holding of a silent public vigil. Since then, Women in Black groups have been developed around the world that engage in a similar form of protest, sometimes in solidarity with the original cause but also in opposition to other events of war and armed conflict.[160] Another example of a more contextualized form of transnational solidarity is the activism by Aboriginal communities in Australia contesting the Australian government's terrible and unjust treatment of asylum seekers through processes of offshore detention. This activism relies explicitly on the unique authority of Indigenous communities as the traditional owners of what is now known as Australia and their continued status as holders of law in Australia, as well as their shared experience of harm perpetrated through the Australian colonial state. As Michael Mansell of the Aboriginal Provisional Government has stated, "as people who know what it's like to be invaded by boat people we are in a better position to judge how the current boat people should be treated," while "giving permission" for asylum seekers and refugees to enter Australia.[161] Such statements could be characterized as externally and internationally oriented yet deeply connected to culture, place, and time—better expressions of the fact that the injustices at issue, in Shaunnagh Dorsett and Shaun McVeigh's words, are "particular wrongs associated with the lives lived in relation with others."[162] There have also been other statements of solidarity between Aboriginal communities and asylum seekers, including their joint statement in opposition to the holding of the Commonwealth Games in the Australian state of Queensland in 2018, dubbed the "Stolenwealth" games in recognition of the continued situation of settler colonialism that persists in that country.[163] These contextualized and highly specific transnational or intercommunal relations differ markedly from the formal relational forms enabled through current conceptualizations of international criminal justice, which configure that enactment of global solidarity as something that is by definition separate from the world with which it engages.

Beyond the Ideal of International Criminal Justice to "Actually Existing Solidarities"

At the twentieth anniversary of the establishment of the ICC, there was celebration but also a focus on the future. Although the achievements of the ICC were applauded, there was also a call from court staff members and advocates for renewed and stronger support for the court. O-Gon Kwon, president of the Assembly of States Parties, proclaimed that "at this important juncture in its history, the Court needs our support more than ever."[164] Fatou Bensouda, the court's prosecutor, stated that "as we commemorate the 20th anniversary of the adoption of the Rome Statute, we owe it to ourselves, our children and future generations to fully support and nurture the ever-evolving international criminal justice system, and the ICC as its central pillar. . . . Let the Rome Statute continue to guide us towards that better future for all."[165] Although these are understandable sentiments from those most invested in the ICC's continued development, they also deserve reflection. It is important to remain aware of the way in which they take international criminal justice as a given and position the ICC as its embodiment. They are statements made at a time when an ethical response to mass harm is frequently equated with the need to support, rather than contest, the ICC's dominance and with the importance of the court having universal jurisdiction (the push for universal jurisdiction is discussed in the Conclusion). Thus, in his address to the Assembly of States Parties, Zeid Ra'ad Al Hussein, the UN High Commissioner for Human Rights, urged those considering withdrawal from the court to "not betray the victims, nor your own people," exemplifying a now popular conflation of the court with the goal of responding ethically and legally to mass harm, suffering, and victims' needs.[166] Such sentiments are problematic in the way that they foreclose debate about and critique of international criminal justice as an idea and a practice.

While there is a diverse and important body of work analyzing the operation of criminal justice institutions over time, this chapter has instead offered a sustained exploration of the *idea* of international criminal justice. I have argued that the current idea and idealization of international criminal justice is problematic, as it pathologizes the national, the local, being cultured, and being political and creates distance, figuring international criminal justice as distinctively other to life as it is lived. Thus, at a time when the primary focus is on strengthening existing international justice institutions or evaluating their limits and possibilities, this chapter also testifies to the need to critically reflect on the very concepts of international criminal justice that are being used and on their contemporary valorization. Building on existing critiques of international criminal justice, I argue that it is neither possible nor ideal to strive for a form of justice that transcends all context and is fundamentally separate from the world around it.

Of course, this is not to suggest that nonnational or regional or transnational courts have no role to play. Indeed, they may have resources, flexibility, and reach that national courts do not have. As has been observed in relation to the ICC, the International Criminal Tribunal for Rwanda, and other hybrid institutions, internationalized justice may also be able to draw on expert and witness testimony that is no longer located in the country that experienced the atrocity, to apprehend alleged offenders who no longer live there, and to provide resources and legal experience that are seen as helpful.[167] That is, as I argued in relation to international crime, the distinction between national and international judicial institutions might be qualitative, focused more on the different roles each might play (rather than the valorization of one at the expense of the other). This also presumably would accord with how they are sometimes regarded by academics, practitioners, and communities. Moreover, my deconstruction of the idea of international criminal justice is not designed to downplay the importance of external engagement with the harm experienced throughout the world. Rather, it is to raise the possibility that such engagement might be grounded, contextual, and collaborative—based on cooperation with, and even deferral to, those who have experienced injustice (at any given moment in time) and those who have not. This sort of collaboration could take different forms, such as compensation, dependent on the wishes of those requesting external assistance.[168] Such engagements would be international in the sense of involving external actors but might avoid any production of the international as a separate and distinct project, with its own personnel and goals.

In her work on internationality, Liisa Malkki refers to the idea of "actually existing solidarities" that exist between people and communities in the world.[169] This is a captivating phrase that speaks of connection but also groundedness, concrete and contextual engagements. Yet it is precisely this form of grounded and material engagement that is fundamentally other to an ideal of international criminal justice, which constitutively separates itself from the world in which it works. Thus, in her research on the idea of solidarity, Uma Kothari asks whether a particular practice "moves us toward solidarities."[170] As international criminal justice develops as its own project—and as one that is defined by its separateness from life as it is lived, particularly as it is lived by those peoples and communities affected by international crime—it can only be distant and disconnected.

Thus, the claim that the ideal of international criminal justice is mythical need not be a negative one. It may also be an emancipatory one, making conceptual and discursive space to reconsider what international criminal justice might look like and mean. This reconsideration would be a dialogue between those who are external to suffering (at any given moment in time) and those who experience it (at any given moment in time). It might be one that acknowledges the ways in which people around the world are currently interconnected, for example through structurally unjust arrangements that benefit some and lead to the exploitation of others.[171] It might facilitate ways of coming together that are not based on national and gender representativeness but are inclusive in different ways. Yet it must be a conversation that also carefully considers the discursive and representational frameworks through which international crime and international criminal justice are currently conceptualized, for they are both problematic and often accepted as ideal—if not also natural and incontestable.

Conclusion

Community Beyond Crime: Untethering International Crime, Justice, and Community

The ambit of this discipline . . . will be the higher universe, with no frontiers, where offences are considered in and of themselves, without regard to territoriality. This idealized world may come about one day.

—Doudou Thiam, "First Report on the Draft Code of Offences Against the Peace and Security of Mankind"

The conquest of the earth . . . is not a pretty thing when you look into it too much. What redeems it is the idea only. An idea at the back of it; not a sentimental pretence but an idea; and an unselfish belief in the idea—something you can set up, and bow down before, and offer a sacrifice to. . . .

—Joseph Conrad quoted in Edward Said, *Culture and Imperialism*

THE IDEA OF DISTINCTLY INTERNATIONAL FORMS of crime and justice whose criminalization represents the sentiment of "our" common humanity is a powerful one. The idea of international crime—of unparalleled monstrosity and incontestable evil—seems to do justice to the atrocities it names: genocide, crimes against humanity, war crimes, and aggression. The denunciation of such harms as especially heinous and horrible feels as though it represents the most adequate way to acknowledge the unjustified suffering of victims and victim-survivors. As its complement, the ideal of international criminal justice—of gold-standard justice that exemplifies best practice and arises from nowhere, yet speaks in everyone's name—appears to constitute a "fitting" response.[1] This ideal is a system of justice "with no frontiers" that will intervene in the face of state failure and transcend culture, politics, and geography to offer an official and denunciatory response to crimes of the powerful "without regard to territoriality." The ideas of international crime and international justice are beautiful, or at least captivating and motivating. In Joseph Conrad's words, they represent "something you can set up, and bow down before." Despite the ambiguities surrounding their precise definitions, they are incontestable ideals that exercise a hold in this historical moment.

There is also clearly an ethical claim embedded in these ideas: to acknowledge suffering, enact justice, and represent community. They boast important relational potentials for connecting people and communities around the world and enacting and testifying to the existence of a cohesive global community (Chapter 1). The concept of crimes against humanity has affective resonance, inspiring continued inquiries into its essence and significance (Chapter 3). International criminal justice has been a subject of more critique, yet it still maintains an important role in dominant imaginaries of a more progressive and humanitarian world (Chapter 4). Thus, to write of international crime and justice is not just to write of legal provisions and criminal courts; it is also to conjure up powerful ideas of a global and contemporary international community, united through its opposition to harm and suffering and committed to establishing legal institutions and statutes that embody its will. Moreover, these ideas of international crime and justice are emphatically central, not secondary, to the practice of international criminal justice mechanisms, inspiring and legitimating them. In its current instantiation, the practice of international criminal justice is unintelligible without these ideas of the most serious international crimes that demand an external and uninvested legal response. Their content and affective hold are integral to what international criminal justice means, and they enable the proscription of certain crimes, the prosecution of certain defendants, and the establishment of certain tribunals to appear as a humanitarian and progressive enterprise. For this, it is claimed, constitutes "the cause of all humanity."[2]

However, I have argued in this book that these ideas of international crime and international criminal justice are problematic. I have suggested that the frameworks currently used to understand what international crime and justice are as well as why they are important requires interrogation and unsettling. These frameworks condemn harm, legitimatize new judicial institutions, and foster new forms of global interconnection, but they also create social and relational distance and inaugurate new forms of power. They spectacularize events of suffering, hierarchize different types of harm, and resituate internationalized harm in a different spatial and subjective context. They foster an ideal of justice that is, by definition, fundamentally disconnected from the everyday. They sit alongside other socio-legal processes of internationalization that facilitate the appropriation of specific events of harm as crimes against "us" all. And although the notion of international criminal justice—presented in the opening quote to this chapter—as a "higher universe, with no frontiers, where offences are considered in and of themselves, without regard to territoriality" is inspiring and affectively moving, it names a broader way of thinking in which international crime is understood to affect generalized, often anonymized, groups of people, and international justice is seen as an enterprise undertaken by those who are constitutively external and other. As such, the problem is not only that current legal definitions of international crime might be problematic, or that international justice institutions in practice have suffered from a range of deficits and unintended consequences. It is also that there are significant issues embedded in even the dominant ideas of international crime and international criminal justice. To apply Conrad's words somewhat differently, the ideas of international crime and international criminal justice are both captivating and problematic; they are not as full of humanitarian promise and as aspirational as they appear at first glance.

In the more sustained exploration of the ideas of international crime and international justice that I have offered in this book, I have sought to identify three key difficulties with these notions that emerged from my case studies. First, the notions function to create ethical and relational distance between those who suffer and those who do not, at any given moment in time. The presentation of international crime through spectacularizing rhetoric potentially makes it more difficult for external parties to comprehend and connect with the lives of those who have experienced the most heinous forms of degradation and injustice. This is not to say that the experiences of those harmed by international crime must be made fully knowable to others. Indeed, there is an ethics associated with the recognition of the uncontainability of such events of suffering.[3] Rather, it is to highlight the ethical implications of the vivid iconography associated with descriptions of international crime, which may make it more difficult for external parties to appreciate the lives of those who have experienced mass harm as livable lives, characterized by strength, resilience, and agency as well as suffering and pain.

Meanwhile, through the hierarchization of suffering, other serious harms (such as those endured in Rwanda's civil war) become difficult to see and appreciate. Through the generalization of internationalized injury, the focus shifts from the direct victims of such injustices—apprehended as they are as members of a group or community—to a broader humanity and state of peace and security. Meanwhile, the figuring of international criminal justice as an idealized form of redress magically transcending geography, culture, and politics to speak in the name of a common humanity serves to fundamentally disconnect this enterprise from any context and community—particularly those most affected by international crime. Furthermore, in practice, there can be a distinct cultural dynamic to this distancing. For example, with respect to the Rwandan genocide in which Rwandan victims and survivors are often lost in the way in which this event has been constructed as a distinct moment in global socio-legal history.[4]

In these ways, the ideas of international crime and justice serve to disconnect these phenomena from life as it is practically lived throughout the world, from the everyday, and actually stymie the development of more contextual, grounded relations between one community and another that are located in time, place, and culture.[5] The ideas do not acknowledge the fact that if one bows (or is required to bow) in a courtroom to the image of international criminal justice, this is an act and an injunction located in a particular time and space. More substantively, such concepts of international crime and justice do not enable a form of thick relations situated at a particular historical moment between different peoples, but instead tend toward a hardening of somewhat one-dimensional subject positions. External parties are invited to relate to the harm experienced by others only as external parties who are always placed outside the site of harm, always other to suffering victims. Hence, at an exhibition in the foyer of the International Criminal Court (ICC) in 2017, visitors were invited to record a video with a message for the victims of international crime: "If you could send a message to those who suffered from crimes, what would you say?" This invitation does not address visitors as parties who also may suffer or have suffered, and suffering itself is not universalized or at least found in different forms in different places.[6] Rather, there are those who suffer and those who respond, a distinction that gestures toward the relational distance embedded at the heart of what international crime and justice have come to mean. Yet victimization does not have to be correlated with a specific subject position; it can also be understood as a transient and situational experience, one that is often traceable to external structural, historical, political, legal, and economic factors. Indeed, given the unequal positions of those who have suffered and those who respond, the ICC exhibition can prompt more than a recognition of the discursive demarcation between victims of international crime and external parties. It can also provoke a consideration of the investment that this always external "we" might have in current conceptualizations of international criminal justice, and on how those positioned as nonsufferers might gain from this identity that downplays their relation to local and global sites of suffering and affords them the power of being positioned as outside the site of international crime but potentially in the space of international justice.[7]

Second, I have demonstrated that there is a power dynamic to current conceptualizations of international crime and justice that authorize power and are marked by appropriative tendencies. At its heart, defining international crime and justice in terms of scalar height is a technique of power, situating them as higher and more privileged than other forms of crime and justice. It accords with a broader privileging of the notion of the international or internationality, which is often conceptualized in idealized terms. Meanwhile, the construction of a mythical ideal of a best-practice and transcendent justice project through a negative contrast with the national and the local also inaugurates inequalities. This myth is also powerful in the sense that it has served to legitimate the development of institutions, professions, and disciplines that now have their own interests, concerns, and needs. In addition, there is a tendency for discursive frameworks regarding international crime to effect an appropriation—through resituating so-called international crimes in a more generalized sociopolitical context and reconceptualizing the suffering and harm experienced by specific people at specific times in specific places as a crime against "us" all or "the world's property."[8] This tendency can be seen in the broader frameworks for thinking about international crime, as well as how they play out in particular contexts. It is in this sense that the post hoc internationalization of the Rwandan genocide entailed its appropriation as an event relating to, and affecting, others. Even the name "Rwanda" now signifies (for non-Rwandans at least) something other than just the Rwandan nation and people.

A third key point has been that it is not only the content of notions of international crime and justice that is problematic, but also their social, legal, and political valorization. On the one hand, the contemporary privileging of the ideas of international crime and justice (as unique, important, and humanitarian, for example) seems an intuitive and proper response to the gravity of their referents. Just as the behavior it names is of utmost importance, so too should the idea of international crime appear as a debated yet somehow real and significant incontestable. Similarly, just as international criminal justice seeks to respond to such unimaginable suffering, so too should the idea of international criminal justice be held up as an innately humanitarian and benevolent ideal. Indeed, such is the current socio-legal privileging of these ideas themselves—as distinct from the injuries and practices that they name—that my critique of them might be regarded as unethical. That is, while it is more commonplace to question the ways in which these terms are defined, it still feels like a controversial move to question the very utility and significance of the terms themselves. Why would anyone impugn these inherently humane ideals? What is the point of calling into question these concepts, which seek to call out harm, demonstrate its importance, and legitimize its redress?

On the other hand, the idealization and spectacularization of notions of international crime and justice are implicated in their problematic ethical and relational effects. The valorization of international crime—its scalar positioning as the worst, most important, and top of the hierarchy—is intricately related to the distance created between this notion and life as it is lived. In turn, such privileging is connected to the resituating of international crime among conventionally grander concepts of humanity as a whole or civilization itself. It is also implicated in their exclusivity and the concomitant downplaying of other violence, such as in the policing of the use of the term *genocide* so that it is not (according to some) improperly applied.[9] Meanwhile, the idealization of international criminal justice as a transcendent global project is firmly implicated in its definition as other to everyday life. Despite the impossibility or undesirability of ever realizing such a type of justice, the idealization of international criminal justice in this way has been crucial to its demarcation as distinctive and the related legitimation of a new, powerful infrastructure of punitive criminal justice. It is in this sense that the valorization of international crime and justice is itself problematic and cannot be separated from the current ethical and relational difficulties associated with these notions. The more that these forms of crime and justice are valorized, the more these ideas are located elsewhere—that is, as constitutively other to the everyday and the knowable, and as related to others and broader global projects. Their valorization is thus not simply a side effect or natural consequence of the inherent nature of what they name. Rather, it is an act of socio-legal construction, with powerful effects. It is through their privileging that ideas of international crime and justice come to possess social, legal, and political power. Furthermore, it is their power, rather than their inherent meaning, that makes it potentially dangerous to question their utility and query whether these are ideals worth striving for.

It is because of the intersection between their privileging, on the one hand, and their power and problematic effects, on the other hand, that I have sought to critique their valorized character. For although it may seem right to privilege these forms of crime and justice, there is nothing certain or stable about doing so. Hence, I have emphasized the possibilities that inhere in the broader circulation and use of the term *genocide* outside its strict legal definition. It is important to emphasize these possibilities—not to question the significance of any event to which they are applied, but to demonstrate that such extralegal applications may enable more expansive affective and ethical connections than the label of *genocide* might legally allow. And more expansive engagements might testify to both the limited nature of legal frames (and their conventional applications) and their failure to maintain a decisive voice on what suffering should matter. I have also sought to underscore the unrealizable and undesirable nature of the common ideal of a transcendent and unlocated justice. Again, this is not to impugn the acceptance by outsiders of a role and responsibility in acknowledging and redressing harm that occurs elsewhere, but to enable the possibility of more grounded and contextual engagements between communities and peoples. These may be based on shared experiences of exploitation or even an acknowledgment of the structural injustices that enable discrete events of harm but that external parties might bear some responsibility for. To question the valorized and privileged character of international crime and justice in this way is thus designed to enable new forms of recognizing and engaging with the suffering of others, rather than to downplay its broader import.

However, it is necessary to acknowledge that many of the problematic tendencies associated with the current content and valorization of international crime and justice are connected to the limitations associated with other socio-legal projects and discourses. Despite claims about the groundbreaking character of this new field of international criminal justice, it is based on conventional ideas of what internationality means. The international is often defined as both distinctively other to the national and the local and as somewhere higher and more important to everyday life, while internationality is a quality frequently associated with abstract and general states and subjectivities (humanity, the international community, and global peace and security), and one that loses specificity.[10] The international is often a site of privilege and power and has been critiqued as an idealized notion.[11] Thus, understandings of international crime and justice are representative of broader discourses of internationality and raise many similar ethical and conceptual problems for consideration.

Moreover, techniques of generalization and the inability to adequately register and respond to the specificity and uniqueness of every case of harm is a key feature of law and legal process. Law is about the application of general rules, regardless of the injustice that might be caused to a particular person in a particular case.[12] And criminal justice everywhere involves an appropriation, whereby an offense perpetrated against a particular person at a particular time and place is rescripted as an offense against a broader community, in whose name prosecution is undertaken.[13] For this and other reasons, it is always ethically complex to found community and human interconnection through the image of crime. Meanwhile, humanitarian discourse and practice more broadly has been critiqued for its foundational inequalities and for also being dependent—as I have argued in relation to international crime and justice—on a hierarchical distinction between those who suffer and those who do not, with the valorization of the latter as inherently benevolent and good and fundamentally external to suffering rather than implicated in it.[14] These connections between international crime and justice and notions and practices of internationality, law, criminal justice, and humanitarianism more generally do not excuse the shortcomings associated with the ideas of international crime and justice that I have charted in this book. Instead, the connections merely situate these shortcomings as properly related to broader socio-legal tendencies and discourses that also require attention. There are other global projects to which current ideas of international criminal justice are related, which also bear mentioning before concluding this book.

Colonial Remnants

As I have alluded to throughout this book, a further, troubling dimension to contemporary understandings of international crime and justice is their resonance with colonial modes of imagining (and configuring) the international. That is, there are similarities between colonial understandings of the world and the relations between people within it, and the image of the same that is produced through the dominant approaches to international crime and justice charted in this book. Dominant imaginings of international criminal justice, for example, reflect the "dynamic of difference"—charted by Antony Anghie—that characterized colonial engagements with other cultures and that informed, and continues to shape, the structure of international law.[15] Anghie defines this dynamic as "the endless process of creating a gap between two cultures, demarcating one as 'universal' and civilized and the other as 'particular' and uncivilized." Such a dynamic can also be traced through dominant conceptualizations of international criminal justice, whose transcendent identity is produced only through its repeated distinction from those places and peoples who are limited to their social, cultural, political, and geographical context and its related repudiation of its own particularity. Moreover, this distinction is hierarchical, with the local and particular portrayed as sites of lack and pathology in contrast to the valorized international that is produced as their other. Furthermore, like colonial modes of global relation before it, the power and self-interest of international criminal justice are also downplayed through its popular presentation as not only objective but also innately progressive and humanitarian.[16] Meanwhile, the whole discursive framework of international crime and justice relies, I have argued, on an appropriative tendency, whereby the experiences of specific groups and individuals are reconceptualized as crimes against humanity and resituated in the global socio-legal sphere in the name of imagining global community.[17]

To make this observation is not to claim that international criminal justice is a neocolonial enterprise. Rather, it is to point to the resonances between the way colonial frameworks and notions of international criminal justice, respectively, make it possible to know the world and pursue a globally oriented project. It is to claim that—when taken together— understandings of international crime and justice figure the international and envision global relations in a colonial mode. In so doing, they demonstrate what Ann Laura Stoler and Anghie have argued about the endurance of colonial structures and forms—in human relations; geography; politics; and, importantly, international law. These "imperial remains" are more than the ongoing legacy of past colonial acts whose effects are still felt to this day. "Imperial remains" can instead be understood as forms of colonial power that have endured beyond the formal end of colonialism, "exerting material and social force in the present" and having the capacity to be revived in new ways.[18] They are signs and symptoms of how "the colonial order of things" lives on despite the formal end of colonial practice.[19]

Colonial repetitions, in this sense, can arguably be traced through the image of the world and global relations offered through dominant approaches to international criminal justice. In addition to those already discussed in this book and mentioned above, it is possible to point in this respect to the repeated use by the ICC of cartographical imagery to situate itself as a global institution and understand what internationality means. On its home page, for example, under the heading "Situations and Cases," is a world map. Countries in which there is a current investigation are shaded in dark blue, whereas countries in which there is a preliminary investigation are shaded in light blue.[20] This map acts as a signifier of the court's internationality by giving a sense of the global and expansive scope of the court's work, well beyond its primary physical location in The Hague. It thereby legitimates a mode of conceiving of internationality as a geographically structured concept, while situating the court as a global institution that considers the world as a whole as under its purview. In the wake of the colonial enterprise, however, any attempt to map the world is a political assertion of power. The practice of cartography was central to colonialism: such pictorial, but ultimately geopolitical, images of the world were central to establishing a colonial knowledge of global space and instantiating it as objective and factual.[21] They were also crucial to establishing a vision of one united world, rather than allowing a sense of a diversity of worlds and acknowledging the variety of coexisting transnational legal jurisdictions (such as the Indigenous, Islamic, and Chinese legal orders) beyond European international law.[22]

This tendency to map is exacerbated by the current focus of the court and its supporters on the need for it to have universal jurisdiction to instantiate itself as a genuinely global institution. On its website, the court now emphasizes "the importance of redoubling our efforts to ensure the continued expansion of the family of States" associated with it.[23] Meanwhile, in its campaign called Global Justice for Atrocities, the Coalition for the International Criminal Court frames as "the problem: uneven global access to justice for war crimes, crimes against humanity and genocide," which leads to the "the solution: universal ICC membership."[24] Such statements link jurisdictional reach with the quality of internationality, invoking—to new ends—a colonial focus on territorial expansion as a key mode of power. They fail to acknowledge that international institutions are not outside of the history of colonial relations but rather have played an active role in colonialism's past and present manifestations.[25]

To be sure, these connections between current approaches to international crime and justice and previous colonial frameworks are provisional resemblances. Yet they demonstrate the endurance of colonial iconographies of globality and global interrelations in contemporary international endeav-ors.[26] They reinvigorate and lend credence to claims of the continued rel-evance of colonialism to the ICC's operation—not because they demonstrate its intention to discriminate, but because they underscore the significance of its culturally skewed operations to date. Regardless of whether the over-whelming focus of the court to date on African conflicts and defendants is due to its bias, countries' self-referral, legitimate prosecutorial decisions, or otherwise, it is problematic that the operations of this international court have been so culturally particular. We all live in a world forever marked by colonialism and need to be cognizant of the diffuse and sometimes ambiguous ways in which colonialism lives on.[27] It matters that on the ICC's website, and in its pamphlets and exhibitions, the current imaginary of international criminal justice consists of images of African defendants in the dock and African victims and communities whose suffering and criminality are thus figured as key bases on which contemporary claims to global community are being founded. In its status as a dominant and mainstream international institution, the ICC produces imagery of what the international is and means.[28] It is only because we all live in a postcolonial world that claims of neocolonialism can be made, and that they must be heard and responded to in a way that recognizes the enduring structural and historical injustice of the colonial project.

Of course, in some ways, this claim of a colonial dynamic in cur-rent conceptualizations of international crime and justice is stronger in an analysis such as mine—which focused, in Chapter 2, on the globaliza-tion and Western appropriation of an African event (namely the Rwandan genocide) and, in Chapter 4, on an international justice institution that has mainly prosecuted African defendants. Indeed, the Rwandan genocide is an exemplary case study of the global recognition of genocide and the self-interested mode of external engagement this can entail. So too, especially at this historical moment, is the ICC a particular, albeit iconic, form of international justice because of its predominant focus on African contexts. In practice, not all events of genocide, mass harm, and systematic persecu-tion are widely recognized and condemned, and other international justice institutions have focused on non-African contexts. It is in this sense, as I noted in the Introduction, that this book offers some general arguments but acknowledges that they only stem from, and are most accurate in rela-tion to, the three case studies I considered. That said, however, I hope that the argument offered here about colonial tendencies is understood as one that relates more broadly to the *form* of imagining the international that emerges from the three case studies I discussed, which collectively figure the international as elsewhere, relating to others; and beyond politics, culture, and history, compared to a grounded, pathologized local whose experiences are regarded, or appropriated, as globally resonant in the name of affirming a common humanity—a form that resembles and repeats colonial imaginings of the same.

In terms of the focus of this book, the resemblances between colonial global frameworks and ideas of international crime and justice simply serve as another reason why these notions deserve close interrogation. It is not enough to excuse their shortcomings through references to good intentions or humanitarian designs. Rather, it is important to remain aware, as Judith Butler cautions, that there are "form[s] of global responsibility" that are "irresponsible," involving "imperialist appropriation and its politics of imposition."[29] The colonial tendencies of dominant approaches to international criminal justice may underscore the importance of a fuller acknowledgment, as Anghie's work powerfully highlights, of the implication of both international law and international institutions in colonial and imperial practice, again serving as a reminder of the dangers of conceiving of international or globally oriented projects as somehow innately humanitarian. International institutions, in particular, do not sit outside of either politics or colonial history; rather, they can act in ways complicit with colonial and discriminatory ways of understanding the world and the diverse cultures within it.[30]

As I argued in Chapter 2, it is not enough to care about and engage with the suffering of others. In addition, it matters *how*, and on what terms, this is done. It is in this sense that postcolonial theory—as drawn on throughout this book—does not speak to the impossibility of global interconnection but presents the challenge to pursue it with a keen awareness of all the historical and contemporary difficulties of doing so. Given the advent of colonialism, subsequent attempts to figure and pursue international interrelation must actively engage with the colonial project and its enduring effects rather than seek to draw a line between the past and the present.[31]

What Remains

In offering this analysis of the ideas of international crime and justice, my aim is not to call into question the reality of certain experiences of harm and their broader ethical significance. Nor is it to imply that there should be no form of supranational or transnational justice processes or that mass harms, such as genocide and crimes against humanity, do not deserve specific names that recognize their qualitatively unique nature. It is important to appreciate both the demand for these ideas of international crime and justice and the practices they name, as well as the hard work of those seeking to enact them. International crime—in its valorized status—is a label that advocacy organizations and victim-survivors choose to apply to experiences of harm, for many reasons. In addition, people and communities that have experienced injury and injustice call for international justice. To provide just a few examples of the demand for international justice, the Cambodian and Sierra Leonean hybrid tribunals and the Rwandan international tribunal were initially requested by the relevant national governments, the Special Tribunal for Lebanon was called for by the victim's son, and there was civil society advocacy for an international tribunal for the atrocities perpetrated in East Timor in 1999.[32] International criminal justice has also been called for, and enacted in the form of people's tribunals, over time by civil societies around the world; and civil society has also been integral to its contemporary establishment.[33] Meanwhile, the ICC website states that the Office of the Prosecutor has received over 12,000 communications since it started operations.[34] My critique of international criminal justice is also not meant to downplay the value of the hard work of international justice and related organizations that draw broader attention to crimes and offer some form of justice-based response—organizations and practitioners who may operate with much more grounded and contextual understandings of what international criminal justice is and how it works. Nor is it meant to deny the significance of a regime of accountability for state and large-scale harms, which may have external elements given the nature of these harms as perpetrated by those in control of particular geopolitical regions.

At issue in this book has also not been the question of whether suffering matters and deserves a response. Rather my focus has been to resist any conflation of international criminal justice and humanitarianism in order to interrogate the actual ways in which notions of international crime and international justice make it possible to understand and relate to suffering in the world. I have argued that ideas of international crime and justice are both affectively engaging and relationally productive. Given their prominent presentation as uniquely humanitarian, international, and distinctive, this book sought to contribute a sustained analysis (and ultimately a critique) of the nature and implications of both the content of ideas of international crime and justice and their social, legal, and political valorization. The purpose of doing so is to provide continued conceptual space to explore, negotiate, and recognize alternative ontologies of international engagement and approaches to responsibility and interrelation.[35] To acknowledge the problems that mark contemporary approaches to what kind of harm matters and why, as well as what international justice means, is a step toward different ways of engaging with and responding to the suffering of each other. These ways might be named translocalism (the connecting of different locals), reparative transnationalism (practices directed toward a sense of transnational belonging), or "situated forms of worldliness."[36] They might take place definitively outside law (through literature, performance, or aid) or with or alongside it. But this would be a project of cross-cultural engagement and collaboration that might take time and unfold over the *longue durée*, with a cognizance of the various histories that inform it.[37] It also might be a project that is already occurring, in diverse ways and in specific, grounded relations that currently exist between those who are suffering and those who are not (or between just those who are suffering in different locations). Indeed, my hope, as I have articulated it throughout the book, is for forms of relation that are, first, premised on an ability to register the importance of specific lives and histories and, second, integrally shaped by those who have experienced harm (at any moment in time) as well as those who respond to them.

For my part, as well as being cognizant of the problems with the current idealizations of international crime and justice, I am not sure whether notions of international crime and international justice can ever hold the ethical weight currently attributed to them.[38] This is a somber realization for people such as myself, who were previously inspired by the ethical promise and humanitarian imagery associated with these ideas. Yet untethering the practice of international criminal justice from these contemporary ideals of international crime and justice may enable both the continuance of external justice-based practices of responsibility and the creation of different and more historically transformative projects of human interconnection and humanitarian response (as well as the continuance of existing ones). To acknowledge the incongruity of positioning punitive practices of criminalization and punishment as sites at which to imagine an interconnected global community may be a precondition for more ethical engagements with the suffering that occurs throughout the world and all of our complex relations to it.

Notes

Introduction

1. Mr. Justice Jackson quoted in International Military Tribunal (Nuremberg), *Trial of the Major War Criminals Before the International Military Tribunal*, 2:98–99 (emphasis added).

2. Benjamin Ferencz, "Ferencz Closes Lubanga Case for ICC Prosecution."

3. "Stop Rape Now"; Save Darfur Coalition, "Save Darfur.org."

4. See Chapter 2; Alexander, "On the Social Construction of Moral Universals"; Mamdani, *Saviors and Survivors*, part 1. See also Meister, *After Evil*.

5. Amnesty International, "'We Are at Breaking Point,'" 9.

6. Gearóid Tuathail's work has been crucial to my understanding of how a sense of social and relational distance is constructed and can affect how external parties understand what events of suffering are "proximate" (see *Critical Geopolitics*, chapters 1 and 6). On the cognitive and affective force of the discursive frames through which violence is depicted, see also Butler, *Frames of War*, introduction and chapter 1; Doty, *Imperial Encounters*, introduction.

7. See Chapter 2; Alexander, "On the Social Construction of Moral Universals."

8. See, for example, Boltanski, *Distant Suffering*; Chouliaraki, *Spectatorship of Suffering*; Moeller, *Compassion Fatigue*.

9. Rome Statute of the International Criminal Court, preamble. See also Cassese, "Rationale for International Criminal Justice"; United Nations, "Presidents of the International Court of Justice, International Criminal Court Present Reports to General Assembly"; Haveman and Smeulers, "Criminology in a State of Denial".

10. Kofi Annan, quoted in International Criminal Court, "About"; Annan, "Secretary General's Statement to the Inaugural Meeting of Judges of the International Criminal Court." For discussion of this terminology, see (among others) Mégret, "In Whose Name?"; Tallgren, "Voice of the International."

11. The first quote is from International Criminal Court, "About." The second and third quotes are from Coalition for the International Criminal Court, "Fight for Global Justice" and "Explore the International Criminal Court System," respectively.

12. See related discussions in Da Silva, "Many Hundred Thousand Bodies Later," 167; Tallgren, "Sensibility and Sense of International Criminal Law," 593.

13. Cassese, "Rationale for International Criminal Justice," 128; Owada, "International Court of Justice," 137; Koller, "Faith of the International Criminal Lawyer," 1021–22. See also Drumbl, "International Criminal Law"; Simpson, *Law, War and Crime*, preface.

14. See Kendall, "Beyond the Restorative Turn"; Kendall and Nouwen, "Representational Practices at the International Criminal Court."

15. Césaire, *Discourse on Colonialism*; Said, *Orientalism*; Anghie, *Imperialism, Sovereignty and the Making of International Law*; Orford, *Reading Humanitarian Intervention*; Pahuja, *Decolonising International Law*; Douzinas, *Human Rights and Empire*; Mutua, "Savages, Victims, and Saviors." See also Feldman and Ticktin, *In the Name of Humanity*, introduction.

16. See particularly the work of postcolonial feminists on this point, including Mohanty, "Under Western Eyes"; Moreton-Robinson, *Talkin' Up to the White Woman*; hooks, *Talking Back*; Lorde, *Sister Outsider*; Mertens and Pardy, "'Sexurity' and Its Effects in Eastern Democratic Republic of Congo."

17. Césaire, *Discourse on Colonialism*; Ahluwalia, "Fanon's Nausea," 345–46; Orford, *Reading Humanitarian Intervention*, 33–34.

18. See Said, *Orientalism*; Orford, *Reading Humanitarian Intervention*; Douzinas, *Human Rights and Empire*; Mutua, "Savages, Victims, and Saviors"; Mamdani, *Saviors and Survivors*; Abu-Lughod, "Seductions of the 'Honor Crime'"; Pupavac, "Misanthropy Without Borders."

19. See, for example, Mbembe, *On the Postcolony*; Bhabha, *Location of Culture*; Said, *Orientalism*; Wolfe, "History and Imperialism"; Hall, "West and the Rest."

20. Shohat and Stam, *Unthinking Eurocentrism*; Anghie, *Imperialism, Sovereignty and the Making of International Law*; Darby, introduction.

21. Stoler, "Imperial Debris," 195. See also Mertens, "Frames of Empire"; Anghie, *Imperialism, Sovereignty and the Making of International Law*.

22. Anghie, *Imperialism, Sovereignty and the Making of International Law*, 2.

23. Hagan and Levi, "Justiciability as Field Effect," especially 373; Aas, *Globalization and Crime*; Lohne, "Penal Humanitarianism Beyond the Nation State"; Kendall, "Beyond the Restorative Turn," 353. See also Drumbl, *Atrocity, Punishment and International Law*; Simpson, "Atrocity, Law, Humanity."

24. In relation to international crime, see in particular Clarke, "Rethinking Africa Through Its Exclusions" and *Fictions of Justice*, introduction; Hagan and Levi, "Justiciability as Field Effect."

25. Here I draw on Fitzpatrick, *Mythology of Modern Law*, and Anghie, *Imperialism, Sovereignty and the Making of International Law*.

26. Alison Young, *Imagining Crime*, 9. I draw on Young's cultural criminological work to advance this argument in Chapter 1. See also Addis, "Imagining the International Community"; Simpson, "Atrocity, Law, Humanity."

27. An acknowledgment of the temporal specificity of suffering is an important way of resisting discourses that fix suffering to certain places and people and conflate people with their experiences of suffering. See also Butler, "Rethinking Vulnerability and Resistance," 25.

28. International Law Commission, "Report of the International Law Commission on the Work of Its Thirty-Fifth Session" (hereafter, such reports will appear as ILC, "Report of the ILC, 35th Session), 14, and "Report of the ILC, 36th Session," 17.

29. Thiam, "Second Report on the Draft Code of Crimes Against the Peace and Security of Mankind," 96 (hereafter, such reports will be referred to simply as "Second Report" and so on); see also "First Report", 147.

30. My reference to livable lives draws from Butler, *Frames of War*, 42–43. See also Butler, *Precarious Life*, preface.

31. My concern with connecting with the specificities of life as it is lived complements the existing excellent work in this field. See particularly Malkki, "Things to Come"; Ndebele, "Rediscovery of the Ordinary"; J. Evans, "Ethos of the Historian"; Dorsett and McVeigh, *Jurisdiction*; Stauffer, *Ethical Loneliness*.

32. Thiam, "Second Report," 93.

33. International Criminal Court, "Interacting with Communities Affected by Crimes."

34. For the excellent scholarship that has demonstrated how this plays out in practice in specific sociohistorical case studies, see (for example) Clark, *Distant Justice*; Kelsall, *Culture Under Cross-Examination*; Stover and Weinstein, *My Neighbor, My Enemy*; Kent, *Dynamics of Transitional Justice*. My claim, however, is not an empirical claim about the distance that actually exists, but a discursive argument about how this sense of distance is embedded in the very idea of international criminal justice (see also Clark, *Distant Justice*, chapter 2).

35. On "cultural appropriations of suffering", see Kleinman and Kleinman, "Appeal of Experience; The Dismay of Images: Cultural Appropriations of Suffering in Our Times." To be clear, this is an argument about representation and the way in which cultural representations of international crime discursively appropriate, rather than a claim about how those who come into contact with international criminal justice understand this project and how it engages with the specificity of their experiences.

36. For related discussions, see Dixon and Tenove, "International Criminal Justice as a Transnational Field"; Drumbl, "International Criminal Law."

37. See Fournet, *Crime of Destruction and the Law of Genocide*, 1; Henry, *War and Rape*, 5–6.

38. For a critique of narratives of humanitarian intervention "to ensure that 'humanitarian intervention' has a more radical meaning," see Orford, *Reading Humanitarian Intervention*, 37.

39. J. Evans, "Ethos of the Historian," 137. See also Dorsett and McVeigh, *Jurisdiction*, chapter 7; Malkki, "Things to Come"; Ndebele, "Rediscovery of the Ordinary."

40. Chouliaraki, *Spectatorship of Suffering*; Razack, "Stealing the Pain of Others"; Malkki, "Things to Come" and "Speechless Emissaries"; Dean, "Empathy, Pornography, and Suffering"; Boltanski, *Distant Suffering*; Kleinman and Kleinman, "Appeal of Experience"; Feldman and Ticktin, *In the Name of Humanity*; Wilson and Brown, introduction; Crawley and Simić, "Unintended Consequences"; Kennedy, "Reparative Transnationalism"; Bennett and Kennedy, *World Memory*; Fassin, "Humanitarianism as a Politics of Life"; Hesford, *Spectacular Rhetorics*; Abu-Lughod, "Seductions of the 'Honor Crime.'"

41. Among an ever-growing body of work, see, for example, Schwöbel, *Critical Approaches to International Criminal Law*; Mamdani, *Saviors and Survivors*; De Vos, Kendall, and Stahn, *Contested Justice*; Simpson, *Law, War and Crime*; Clarke, Knottnerus, and de Volder, "Africa and the ICC"; Elander, *Figuring Victims in International Criminal Justice*; R. Hughes, "Ordinary Theatre and Extraordinary Law at the Khmer Rouge Tribunal"; Nouwen

and Werner, "Monopolizing Global Justice"; Orford, *Reading Humanitarian Intervention*; Stover and Weinstein, *My Neighbor, My Enemy*; Anghie, *Imperialism, Sovereignty and the Making of International Law*; Clark, *Distant Justice*; Tallgren, "Sensibility and Sense of International Criminal Law"; Mégret, "What Sort of Global Justice Is 'International Criminal Justice'?"; Kendall and Nouwen, "Representational Practices at the International Criminal Court"; Drumbl, *Atrocity, Punishment and International Law*; Henry, *War and Rape*; Balint, *Genocide, State Crime, and the Law*; Burgis-Kasthala, "Defining Justice During Transition?"

42. See, among others, Kelsall, *Culture Under Cross-Examination*; Clarke, *Fictions of Justice*; Branch, "International Justice, Local Injustice"; Kamatali, "Challenge of Linking International Criminal Justice and National Reconciliation"; Fletcher and Weinstein, "World unto Itself?"; Clark, *Distant Justice*.

43. Dixon and Tenove, "International Criminal Justice as a Transnational Field"; de Lint, "Introduction"; Nouwen and Werner, "Doing Justice to the Political"; De Vos, Kendall, and Stahn, *Contested Justice*.

44. Clarke, *Fictions of Justice*; Mamdani, *Saviors and Survivors*; Kelsall, *Culture Under Cross-Examination*; R. Shaw, "Memory Frictions."

45. Kendall and Nouwen, "Representational Practices at the International Criminal Court"; Elander, *Figuring Victims in International Criminal Justice*; Human Rights Center, *Victims' Court?*; Fletcher, "Refracted Justice"; Clarke, Knottnerus, and de Volder, "Africa and the ICC."

46. Mégret, "In Whose Name?"; Tallgren, "Voice of the International"; Schwöbel-Patel, "Spectacle in International Criminal Law."

47. See, for example, Elander, *Figuring Victims in International Criminal Justice*; Tallgren, "Voice of the International"; Stolk, "Solemn Tale of Horror"; Werner, "Reckoning"; Kendall and Nouwen, "Representational Practices at the International Criminal Court."

48. Hagan and Levi, "Justiciability as Field Effect"; Lohne, "Penal Humanitarianism Beyond the Nation State."

49. See Drumbl, "Toward a Criminology of International Crime," and Lohne, "Penal Humanitarianism Beyond the Nation State." See also other critical international criminal justice scholars who have questioned both the contemporary idealization of international criminal justice as a way of addressing mass atrocity and its modes of legitimation: see Damaška, "What Is the Point of International Criminal Justice?"; Drumbl, *Atrocity, Punishment and International Law* and "Tragic Perpetrators and Imperfect Victims."

50. For the commission's work on developing a *Draft Code of Crimes Against the Peace and Security of Mankind*, see Chapter 3 of this book as well as International Law Commission, "Analytical Guide to the Work of the International Law Commission: Draft Code of Crimes Against the Peace and Security of Mankind (Part I)"and "Analytical Guide to the Work of the International Law Commission: Draft Code of Crimes Against the Peace and Security of Mankind (Part II)." There is also a significant body of philosophically oriented work focused on interrogating what constitutes a crime against humanity, which has not produced one generally accepted definition. See, for example, Simpson, *Law, War and Crime*, chapter 2; May, *Crimes Against Humanity*; Vernon, "What Is Crime

Against Humanity?"; Luban, "Theory of Crimes Against Humanity"; and more generally Chapter 3 of this book.

51. Christie, *A Suitable Amount of Crime*, 6 and 3. See also S. Cohen, *Against Criminology*.

52. Clarke, *Fictions of Justice*; Mamdani, *Beyond Nuremberg*; Nouwen and Werner, "Monopolizing Global Justice"; Drumbl, *Atrocity, Punishment and International Law*. See also Findlay and Henham, *Beyond Punishment*.

53. Internationalism, universalism, globalism, cosmopolitanism, humanism, and transnationalism are diverse and sophisticated fields in their own right that cannot be contained by any one definition or text. However, comparatively speaking, it might be possible to broadly characterize internationalism (defined by Malkki in the coming pages) as a philosophy of global interrelation and of working together toward common, international goals; universalism as relating to the idea that certain principles and truths, such as human rights, are applicable across the world as a whole without exception; globalism as concerned with the world as a whole entity; cosmopolitanism as focused on the possibility of conceiving of peoples as also part of a global community—"citizens" of the world (as well as or before being national citizens); humanism as relating to the existence of a shared human essence; and transnationalism as relating to cross-border and interstate cooperation, flows, and issues. These brief descriptions simply illustrate, however, how such a typology is unduly reductive and unhelpful in thinking through the complexity of social problems. They do give a sense of the range of different theoretical perspectives—often with disciplinary variants—that address questions of human and communal interaction and engagement across the world. For some texts that focus on these terms as relevant to the topics of international justice and responsibility, see, for example, in order: Malkki, "Citizens of Humanity"; Sluga and Clavin, *Internationalisms*; Teitel, "Universal and the Particular in International Criminal Justice"; Dirlik, "Is There History After Eurocentrism?"; Nussbaum, *For Love of Country?*; Cheah and Robbins, *Cosmopolitics*; Césaire, *Discourse on Colonialism*; Ahluwalia, "Fanon's Nausea"; Friedrichs, "Transnational Crime and Global Criminology"; Vertovec, "Conceiving and Researching Transnationalism."

54. A. Roberts, *Is International Law International?*, 5–6.

55. Malkki, "Citizens of Humanity," "Things to Come," and "Speechless Emissaries." The quote in the following sentence in text comes from "Citizens of Humanity," 45.

56. Malkki, "Citizens of Humanity," 41.

57. Englund quoted in Malkki, "Commentary," 336. Feldman analyzes the international community as a constructed notion, one enlivened by and produced through the work of United Nations peacekeeping forces in their work in the Gaza Strip in "Ad Hoc Humanity."

58. See also Darian-Smith, "Laws & Societies in Global Contexts"; Darian-Smith and McCarty, "Beyond Interdisciplinarity: Developing a Global Transdisciplinary Framework."

59. See, for example, Massey, *For Space*; Tuathail, *Critical Geopolitics*; De Sousa Santos, "Law"; Riles, "View from the International Plane"; R. Hughes, "Abject Artefacts of Memory"; Ferguson and Gupta, "Spatializing States"; Philippopoulos-Mihalopoulos, "Law's Spatial Turn"; Darian-Smith, *Laws and Societies in Global Contexts*.

60. Riles, "View from the International Plane," 49.

61. On the geopolitical construction of distance and proximity, see Tuathail, *Critical Geopolitics*, chapter 6.

62. See Aas, *Globalization and Crime*; McCulloch, "From Garrison State to Garrison Planet"; Escobar, "Beyond the Third World."

63. Riles, "View from the International Plane," 48.

64. Feldman and Ticktin, *In the Name of Humanity*, introduction.

65. As explained in Chapter 4, I started this project by conducting interviews with people working in and alongside international criminal justice institutions. My interviewees often indicated that it was interesting to reflect on how and why crime and justice are international, but they did not have definite or consistent answers to such questions.

66. Dixon and Tenove, "International Criminal Justice as a Transnational Field"; Nouwen and Werner, "Monopolizing Global Justice."

67. Sagan, "African Criminals / African Victims," 20. See also Simpson, *Law, War and Crime*, preface; Hagan and Levi, "Justiciability as Field Effect," 377; Gearin and Brown, "Rudd Says Australia Condemns Syrian Regime's Chemical Weapons Attack in Damascus"; Rigney, "Asylum-Seeker Policy Could Amount to Crime."

68. AFP/Reuters, "Michael Kirby Recommends UN Refer North Korea to International Criminal Court over Rights Abuses"; Amnesty International, "Dozens of Countries Call on UN to Refer Syria to International Criminal Court"; Black, "Russia and China Veto UN Move to Refer Syria to International Criminal Court"; Buncombe, "UN Chief Wants Syria Crisis Referred to International Criminal Court"; Human Rights Watch, "UN Security Council Should Seek Justice for Myanmar Atrocities." See also Teitel, "Universal and the Particular in International Criminal Justice," 285.

69. Fitzpatrick, *Mythology of Modern Law*.

70. Featherstone, *Solidarity*, 4; Malkki, "Things to Come," 439. See also Malkki, "Commentary." And on the possibility of reparative transnationalism, see Kennedy, "Reparative Transnationalism."

71. See, for example, Kent, *Dynamics of Transitional Justice*; Elander and Hughes, "Internationalising Criminal Justice"; R. Hughes, "Ordinary Theatre and Extraordinary Law at the Khmer Rouge Tribunal"; Elander, *Figuring Victims in International Criminal Justice*; Peskin, *International Justice in Rwanda and the Former Yugoslavia*; Kendall, "'Hybrid' Justice at the Special Court for Sierra Leone"; Mertens and Pardy, "'Sexurity' and Its Effects in Eastern Democratic Republic of Congo"; Malkki, "Speechless Emissaries"; Feldman, "Ad Hoc Humanity"; Burgis-Kasthala, "Defining Justice During Transition?"; Nouwen, *Complementarity in the Line of Fire*. See also the following previously cited works: Kelsall, *Culture Under Cross-Examination*; Clarke, *Fictions of Justice*; Branch, "International Justice, Local Injustice"; Kamatali, "Challenge of Linking International Criminal Justice and National Reconciliation"; Fletcher and Weinstein, "World unto Itself?"; Clark, *Distant Justice*; Mamdani, *Beyond Nuremberg*; Nouwen and Werner, "Monopolizing Global Justice"; Drumbl, *Atrocity, Punishment and International Law*. In relation to the practical application of a concept of distant justice, Clark's recent *Distant Justice* is particularly significant.

72. Scott, *Question of Ethics*, 1.

Chapter 1

1. For a related argument, see Addis, "Imagining the International Community."

2. The term *crimino-legal* can be traced to Alison Young's work in which she, drawing on Peter Rush's articulation of it, uses the term to describe the "crimino-legal complex"—which she defines as the "collapse and confusion of criminology and criminal law that has been gradually occurring since the 1940s" (*Imagining Crime*, 2). Here, I draw on this term to also discuss the intersections between the criminological and the legal, albeit in a different way.

3. Such representations of international crime and justice "write" proximity in the sense discussed by Tuathail (*Critical Geopolitics: The Politics of Writing Global Space*, chapters 1 and 6).

4. Vernon helpfully draws attention to the particularity of using the "figure of *crime*" specifically to grapple with the notion of inhumanity, through the idea of "crimes against humanity" ("What Is Crime Against Humanity?," 231).

5. See A. Young, *Imagining Crime*, 10.

6. Cassese, "Rationale for International Criminal Justice," 128; Owada, "International Court of Justice," 137; Fernández de Gurmendi, "15 Years of ICC."

7. Thiam, "Second Report on the Draft Code of Offences Against the Peace and Security of Mankind," 96. And in this way it remains, like crime more broadly, an object of fascination in social and legal discourse: with respect to noninternational crime (see A. Young, *Imagining Crime*, chapter 1).

8. See, for example, Haveman and Smeulers, "Criminology in a State of Denial," 8; Waldorf, "Mass Justice for Mass Atrocity," 2. Regarding the distinctiveness and newness of international crimes, see International Law Commission, *Yearbook of the International Law Commission, 1950*, 1:112.

9. Arendt, *Eichmann in Jerusalem*, 272. Her sentiments are echoed by numerous others. See, for example, International Law Commission, *Yearbook of the International Law Commission, 1949*, 220 ("violation of international law was a violation of the international public order and not of the national public order"); Cassese, "Rationale for International Criminal Justice," 127.

10. See, for example, Haveman, Kavran, and Nicholls, *Supranational Criminal Law: A System Sui Generis*; Haveman and Smeulers, "Criminology in a State of Denial," 15–16.

11. This is evident, for example, in the self-referential definition of international crime as simply an offense proscribed by international law and international justice as institutions developed through international laws and treaties (discussed in Chapters 3 and 4). See also International Law Commission, "Report of the International Law Commission on the Work of Its Thirty-Fifth Session," 15; Thiam, "Fourth Report on the Draft Code of Offences Against the Peace and Security of Mankind," 70.

12. See de Lint, "Introduction," 1 and 7; Dorsett and McVeigh, *Jurisdiction*.

13. Ferguson and Gupta, "Spatializing States," 982.

14. Cassese, "Rationale for International Criminal Justice," 127; Simpson, *Law, War and Crime*, 30.

15. Teitel, *Transitional Justice*, 33.

16. Rome Statute of the International Criminal Court (hereafter, Rome Statute), preamble.

17. Rome Statute, preamble.

18. Luban, "Theory of Crimes Against Humanity," 125–27.

19. See, in particular, Addis, "Imagining the International Community"; Buchanan and Pahuja, "Law, Nation and (Imagined) International Communities"; Malkki, "Citizens of Humanity." For a discussion of the production of the victim of international crime, see Elander, *Figuring Victims in International Criminal Justice*, chapter 1. For a discussion of the socializing effect of international criminal law, see Koller, "Faith of the International Criminal Lawyer," 1058; see also 1057–60.

20. See Delaney, Ford, and Blomley, "Preface," xvi; Massey, *For Space*; Tuathail, *Critical Geopolitics*, chapter 6; Darian-Smith, *Laws and Societies in Global Contexts*, 167.

21. Ferencz, "Ferencz Closes Lubanga Case for ICC."

22. See also Werner, "Reckoning." Of course, this is not the only site at which international community is imagined.

23. This is so despite the different trajectories of the emergence and codification of these two concepts. Thank you to Willem de Haan and others at the Centre for International Criminal Justice seminar series at the Vrije Universiteit, Amsterdam, for drawing my attention to this point.

24. DeChaine, "Humanitarian Space and the Social Imaginary," 357 and 364. See also Debrix, "Deterritorialised Territories, Borderless Borders."

25. A. Young, *Imagining Crime*, 2; see also 15–19. However, her discussion is more focused on the role of the scapegoat and the expulsion of the criminal in the constitution of identity and community than the present discussion (see ibid., 9). For a related discussion in the international sphere, see Tallgren, "The Voice of the International," 147–48.

26. United States Holocaust Memorial Museum, "Why We Remember the Holocaust."

27. Teitel, "For Humanity," 225–26.

28. A. Young, *Imagining Crime*, 4–5.

29. A. Young, *Imagining Crime*, 4–5 and 9.

30. Addis, "Imagining the International Community," 160.

31. Cassese, *International Criminal Law*, 325. See also Jallow, "International Criminal Tribunal for Rwanda, Prosecutor," 149; International Criminal Court, "Understanding the International Criminal Court," 3.

32. In relation to the question of jurisdiction more specifically, see Dorsett and McVeigh, *Jurisdiction*, 125–26.

33. Quoted in Schabas, *Genocide in International Law*, 14.

34. International Criminal Court, "Justice Matters."

35. Kendall and Nouwen, "Representational Practices at the International Criminal Court," 253 and 256. See also Dixon and Tenove, "International Criminal Justice as a Transnational Field," 408.

36. Kendall and Nouwen, "Representational Practices at the International Criminal Court," 239, footnotes in quoted text are omitted. See also International Criminal Court, "Understanding the International Criminal Court," 35.

37. The court has jurisdiction over the crimes of genocide, crimes against humanity, war crimes, and the crime of aggression (although it has only conditional jurisdiction over aggression).

38. Hagan and Levi, "Justiciability as Field Effect," 377–78. More generally, see also Simpson, *Law, War and Crime*, preface; Sagan, "African Criminals / African Victims."

39. See Koskenniemi, "Legal Cosmopolitanism," 12–13.

40. Akhavan, "Beyond Impunity," 8.

41. Song, "Statement by ICC President Sang-Hyun Song."

42. Simpson, *Law, War and Crime*, 1.

43. Massey, *For Space*, 61; see also 9.

44. See also Tuathail, *Critical Geopolitics*, chapters 1 and 6 and the discussion of his work in Chapter 2.

45. Winter, "The Special Court for Sierra Leone, President," 155.

46. On humanitarianism, see Wilson and Brown, introduction, 2–3 and 19–20.

47. United Nations, "General Assembly Meets to Mark Day of Reflection on 1994 Rwanda Genocide"; Annan, "Rwanda Genocide 'Must Leave Us Always with a Sense of Bitter Regret and Abiding Sorrow'"; Ki-Moon, "Remarks at the Commemoration of the 20th Anniversary of the Rwandan Genocide."

48. D. Robinson, "Dutch Still Grapple with the Shame of Srebrenica"; UN News, "UN Officials Recall 'Horror' of Srebrenica as Security Council Fails to Adopt Measure Condemning Massacre"; Annan, "Srebrenica Tragedy Will Forever Haunt United Nations History, Says Secretary-General on Fifth Anniversary of City's Fall." See also CBS News, "The Shame of Srebrenica"; Eliasson, "UN 'Failed to Protect' People of Srebrenica, Deputy Secretary-General Says at Genocide Commemoration, 'There Will Be Justice for Crimes Committed.'"

49. Wilson and Brown, introduction, 19. On the significance of and demand for "affective justice," see Rush, "Preface," vii.

50. The Responsibility to Protect doctrine is a global norm, according to which states have a responsibility, rather than a right, to intervene in the internal affairs of another state if the latter state is unable or unwilling to protect its nationals from sufficiently grave harm and suffering. See United Nations, "Responsibility to Protect"; International Commission on Intervention and State Sovereignty, "The Responsibility to Protect: Report of the International Commission on Intervention and State Sovereignty"; G. Evans and Sahnoun, "The Responsibility to Protect."

51. Dorsett and McVeigh highlight the interpersonal and subjective effects of the productions of legal jurisdiction that shape the nature and "quality" of the lawful relations that exist in the jurisdictional spheres they envisage and authorize (*Jurisdiction*, 10 and 16).

52. On the affective and ethical consequences of representation, which shape whose lives can be "seen, felt, and known," see Butler, *Precarious Life*, xx. See also Butler, *Frames of War*, 1 and 13.

53. Koller cautions that "one must be mindful of the potential negative effects of building a community through the law" ("Faith of the International Criminal Lawyer," 1062; see also

1062–67). See also, more generally, Hagan and Levi, "Justiciability as Field Effect: When Sociology Meets Human Rights."

54. Simpson, *Law, War and Crime*, 10; Green and Ward, *State Crime*; Balint, Lasslett, and MacDonald, "'Post-Conflict' Reconstruction."

55. Henry, *War and Rape*, 3.

56. Criminology has prioritized much more the discussion of state, structural, and institutional responsibility as central to any discussion of international crime and mass harm. See Haveman and Smeulers, "Criminology in a State of Denial," 8; Balint, *Genocide, State Crime, and the Law*; Friedrichs, "Transnational Crime and Global Criminology," 10; Green and Ward, *State Crime*. Regarding the importance of structural harm in particular, see Balint et al., *Keeping Hold of Justice*; Balint, Evans, and McMillan, "Rethinking Transitional Justice, Redressing Indigenous Harm." And in relation to international criminal justice specifically, see Clarke, "Rethinking Africa Through Its Exclusions" and *Fictions of Justice*.

57. For rigorous accounts of the significance of these factors to the genocide, see, respectively, Mamdani, *When Victims Become Killers*; Uvin, *Aiding Violence* and "Reading the Rwandan Genocide"; Melvern, *A People Betrayed*. On the supply of arms specifically, see Melvern, 5 and 182–83.

58. An earlier version of my argument (published as "Imagining the International: The Constitution of the International as a Site of Crime, Justice and Community," in *Social and Legal Studies* 25, no. 2 [2016]: 163–80) was written in a way that implied that corporations are not covered by international criminal justice, which deserves clarification.

59. Kendall and Nouwen, "Representational Practices at the International Criminal Court," 241.

60. Kendall and Nouwen, 244–45.

61. International Criminal Court, "Victims."

62. These words are borrowed from Butler, *Precarious Life*, xx. See also Butler, *Frames of War*.

63. See, for example, Kamatali, "The Challenge of Linking International Criminal Justice and National Reconciliation," 132.

64. These are the rules displayed at the court and noted in its publications. For example, "in the interests of public order, minors under the age of sixteen are not allowed in the Court building" (International Criminal Court, "Understanding the International Criminal Court," 44). See also International Criminal Court, "Visit Us" and "ICC Rules of Decorum."

65. International Criminal Court, "ICC Rules of Decorum." For a complementary discussion of the ECCC, see Elander and Hughes, "Internationalising Criminal Justice."

66. As Drumbl has shown in relation to child soldiers more generally, this is a disempowering approach to children that enables them to appear as passive victims but not as agents (*Reimagining Child Soldiers in International Law and Policy*). For the potential of space to be exclusionary and embody power relations, see Merry, "International Law and Sociolegal Scholarship," 159–60.

67. Werner, "Reckoning," 173. See also Koller, "Faith of the International Criminal Lawyer," 1059, note 150.

68. Carpenter, quoted in Crawley and Simić, "Unintended Consequences," 93. See also Crawley and Simić more generally.

69. Kendall and Nouwen, "Representational Practices at the International Criminal Court," 259.

70. Butler, Gambetti, and Sabsay, introduction. Butler's chapter in this collection also demonstrates that "vulnerability is not a subjective disposition" ("Rethinking Vulnerability and Resistance," 25).

71. Arendt, *Eichmann in Jerusalem*, 269.

72. Simpson, *Law, War and Crime*, 51.

73. See also Dorsett and McVeigh, *Jurisdiction*, 128. For a consideration and critique of this framing of crimes against humanity, see Luban, "Theory of Crimes Against Humanity," 88 and 124; and, in a noninternational law context, Malkki, "Things to Come" and "Commentary." See also Elander, *Figuring Victims in International Criminal Justice*, 18–19.

74. Regarding the "global carceral complex" justified in part through the "war on terror," see McCulloch, "From Garrison State to Garrison Planet." See also Lohne, "Penal Humanitarianism Beyond the Nation State."

75. Sandström, "Report on the Question of International Criminal Jurisdiction," 19.

76. International Criminal Court, Regulations of the Registry, section 4, and "Permanent Premises of the ICC."

77. For an interesting and related discussion of the nature of the international community produced through the notion of universal jurisdiction, see Addis, "Imagining the International Community."

78. For a related discussion, see Teitel, "Humanity's Law," 376–77.

79. For a related discussion of the "impoverished, pale version of community" that is founded on "fear, alienation," and victimization, see A. Young, *Imagining Crime*, 10.

80. See Werner, "Reckoning."

81. A. Young, *Imagining Crime*, 18–19.

82. See also Dixon and Tenove, "International Criminal Justice as a Transnational Field."

83. Massey, *For Space*, 85.

84. See Social Science Bites, "Doreen Massey on Space."

85. See, for example, Clarke, "Rethinking Africa Through Its Exclusions"; Mamdani, "The New Humanitarian Order"; Clarke, Knottnerus, and de Volder, "Africa and the ICC."

86. The insightful volume edited by Ilana Feldman and Miriam Ticktin (*In the Name of Humanity*) uses this common phrase as a point of departure for an interdisciplinary inquiry into the way in which humanity is configured and invoked across a range of different social, political, and legal spheres.

87. See International Criminal Court, home page: "Situations and Cases," and "Situations Under Investigation."

88. See Douzinas, *Human Rights and Empire*; Fassin, "Humanitarianism as a Politics of Life"; Mutua, "Savages, Victims, and Saviors"; Orford, *Reading Humanitarian Intervention*

89. For a more general discussion on the gendered and racialized nature of legal space, see Merry, "International Law and Sociolegal Scholarship," 159–60.

90. Massey, *For Space*, 9.

91. Justice Hans-Peter Kaul of the court writes: "On 1 July 2002, the date the Rome Statute entered into force, a so-called 'ICC Advance Team,' composed of the first five members of the staff of the future ICC, entered a completely empty office building in The Hague" ("The International Criminal Court," 575).

92. A. Young, *Imagining Crime*, 16.

Chapter 2

1. For the first quote see J. Roberts, "Sudan"; for the second quote, see Evans and Sahnoun, "Responsibility to Protect," 100. See also Grewal, "Somalia 'Is Not a Human Place.'"

2. United Nations, "Outreach Programme on the Rwanda Genocide and the United Nations: Background Information" and "International Residual Mechanism for Criminal Tribunals." See also Welsh, "Rwanda Effect."

3. Gourevitch, *We Wish to Inform You That Tomorrow We Will Be Killed with Our Families*, 350.

4. On the social production of proximity and distance, see Tuathail, *Critical Geopolitics*, 192–93 and 220–21.

5. See, among many others, Tasma, *Opération Turquoise*; Braeckman, *Rwanda*; Des Forges, *Leave None to Tell the Story*; Ferroggiaro, *U.S. and the Genocide in Rwanda*; Barker, "Ghosts of Rwanda"; Gourevitch, "Genocide Fax"; Kabera, *Keepers of Memory*; Melvern, *People Betrayed* and *Conspiracy to Murder*; African Rights, *Rwanda*; Power, *"Problem from Hell"*; Saint-Exupéry, *L'inavouable*; Raymont, *Shake Hands with the Devil*; Harrison, "Rwanda"; Silver, *Last Just Man*; Ibuka, *Rwandan Genocide*; Robinson and Loeterman, "Triumph of Evil"; Glucksmann and Hazan, *Tuez-les tous!*; Robinson, "When Good Men Do Nothing."

6. Barker, "Ghosts of Rwanda."

7. Melvern, *People Betrayed*, 227.

8. Power, *"Problem from Hell,"* 508 and 357. For an extended analysis of these nonfiction texts, read McMillan, "'Our' Shame," in conjunction with this chapter (which contains some updated and corrected information).

9. Straus, "Historiography of the Rwandan Genocide," 517 and 537; Uvin, "Reading the Rwandan Genocide," 76–77 and 99.

10. See, for example, Destexhe, *Rwanda and Genocide in the Twentieth Century*, 60; Bassiouni, "Establishment of the International Criminal Court (ICC)," 241.

11. Grünfeld and Huijboom, *Failure to Prevent Genocide in Rwanda*, xv.

12. Barnett, *Eyewitness to a Genocide*, 161.

13. See, for example, Hughes, *100 Days*; Favreau, *Sunday in Kigali*; Ruhorahoza, *Grey Matter*; George, *Hotel Rwanda*; Raymont, *Shake Hands with the Devil*; Caton-Jones, *Shooting Dogs*; Peck, *Sometimes in April*.

14. See, for example, Bazambanza, *Sourire malgré tout*; Benaron, *Running the Rift*; Combres, *Broken Memory*; Courtemanche, *Sunday by the Pool in Kigali*; Diop and McLaughlin, *Murambi*; Jansen, *Over a Thousand Hills I Walk with You*; Pierce, *Speak Rwanda*; Stassen, *Deogratias*; Tadjo, *Shadow of Imana*.

15. See, for example, Dallaire with Beardsley, *Shake Hands with the Devil*; Gourevitch, *We Wish to Inform You That Tomorrow We Will Be Killed with Our Families*; Hatzfeld, *Life Laid Bare*; Keane, *Season of Blood*; Mushikiwabo and Kramer, *Rwanda Means the Universe*; Rusesabagina and Zoellner, *Ordinary Man*.

16. Dallaire with Beardsley, *Shake Hands with the Devil*, xi.

17. Wilson and Brown, introduction.

18. See, for example, Chishugi, *Long Way from Paradise*; Ilibagiza and Erwin, *Left to Tell*; Kayimahe, *France-Rwanda*; Mushikiwabo and Kramer, *Rwanda Means the Universe*; Rusesabagina and Zoellner, *Ordinary Man*; Nganemariya, *Miracle in Kigali*; Umutesi, *Surviving the Slaughter*. In addition to such Rwandan memoirs, there are also an increasing number of websites containing visual and written survivor testimonies. See, for example, Genocide Archive of Rwanda, "Welcome to the Genocide Archive of Rwanda"; Rwandan Stories, home page; Foundation Rwanda, home page; Voices of Rwanda, "About Voices of Rwanda."

19. See also the following photographic books and exhibits: Jaar, *Let There Be Light* and Peress, *Silence*. For theater productions, see discussions in Dauge-Roth, *Writing and Filming the Genocide of the Tutsis in Rwanda*; Kalisa, "Theatre and the Rwandan Genocide."

20. See, for example, George, *Hotel Rwanda*; Caton-Jones, *Shooting Dogs*.

21. George, *Hotel Rwanda*.

22. Clinton, "Remarks by the President to Genocide Survivors," quoted in McMillan, "Regret, Remorse and the Work of Remembrance," 85.

23. Annan, "Rwanda Genocide 'Must Leave Us Always with a Sense of Bitter Regret and Abiding Sorrow.'" See also Annan, "Secretary-General, in 'Mission of Healing' to Rwanda."

24. On this argument and for a broader analysis of these statements of regret, see McMillan, "Regret, Remorse and the Work of Remembrance."

25. Wroughton, "World Bank Chief Apologizes over Rwanda Genocide"; Verhofstadt, "Discours du Monsieur le Premier Ministre Guy Verhofstadt"; Mbeki, "Statement of the President of the Republic of South Africa."

26. However, the former French president, Nicolas Sarkozy acknowledged that his country had made "errors" with respect to the genocide (Lichfield, "Sarkozy Admits France's Role in Rwandan Genocide"), and President Emmanuel Macron recently established a French commission to research and report on the country's role in the 1994 genocide (Chrisafis, "Macron Asks Experts to Investigate French Role in Rwandan Genocide").

27. Belgian Senate, *Parliamentary Commission of Inquiry Regarding the Events in Rwanda*; Assemblée Nationale, *Mission d'information sur le Rwanda*.

28. United Nations, "Report of the Independent Inquiry into the Actions of the United Nations During the 1994 Genocide in Rwanda"; International Panel of Eminent Personalities to Investigate the 1994 Genocide in Rwanda and the Surrounding Events, *Rwanda*. For another earlier and rigorous inquiry, see Eriksson et al., *International Response to Conflict and Genocide*.

29. For examples of references to "errors," "deficiencies," and "failures," see Assemblée Nationale, *Mission d'information sur le Rwanda*, 3.II.A; Belgian Senate, *Parliamentary Commission*

of Inquiry Regarding the Events in Rwanda, paragraph 4.4; United Nations, "Report of the Independent Inquiry into the Actions of the United Nations During the 1994 Genocide in Rwanda," 35.

30. Balint, Evans, and McMillan, "Justice Claims in Colonial Contexts."

31. Borton and Eriksson, *Lessons from Rwanda*, annex 3.

32. Melvern, "France and Genocide." There was also a second counterinquiry initiated in France (see de Geouffre de la Pradelle, "Introducing the Ongoing Citizen Inquiry Commission"). And a third independent inquiry was commissioned by the Rwandan government (see Moore, "Rwanda Accuses France of Complicity in 1994 Genocide"). At the time of writing, the latest inquiry is the one initiated by France in 2019 (see Chrisafis, "Macron Asks Experts to Investigate French Role in Rwandan Genocide").

33. See, for example, Center for Human Rights and Humanitarian Law, "The Rwanda Commemoration Project"; Survivors Fund, "Learn."

34. For museum websites, see Kigali Genocide Memorial, "Place for Remembrance and Learning"; Imperial War Museums, home page. For the traveling exhibitions facilitated through the United Nations, see United Nations, "Outreach Programme on the Rwanda Genocide and the United Nations: Home Page."

35. See more information at "Remembering Rwanda."

36. United Nations, "Outreach Programme on the Rwanda Genocide and the United Nations: Commemorations."

37. See United Nations, "Outreach Programme on the Rwanda Genocide and the United Nations: Home Page." The program is now also focused on assisting survivors in the wake of the genocide.

38. United Nations, "Outreach Programme on the Rwanda Genocide and the United Nations: About."

39. Howard-Hassmann, "Genocide and State-Induced Famine," 492.

40. Regarding the Holocaust, see Alexander, "On the Social Construction of Moral Universals," 6 and 27–29; Novick, *Holocaust in American Life*, 19–20; Schaffer and Smith, *Human Rights and Narrated Lives*, 20–21.

41. International Panel of Eminent Personalities to Investigate the 1994 Genocide in Rwanda and the Surrounding Events, *Rwanda: The Preventable Genocide*; Straus, "Historiography of the Rwandan Genocide," 533.

42. However, with the passage of time, there is a sense that the international failure has been dealt with (academically and politically), while the genocide and its aftermath have come to assume more prominence in academic work.

43. See McMillan, "'Our' Shame."

44. Melvern, *People Betrayed*, 236.

45. United Nations, "Report of the Independent Inquiry into the Actions of the United Nations During the 1994 Genocide in Rwanda," 30.

46. See Clinton in Barker, "Ghosts of Rwanda."

47. Annan, "Rwanda Genocide 'Must Leave Us Always with a Sense of Bitter Regret and Abiding Sorrow.'"

48. Kagame, "Speech by President Kagame at the 17th Genocide Commemoration Ceremony," "Speech by President Kagame at the 15th Commemoration of the Genocide Against the Tutsi," and "Speech by His Excellency Paul Kagame at the 10th Anniversary of the Genocide in Rwanda"; Rombouts, *Victim Organisations and the Politics of Reparation*, 163.

49. Kigali Memorial Centre, *Jenoside*, 26–28.

50. Rombouts, *Victim Organisations and the Politics of Reparation*, 487. It is important to note that it has been argued that, in practice, this Rwandan framing of "Rwanda" as the preventable genocide has had significant implications for what and whose suffering during the conflict has been officially and socially recognized at the national level. That is, a focus on the genocide as the defining feature of the 1994 violence (often referred to as the "Tutsi genocide") has led to a downplaying of the suffering and loss occasioned by the contemporaneous civil war and particularly the harms experienced by Rwandan Hutus as part of that war or due to their resistance to the genocide. See Cameron, "'Second Betrayal?,'" 3–7.

51. Meierhenrich, "Topographies of Remembering and Forgetting," 292.

52. Kagame, "Speech by His Excellency Paul Kagame at the 10th Anniversary of the Genocide in Rwanda" and "Commemoration of the 14th Anniversary of Tutsi Genocide"; Straus and Waldorf, "Introduction," 13–14.

53. Waldorf, "Instrumentalizing Genocide," 53–54; see also Straus and Waldorf, "Introduction," 11–14.

54. Zorbas, "Aid Dependence and Policy Independence," 104–6.

55. Rombouts, *Victim Organisations and the Politics of Reparation*, 305.

56. J. Roberts, "Sudan"; Grewal, "Somalia 'Is Not a Human Place'"; "Stop Another Rwanda in Sudan"; Blair, "If Darfur Is Not to Be Another Rwanda"; Merrick, "Burma Risks Becoming 'the Next Rwanda' as Violence Grows"; Associated Press, "'We Will Not Let Aleppo Become Another Rwanda.'"

57. Huyssen, *Present Pasts*, 14; Levy and Sznaider, "Memory Unbound," 99.

58. For example, Kagame argued for international and African intervention in Libya by invoking the memory of "Rwanda" as the "preventable genocide" ("Africa").

59. "Obama Strikes the Right Note." This decision has also been presented as a product of the support of three senior women in his administration whose different connections to the international failure to halt the Rwandan genocide led them to advocate for international intervention in Libya—namely, Hillary Clinton (whose husband's administration has been condemned for its response to the genocide and who has publicly expressed her regret regarding the international failure), Samantha Power (a journalist and public policy academic, whose account of the international failure has been broadly acclaimed), and Susan Rice (who was a member of the National Security Council during the Clinton government's failure to intervene in the Rwandan genocide). See Jackson, "One Reason for Obama's Decision on Libya"; Stolberg, "Still Crusading, but Now on the Inside"; Calabresi, "Susan Rice"; Harris, "Clinton Cites Rwanda, Bosnia in Rationale for Libya Intervention."

60. Power, *"Problem from Hell,"* 511.

61. See, for example, Power, "Remember Rwanda, but Take Action in Sudan"; Dallaire, "Looking at Darfur, Seeing Rwanda."

62. Mamdani, *Saviors and Survivors*, 66. See also Dawes, *That the World May Know*, 72. "Rwanda" has also been invoked on subsequent anniversaries to argue for a more robust international response to the atrocities in Darfur. See United Nations, "On Remembrance Day for Rwanda's Genocide Victims, UN Urges Action on Darfur."

63. With respect to the Holocaust, James Young writes about the impact of understandings of the past on the present (*Writing and Rewriting the Holocaust*, 10–11). See also Novick, *Holocaust in American Life*, 4–5.

64. See Mamdani, *Saviors and Survivors*, 22–24 and 37–38. In relation to Darfur, a UN commission of inquiry found that the conflict did not fit the definition of a genocide, even though war crimes and crimes against humanity had been committed in the region (see United Nations, "UN Commission Finds Sudanese Government Responsible for Crimes in Darfur"). Meanwhile, Straus argues that despite the political willingness to accept this designation of the killings, the international response to Darfur has not been more effective ("Historiography of the Rwandan Genocide," 534).

65. See discussion of Tuathail's work on Bosnia (*Critical Geopolitics*) below in this chapter.

66. See Rothberg, *Multidirectional Memory*, 18–19; see also 3.

67. Butler, *Frames of War*, 1–15. On the affective nature of crime, law, and representations of suffering, see, for example, A. Young, *Scene of Violence*, chapter 1; Buchanan and Johnson, "Strange Encounters"; Schaffer and Smith, *Human Rights and Narrated Lives*, chapter 1 and introduction; Reichman, *Affective Life of Law*, chapter 1.

68. On affect more generally, see Buchanan and Johnson, "Strange Encounters," 36; A. Young, *Scene of Violence*, 9.

69. Regarding the centrality of affect to the construction of meaning and the process of thinking, see, respectively, A. Young, *Scene of Violence*, 9; Buchanan and Johnson, "Strange Encounters," 36.

70. See also Schaffer and Smith, *Human Rights and Narrated Lives*, 6.

71. Alexander, "On the Social Construction of Moral Universals," 30–31 and 55.

72. Wilson and Brown, introduction, 22–25.

73. Mbembe, *On the Postcolony*, 8.

74. Barnett, *Eyewitness to a Genocide*, 18.

75. Grünfeld and Huijboom, *Failure to Prevent Genocide in Rwanda*, xv.

76. Mamdani writes about how some existing analyses of the genocide downplay the agency, and thus the responsibility, of the Rwandan people (*When Victims Become Killers*, 196–97). In relation to dominant narratives concerning humanitarian intervention, see Orford, "Muscular Humanitarianism," 695.

77. For alternative accounts to this dominant narrative, see Des Forges, *Leave None to Tell the Story*, 216–21; Kagame, "Speech by His Excellency Paul Kagame at the 10th Anniversary of the Genocide in Rwanda"; Republic of Rwanda National Commission for the Fight Against Genocide, home page. For stories of Rwandan resistance, see Kigali Memorial Centre, *Jenoside*, 30.

78. For broader analyses of this neocolonial iconography, see Orford, *Reading Humanitarian Intervention*; Douzinas, *Human Rights and Empire*; Abu-Lughod, "Seductions of the

'Honor Crime'"; Pupavac, "Misanthropy Without Borders"; Mutua, "Savages, Victims, and Saviors."

79. See PBS, "100 Days of Slaughter." See also Power, *"Problem from Hell"*; Barnett, *Eyewitness to a Genocide.*

80. Wallis, *Silent Accomplice*, x.

81. Uvin, "Reading the Rwandan Genocide," 95–96; Newbury, "Understanding Genocide," 88–91; Mamdani, *When Victims Become Killers*, 9–20; Melvern, *People Betrayed*, 24–36; Orford, *Reading Humanitarian Intervention*, 102–10.

82. Uvin, *Aiding Violence*, 3, and "Reading the Rwandan Genocide," 95–96.

83. See Straus, "Historiography of the Rwandan Genocide," 520–24.

84. Orford, *Reading Humanitarian Intervention*, 87; see also 96–110.

85. Kagame, "Speech by President Kagame at the 15th Commemoration of the Genocide Against the Tutsi."

86. Kagame, "Speech by President Kagame at the 15th Commemoration of the Genocide Against the Tutsi." See also Kagame, "Speech by His Excellency Paul Kagame at the 10th Anniversary of the Genocide in Rwanda"; McNamee, "Reconciling Rwandan Reconciliations," 113.

87. See Kigali Memorial Centre, *Jenoside*, 9. In general, references to the acts of Belgium when it was the colonial power in Rwanda are an exception to the generalized academic focus on just the reaction of always external bystanders during the genocide.

88. Kigali Memorial Centre, 28. See also Kagame, "Speech by President Kagame at the 17th Genocide Commemoration Ceremony," "Speech by President Kagame at the 15th Commemoration of the Genocide Against the Tutsi," and "Speech by His Excellency Paul Kagame at the 10th Anniversary of the Genocide in Rwanda."

89. Kagame, "Remarks by His Excellency Paul Kagame at the 13th Commemoration of Genocide of 1994." See also Kagame, "Speech by His Excellency Paul Kagame at the 10th Anniversary of the Genocide in Rwanda."

90. However, many of these texts are still tailored to Western audiences and markets.

91. Bennett and Kennedy, introduction, 4–9; Schaffer and Smith, *Human Rights and Narrated Lives*, 24.

92. Dawes, *That the World May Know*, 21. On the "narcissism" that underpins contemporary interventions, Ignatieff writes that "we intervened not only to save others, but to save ourselves, or rather an image of ourselves as defenders of universal decencies" (*Warrior's Honor*, 95).

93. Mamdani, *Saviors and Survivors*, 6 and 61–62.

94. Quoted in Mamdani, *Saviors and Survivors*, 54.

95. See, for example, respectively, Power, "Remember Rwanda, but Take Action in Sudan"; Harris, "Clinton Cites Rwanda, Bosnia in Rationale for Libya Intervention"; Marlowe, "Another Rwanda?"; Cole, "Church Council"; Tinsley, "Is Cameroon Gradually Becoming Another Rwanda?". Regarding Myanmar, see Merrick, "Burma Risks Becoming 'the Next Rwanda' as Violence Grows."

96. Levy and Sznaider, "Memory Unbound," 101; Alexander, "On the Social Construction of Moral Universals," 32–34.

97. Mbembe, *On the Postcolony*, 2–3.

98. Orford, *Reading Humanitarian Intervention*, 96–99 and 16–17; Mamdani, *Saviors and Survivors*, 67; Musabende, "Why Libya but Not Rwanda?"

99. Mbembe, *On the Postcolony*, 3.

100. Mamdani, *Saviors and Survivors*, 3.

101. See, in another context, Huyssen, *Present Pasts*, 18. Huyssen describes such constructs as "border-crossing" forms of memory (ibid., 12).

102. Meister, *After Evil*, viii–ix, 144, 155, 163–64, and 2–5. In another and more limited context of legal trials, see Koskenniemi, "Between Impunity and Show Trials," 34 and note 105.

103. International Commission on Intervention and State Sovereignty, "Responsibility to Protect."

104. See Evans and Sahnoun, "Responsibility to Protect," especially 100.

105. Welsh, "Rwanda Effect," 334 and 337–38.

106. More generally, see Riles, "View from the International Plane," 40.

107. Song, "International Criminal Court," 144.

108. In another context, see Koskenniemi, "Between Impunity and Show Trials," 34 and note 105.

109. Levy and Sznaider, *Holocaust and Memory*, 4, 5–6.

110. For an excellent discussion of the potentially appropriative nature of representations of suffering, see Kleinman and Kleinman, "Appeal of Experience."

111. Tuathail, *Critical Geopolitics*, 192–93 and 220–21.

112. Kristof quoted in Mertens, "Frames of Empire: Congo and Sexual Violence," 16. More generally, see ibid., 16–22 and chapters 2–4.

113. Mamdani, *Saviors and Survivors*, introduction and part I.

114. See also R. Hughes, "Abject Artefacts of Memory."

115. In addition to Mamdani's arguments discussed throughout this chapter, see, for example, M. Shaw, "Snare of Analogy."

Chapter 3

1. Ibrahim, "There's Only One Conclusion on the Rohingya in Myanmar."

2. Amnesty International, "'We Are at Breaking Point,'" 9.

3. Regarding the Armenian destruction, see Hovannisian, *Armenian Genocide in Perspective*; Alayarian, *Consequences of Denial*. On the Darfur violence, see Hagan and Rymond-Richmond, *Darfur and the Crime of Genocide*. See more broadly the discussion of this violence in Prunier, *Darfur*; Straus, "Darfur and the Genocide Debate." Regarding Palestinian suffering, see Rashed and Short, "Genocide and Settler Colonialism"; Center for Constitutional Rights, "The Genocide of the Palestinian People." On the need to recognize indigenous harm as genocidal, see Moses, *Genocide and Settler Society*; Cunneen, "Criminology, Genocide and the Forced Removal of Indigenous Children from Their Families"; Balint, "Stating Genocide in Law"; Behrendt, "Genocide"; Woolford and Benvenuto, *Canada and Colonial Genocide*.

4. See, for example, Asquith and Pence, "Why Turkey Won't Say the G-Word When It Comes to the Armenians"; Haltiwanger, "Is Genocide Occurring Against the Rohingya in Myanmar?"; Steele, "Darfur Wasn't Genocide and Sudan Is Not a Terrorist State"; Straus, "Darfur and the Genocide Debate."

5. Barrera, "Former Harper-Era Minister Doubles Down on Calling MMIWG Inquiry Report 'Propagandist.'" See also Woolford, "Canada's MMIWG Report Spurs Debate on the Shifting Definitions of Genocide."

6. From an extensive corpus of literature, see, for example, Geras, *Crimes Against Humanity*; May, *Crimes Against Humanity*; Vernon, "What Is Crime Against Humanity?"; Luban, "Theory of Crimes Against Humanity"; Maier-Katkin, Mears, and Bernard, "Towards a Criminology of Crimes Against Humanity"; Heller, "What Is an International Crime?" On crimes against humanity more broadly, see also, Simpson, *Law, War and Crime*, chapter 2; Waldorf, "Inhumanity's Law"; Van Schaack, "Definition of Crimes Against Humanity"; Bassiouni, *Crimes Against Humanity*. There is also a debate about the definitions of particular crimes, such as genocide. For example, see Straus, "Contested Meanings and Conflicting Imperatives"; Van Schaack, "Crime of Political Genocide"; Churchill, "Genocide"; Curthoys and Docker, "Defining Genocide." The social, political, legal, and academic interest in the category of international crime is both reflective and constitutive of its social and political power.

7. Barnett, *Eyewitness to a Genocide*, 19.

8. Ross, "UN Urged to Label Isis Crimes Against Yazidi Community as 'Genocide.'" For another example, see BBC News, "Downing of MH17 Jet in Ukraine 'May Be War Crime.'"

9. See, for example, Kennedy, "Moving Testimony," 73–75.

10. Fournet, *Crime of Destruction and the Law of Genocide*, xxxi.

11. The first quote is from Schabas, "Genocide and the International Court of Justice: Finally, a Duty to Prevent the Crime of Crimes." The second is from Thiam, "Seventh Report on the Draft Code of Crimes Against the Peace and Security of Mankind" (hereafter, such reports will be referred to simply as "Seventh Report" and so on), 86. See also Barnett, *Eyewitness to a Genocide*, 170; Mamdani, "Politics of Naming"; May, *Crimes Against Humanity*, 3.

12. Rome Statute of the International Criminal Court (hereafter, Rome Statute), Article 5. See also International Criminal Court, "Understanding the International Criminal Court," 1.

13. UN General Assembly, Resolution 174 (II) (November 21, 1947) established the commission, and UN General Assembly, Resolution 177 (II) of the same date requested it to "prepare a draft code of offences against the peace and security of mankind." The general mandate of the commission was to ensure the "progressive development of international law and its codification" (UN General Assembly, Resolution 174 (II) (November 21, 1947). Its members were not simply state representatives but experts in international law, and its members have been predominantly male—with the first female members elected only in 2001 (International Law Commission, "Membership"). The Code was previously known as the "Draft Code of *Offences* Against the Peace and Security of Mankind" (emphasis added).

14. The progress of the commission's work was shaped by requests from the UN General Assembly to rest deliberations while other related matters were resolved, such as the definition

of aggression. The Code was never adopted, and attention shifted to the creation of the ICC—which was informed by the commission's work on the Code and the related topic of international criminal jurisdiction. For a full account of the documents produced through the deliberations over both sessions, see International Law Commission, "Analytical Guide to the Work of the International Law Commission: Draft Code of Crimes Against the Peace and Security of Mankind (Part I)" and "Analytical Guide to the Work of the International Law Commission: Draft Code of Crimes Against the Peace and Security of Mankind (Part II)."

15. Butler, *Frames of War*, particularly the introduction and chapter 1.

16. Butler, *Precarious Life*, chapter 1 and the preface.

17. Butler, *Frames of War*, 1.

18. Luban, "Theory of Crimes Against Humanity," 86.

19. I draw here on Barthes, *Mythologies*; Ndebele, "Rediscovery of the Ordinary."

20. Luban writes, "The phrase 'crimes against humanity' has acquired enormous resonance in the legal and moral imaginations of the post-World War II world" ("Theory of Crimes Against Humanity," 86). See also Simpson, *Law, War and Crime*, chapter 2.

21. Thiam, "Second Report," 99. On distinguishing such harms from "common crimes," see also International Law Commission, "Report of the International Law Commission on the Work of Its Thirty-Eighth Session" (hereafter, such reports will be referred to simply as ILC, "Report of the ILC, 38th Session" and so on), 45.

22. Bassiouni, *Introduction to International Criminal Law*, 139. International criminal tribunals have also differed in terms of their mandate: see Einarsen, *Concept of Universal Crimes in International Law*, 146. See also Luban, "Theory of Crimes Against Humanity," 101; Heller, "What Is an International Crime?," 354.

23. For a sample of terminology, see, for example, Vernon, "What Is Crime Against Humanity?"; Cryer et al, *Introduction to International Criminal Law and Procedure*; Einarsen, *Concept of Universal Crimes in International Law*; Mr. Justice Jackson quoted in International Military Tribunal (Nuremberg), *Trial of the Major War Criminals Before the International Military Tribunal*, 2:98–99; and Thiam, "First Report," 142. These terms are distinct but complementary to other legal terms referring to overriding obligations, important norms, and global jurisdiction regarding certain offenses (such as *jus cogens*, obligations *erga omnes*, and universal jurisdiction).

24. ILC, "Report of the ILC, 36th Session," 12.

25. "The method followed by the Commission in 1954 was a purely enumerative one. The Commission listed a number of acts which, in its view, constituted offences against the peace and security of mankind *but it did not try to establish a link between such acts, except to state that such crimes were crimes in international law*" (ILC, "Report of the ILC, 35th Session," 15 [emphasis added]). See also ILC, "Report of the ILC, 38th Session," 53.

26. ILC, "Report of the ILC, 39th Session," 13. The commission did include an article setting out the broad parameters of the notion of a "crime against the peace and security of mankind," but this was deliberately schematic and more focused on the legal basis of such

harm than its core characteristics. Article 1(2) of the Draft Code provided that "Crimes against the peace and security of mankind are crimes under international law and punishable as such, whether or not they are punishable under national law" ("Draft Code of Crimes Against the Peace and Security of Mankind").

27. ILC, "Report of the ILC, 36th Session," 12. For a related discussion, see ILC, "Report of the ILC, 37th Session," 14. Bassiouni distinguishes between crimes against peace and security and others (*Introduction to International Criminal Law*, 227–30).

28. See, for example, Thiam, "Second Report," 91, and "Third Report," 71.

29. Cryer et al, *Introduction to International Criminal Law and Procedure*, 7.

30. For example, Cassese includes six (*International Criminal Law*, 12), and Bassiouni includes twenty-seven (*Introduction to International Criminal Law*, 142–45).

31. See, for example, Cassese, *International Criminal Law*, 12; Bassiouni, *Introduction to International Criminal Law*, 144–45. Cryer et al refer to the potential of future inclusions (*Introduction to International Criminal Law and Procedure*, 5). Terrorism is also within the mandate of the Special Tribunal for Lebanon (UN Security Council, Resolution 1757). For this tribunal, see Burgis-Kasthala, "Defining Justice During Transition?"

32. Cassese, *International Criminal Law*, 12 and 28.

33. See, for example, Bassiouni, *Introduction to International Criminal Law*, 144–45.

34. It included a separate offense: "crimes against United Nations and associated personnel" ("Draft Code of Crimes Against the Peace and Security of Mankind," Article 19).

35. See Thiam, "Second Report," 96. For a discussion of economic aggression, which is more controversial, see ILC, "Report of the ILC, 36th Session," 16–17. See also Thiam, "Third Report," 71, and "First Report," 142. It is notable that the request from Trinidad and Tobago to recommence discussions regarding an ICC related to its region's experience of the crime of drug trafficking (see United Nations, "Rome Statute of the International Criminal Court").

36. Schabas explains that the court has received communications beyond its mandate relating to "environmental damage, drug trafficking, money laundering, tax evasion and judicial corruption" and "aggression in Iraq" (*Introduction to the International Criminal Court*, 38).

37. Pogge, "Priorities of Global Justice" and "Real World Justice."

38. Van Schaack, "Crime of Political Genocide"; Short, "Cultural Genocide and Indigenous Peoples."

39. White, *Global Environmental Harm*; Beirne and South, *Issues in Green Criminology*.

40. Green and Ward, *State Crime*; Michalowski and Kramer, *State-Corporate Crime*; Clinard and Yeager, *Corporate Crime*; Slapper and Tombs, *Corporate Crime*; Balint, Lasslett, and MacDonald, "'Post-Conflict' Reconstruction, the Crimes of the Powerful and Transitional Justice."

41. Tomuschat, "Document on Crimes Against the Environment," 25. See also Thiam's reference to certain crimes having a "rightful place" in the code ("Seventh Report," 86).

42. See, for example, Thiam, "First Report," 142. See also Vernon, "What Is Crime Against Humanity?," 232; Einarsen, *Concept of Universal Crimes in International Law*, iii and 23; Bassiouni, *Introduction to International Criminal Law*, 137–38.

43. These dynamics, of course, relate to how international crime is defined (my focus here) and applied in practice (affected by jurisdictional limits, prosecutorial policy, available evidence, and so on).

44. For an acknowledgment of a shift in social understandings between the commission's two sessions, see Thiam, "First Report," 144 and 148. See also author's interview with NGO representative 1, April 2014.

45. International Law Commission, *Yearbook of the International Law Commission, 1995* (hereafter, such yearbooks will be referred to simply as "ILC, *Yearbook 1995*" and so on), 1:4.

46. ILC, *Yearbook 1950*, 1:101; ILC, *Yearbook 1995*, 1:11. See also Spiropoulos, "Draft Code of Offences Against the Peace and Security of Mankind," 255.

47. On illegal arms and retaliation, see ILC, *Yearbook 1950*, 1:130–31. On nuclear weapons, see Thiam, "Second Report," 96; ILC, "Report of the ILC, 38th Session," 47. On colonial domination, see Thiam, "Thirteenth Report," 35.

48. ILC, *Yearbook 1950*, 1:151. See also Thiam, "Third Report," 68.

49. Spiropoulos, "Draft Code of Offences Against the Peace and Security of Mankind," 255; ILC, *Yearbook 1950*, 1:119 (in a discussion about the draft of a particular crime). See also Thiam, "Second Report," 91; author's interview with international criminal justice practitioner 1, April 2014; Bassiouni, *Introduction to International Criminal Law*, 147 and 219.

50. Thiam, "Fourth Report," 56 (writing about *crimes against humanity* in particular). It is also described as a "concept . . . so rich in substance" (ibid., 57).

51. Thiam, "Second Report," 90.

52. Thiam, "Third Report," 68; ILC, "Report of the ILC, 39th Session," 13, "Report of the ILC, 35th Session," 14, and *Yearbook 1950*, 1:145. See also ILC, "Report of the ILC, 38th Session," 40 and more generally; ILC, "Report of the ILC, 41st Session," 52; International Law Commission, "Comments and Observations Received Pursuant to General Assembly Resolution 36/106."

53. Rome Statute, Articles 1 and 17(1)(d) (emphasis added). Both the court (ibid., Article 17) and the prosecutor (ibid., Article 15) consider the gravity of a crime in their decisions about whether to proceed with a case. In the case of the prosecutor, gravity is evaluated with reference to the "scale, nature, manner of commission and impact of the crimes" (International Criminal Court, Office of the Prosecutor, "Policy Paper on Case Selection and Prioritisation," 12). This draws on some of the potential bases used to assess "seriousness" that were also discussed by the commission, such as the nature and extent of the crime, the intention informing it, its consequences, and its "especially horrible, cruel, savage and barbarous" nature (these quotes are cited above in this chapter). See also deGuzman, "What Is the Gravity Threshold for an ICC Investigation?"

54. Thiam, "Fifth Report," 2, and "Third Report," 66. As evidence of the circularity of definitions of international crime, its key characteristics are sometimes discussed separately or interdependently—for example, the mass or extent of a crime is discussed as something that determines whether the crime is sufficiently serious to be deemed to be an international crime, as well as being framed as a key characteristic of international crime on its own.

55. Thiam, "Fourth Report," 58–60. This accords with the views of academic scholars. See Luban, "Theory of Crimes Against Humanity," 107; Vernon, "What Is Crime Against Humanity?," 237–38 and 246.

56. Thiam, Seventh Report," 88–89.

57. Thiam, "Seventh Report," 88–89. See also ILC, "Report of the ILC, 38th Session," 45; Thiam, "Third Report," 66.

58. See author's interview with international criminal justice practitioner 2, May 2014.

59. ILC, "Report of the ILC, 36th Session," 12. However, it should be noted that such requirements of systematicity in practice reflect the definitions of genocide and crimes against humanity more than those of other international crimes.

60. Thiam, "Second Report," 93, and "Fourth Report," 58–9. See also May, *Crimes Against Humanity*, 21–22. Commission members also emphasized that international crime was defined by its motive or intention to harm such groups.

61. ILC, "Report of the ILC, 35th Session," 14; Thiam, "Third Report," 66. See also Einarsen, *Concept of Universal Crimes in International Law*, 4; Vernon, "What Is Crime Against Humanity?," 242–46.

62. "Draft Code of Crimes Against the Peace and Security of Mankind," Article 2. For the "hyperbolization of individual agency" in international criminal justice, see Mégret, "What Sort of Global Justice Is 'International Criminal Justice'?," 86. However, many academic commentators see the state character of such crimes as decisive to their nature. See Balint, *Genocide, State Crime, and the Law*; Vernon, "What Is Crime Against Humanity?," 233 and 242; Luban, "Theory of Crimes Against Humanity," 93–94; Haveman and Smeulers, "Criminology in a State of Denial," 13. The commission also arguably leaves the recognition of state responsibility open ("Draft Code of Crimes Against the Peace and Security of Mankind," Article 4).

63. See Bassiouni, *Introduction to International Criminal Law*, 227–31; Drumbl, *Atrocity, Punishment and International Law*, 6.

64. See, for example, Thiam, "Fourth Report," 56–57; ILC, "Report of the ILC, 35th Session," 14–15.

65. Thiam, "First Report," 142 and 143. See also ILC, "Report of the ILC, 35th Session," 14.

66. For the first two quotes, see ILC, "Report of the ILC, 35th Session," 15. For the third quote, see Thiam, "Fourth Report," 73. See also "First Report," 143; the Rome Statute, preamble. May focuses on crimes that "harm humanity" (*Crimes Against Humanity*, 7 and 80).

67. Thiam, "Second Report," 90.

68. ILC, "Report of the ILC, 42nd Session," 17 (in the discussion of whether drug trafficking possessed the characteristics to make it a crime against the peace and security of humankind). See also Haveman and Smeulers, "Criminology in a State of Denial," 16.

69. Thiam, "Second Report," 90; "Third Report," 70–71; "Fourth Report," 57 (quoting the Supreme Court of the British Zone); "Third Report," 69.

70. This discourse resurfaces in the later Rome Statute, which describes the international crimes within its jurisdiction as those that "threaten the peace, security and well-being of the world" (preamble).

71. Comments of the German Democratic Republic in International Law Commission, "Comments and Observations Received Pursuant to General Assembly Resolution 36/106," 276. See also Einarsen, *Concept of Universal Crimes in International Law*, 27–28.

72. At times, it seems that the notion of *crimes against the peace* is associated with aggressive war and that of *crimes against security* with having an "atrocious character" (and hence with war crimes, genocide, and crimes against humanity). See, for example, Thiam, "Third Report," 68. Before moving on, it should be noted that other approaches to defining international crime come up in broader academic literature, such as positivist definitions of international crime as harm proscribed and defined by international law. See Cryer et al, *Introduction to International Criminal Law and Procedure*, 8; Einarsen, *Concept of Universal Crimes in International Law*, 19. According to this account, the distinctiveness of international crime is attributable to its legal basis as a crime that is proscribed through international, rather than national, law (see also Heller's analysis of such definitions in "What Is an International Crime?"). In the commission's debates there are also references to distinctive elements of international crime, such as its collective or complex nature, but these are rarely talked about as definitive of the category in the same way as scalar considerations.

73. Marston, "Social Construction of Scale," 220–21, referring to Howitt.

74. See Delaney and Leitner, "Political Construction of Scale," 93.

75. Riles, "View from the International Plane," 49.

76. De Sousa Santos, "Law," 289. See also Riles, "View from the International Plane," 45 and 49.

77. This even entails a comparison between core and other international crimes. See Thiam, "Second Report," 98–99; ILC, "Report of the ILC, 36th Session," 12; Thiam, "Third Report," 67.

78. ILC, "Report of the ILC, 35th Session," 14.

79. Transnational crime, such as trafficking in people and substances, is presented as more of a sign of the need for cross-jurisdictional cooperation. See, for example, Spiropoulos, "Draft Code of Offences Against the Peace and Security of Mankind," 258.

80. ILC, "Report of the ILC, 35th Session," 14; Thiam, "Fifth Report," 2. See also Thiam, "Second Report," 94 and "Third Report," 70–71; ILC, "Report of the ILC, 42nd Session," 18 (on "raising" harms "to the level of international crimes").

81. This is also reflected in the Rome Statute, which refers to genocide as crime targeting a "national, ethnical, racial or religious group" (Article 6), crimes against humanity as being "widespread" attacks against a "civilian population" (Article 7), and war crimes as being particularly within the jurisdiction of the court when they are committed "as part of a plan or policy or as part of a large-scale commission of such crimes" (Article 8). See also Drumbl, *Atrocity, Punishment and International Law*, 4.

82. Thiam, "Second Report," 93.

83. Butler, *Frames of War*, 6; see also 5. Here I am applying the work of Butler to international criminal justice.

84. On norms of recognition, see Butler, *Frames of War*, 6 and 5.

85. Delaney and Leitner, "Political Construction of Scale," 93; Marston, "Social Construction of Scale," 220.

86. Delaney and Leitner, "Political Construction of Scale," 93; Delaney, Ford, and Blomley, "Preface," xx–xxi; Marston, "Social Construction of Scale," 221.

87. Barthes, "World of Wrestling," in Barthes, *Mythologies*, 13. For an insightful analysis of spectacle, victimhood, and visuality drawing instead on Guy Debord, see Schwöbel-Patel, "Spectacle in International Criminal Law"; and on spectacularization and international justice through the spectacle of victims' suffering, see Clarke, *Fictions of Justice*.

88. Barthes, *Mythologies*, 21 and 17; Ndebele, "Rediscovery of the Ordinary," 143.

89. Thiam, "First Report," 147, and "Second Report," 96.

90. Luban, "Theory of Crimes Against Humanity," 99 (his discussion relates to the idea of crimes against humanity specifically). See also Drumbl, *Atrocity, Punishment and International Law*, 3–4.

91. Thiam, "Second Report," 94 and 93 (emphasis omitted in latter).

92. ILC, "Report of the ILC, 36th Session," 17, and "Report of the ILC, 43rd Session," 102. See also "Report of the ILC, 35th Session," 14; Thiam, "Fourth Report," 57.

93. Barthes clarifies that the spectacular character of representation does not relate to the facticity of what is viewed, but to the fact that it is consumed as spectacle (*Mythologies*, 13). And Ndebele writes of how the crimes of the South African apartheid regime were both "mind-bogglingly spectacular" and represented through spectacle ("Rediscovery of the Ordinary," 143–44). See also Drumbl, *Atrocity, Punishment and International Law*, 3–4 and 8–9.

94. For a related critique of the post-Nuremberg idea of "extraordinary international criminality," see Drumbl, *Atrocity, Punishment and International Law*, 3–4.

95. Ndebele, "Rediscovery of the Ordinary," 150.

96. Barthes, *Mythologies*, 15. See also Rwafa, "Film Representations of the Rwandan Genocide," 397. Rwafa's work alerted me to that of Ndebele.

97. Ndebele, "Rediscovery of the Ordinary," 147; and 143.

98. De Waal, "Writing Human Rights and Getting It Wrong." For a discussion of the spectacle as distancing and simplified, see Malkki, "Speechless Emissaries," 388.

99. Ndebele, "Rediscovery of the Ordinary," 144.

100. See, for example, Drumbl, *Atrocity, Punishment and International Law*, chapter 1, especially 8 (regarding postconflict offending); Smeulers and Hoex, "Studying the Microdynamics of the Rwandan Genocide"; McEvoy and McConnachie, "Victimology in Transitional Justice"; Theidon, "Histories of Innocence."

101. See, for example, McDermott, "Child Victim or Brutal Warlord?"

102. In relation to Sri Lanka, for example, see Maunaguru and de Mel, "Exchange on Transitional Justice in Sri Lanka."

103. See Holá and van Wijk, "Life After Conviction at International Criminal Tribunals," 112. See also Drumbl, *Atrocity, Punishment and International Law*, 15–16. For the work of criminologists who have shown how discourses of monstrosity and exception at the national level can be used to justify serious departures from usual criminal justice principles, see McDonald, "Ungovernable Monsters." Notable in this respect is one special rapporteur's observation that "it should not be forgotten that the crimes covered by the Code were of exceptional gravity and required an exceptional regime" (ILC, *Yearbook 1991*, vol. 2, part 2: 84).

104. See Ní Aoláin, "Women, Security, and the Patriarchy of Internationalized Transitional Justice"; Rose, "Feminist Reconceptualisation of Intimate Partner Violence Against Women"; Manjoo and Mcraith, "Gender-Based Violence and Justice in Conflict and Post-Conflict Areas," 12–13; Boeston, "Of Exceptions and Continuities."

105. See also Ndebele, "Rediscovery of the Ordinary," 155–56.

106. Barthes, *Mythologies*, 23.

107. For example, the International Criminal Court formally focuses on prosecuting those who bear the "greatest responsibility," which has notionally been the focus of most international tribunals to date ("Understanding the International Criminal Court," 5).

108. See also Drumbl, *Atrocity, Punishment and International Law*, 10.

109. Drumbl, *Atrocity, Punishment and International Law*, 8–9 and 21; Smeulers, *Collective Violence and International Criminal Justice*.

110. Smeulers and Hoex, "Studying the Microdynamics of the Rwandan Genocide."

111. Drumbl, *Atrocity, Punishment and International Law*, 8–9.

112. Drumbl, *Atrocity, Punishment and International Law*, 7–9.

113. For a related discussion, see Schwöbel-Patel, "Spectacle in International Criminal Law," 269–70.

114. Hesford, *Spectacular Rhetorics*, 1. On the victims of international crime specifically, see Elander, *Figuring Victims in International Criminal Justice*, chapter 1 and 13–14.

115. Mertens, "Frames of Empire," 40. Mertens was discussing her work in connection to that of Didier Fassin.

116. Butler, *Frames of War*, 42–3. See also Butler, *Precarious Life*, preface.

117. This explains the observation that people accused of international crime may be reluctant to admit their guilt because they are unable to see themselves as the perpetrators of such extreme forms of criminality—an insight emerging from a seminar and question-and-answer session (Scalia, "Legitimacy of International Criminal Tribunals").

118. Butler explains that if particular lives are "from the start, not conceivable as lives within certain epistemological frames, then these lives are never lived nor lost in the full sense" (*Frames of War*, 1; see also 8).

119. Hesford, *Spectacular Rhetorics*, 19. See also Schwöbel-Patel, "Spectacle in International Criminal Law," 268–70 and 272.

120. Hesford, *Spectacular Rhetorics*, 23.

121. Butler, *Frames of War*, 19–23.

122. Butler, *Frames of War*, 3.

123. Butler, *Frames of War*, 14; see also 22. Relatedly, Luban conceptualizes crimes against humanity, specifically, as crimes against "our character as political animals," arguing that they are thus crimes that everyone has an interest in prosecuting since everyone is vulnerable to being a victim of such crimes ("Theory of Crimes Against Humanity," 90–91).

124. See, for example, Butler, *Frames of War*, 31–32; Schwöbel-Patel, "Spectacle in International Criminal Law," 268–69.

125. Dorsett and McVeigh, *Jurisdiction*, 128. See also Meister, *After Evil*, 24.

126. Relatedly, see Vernon, "What Is Crime Against Humanity?," 237–38.

127. Thiam, "Seventh Report," 84. Neil Boister claims that torture does not "shock the conscience of international society sufficiently" (quoted in Heller, "What Is an International Crime?," 409).

128. ILC, "Report of the ILC, 36th Session," 17. See also May, *Crimes Against Humanity*, 4; Luban, "Theory of Crimes Against Humanity," 102.

129. See also Uvin, "Reading the Rwandan Genocide," 91.

130. Mamdani, "New Humanitarian Order."

131. Cameron, "'Second Betrayal?,'" 3–7.

132. Fournet, *Crime of Destruction and the Law of Genocide*, 1. See also Fry, "Nature of International Crimes and Evidentiary Challenges."

133. See Rothberg, *Multidirectional Memory*, 18–19 and 3.

134. See, for example, Uvin, "Reading the Rwandan Genocide," 98.

135. See also Uvin, "Reading the Rwandan Genocide." In its development of the Responsibility to Protect, the International Commission on Intervention and State Sovereignty also does not confine intervention to only genocidal violence ("Responsibility to Protect," xii).

136. De Sousa Santos, "Law," 284; Riles, "View from the International Plane," 45 and 49.

137. De Sousa Santos, "Law," 289.

138. De Sousa Santos, 287; see also 284 and 288.

139. See Riles (discussing Marilyn Strathern's work) in "View from the International Plane," 50.

140. Schwöbel-Patel, "Spectacle in International Criminal Law," 255–56 and 259.

141. In relation to dominant media conceptualizations of refugee populations, see Malkki, "Speechless Emissaries" (the quote is from 378). This sense of zooming out also arguably translates into practice with the process of victims' advocates representing sometimes thousands of victims in the ICC. See Kendall and Nouwen, "Representational Practices at the International Criminal Court," 247–52.

142. Malkki, "Speechless Emissaries," 389. Indeed, Malkki argues in this respect that they are "dehumanizing" (ibid, 390; see also 387 and 378).

143. Emphasis added. See, for example, Thiam, "Second Report," 90; "Third Report," 70–71 and 69; "Fourth Report," 56–57; and "First Report," 143–44.

144. For a related discussion, see Luban, "Theory of Crimes Against Humanity," 88 and 124.

145. Thiam, "Second Report," 90.

146. These crimes are relatable as events that are understood to have taken place on an "international plane." Riles charts a similar dynamic in relation to events in colonial international law discourse ("View from the International Plane," 40 and 43).

147. My focus here is not so much on asserting that there is a proper or real place of international crime as it is on clarifying the effects of the workings of scale.

148. Riles, "View from the International Plane," 47.

149. Thiam, "Second Report," 93. However, he also notes the potential overlap between these categories of offense.

150. Arendt, *Eichmann in Jerusalem*, 269; see also 270–72.

151. Arendt, *Eichmann in Jerusalem*, 272 (emphasis added); see also 270–72. For a similar sentiment, see Cassese, "Rationale for International Criminal Justice," 127.

152. International Panel of Eminent Personalities to Investigate the 1994 Genocide in Rwanda and the Surrounding Events, "*Rwanda,*" paragraph 4.

153. Dorsett and McVeigh make a similar argument about the abstracting of such wrongs as harms against a general legal order (*Jurisdiction*, 128, and chapter 7 generally). On the other hand, there is some reference in the commission's materials to individuals being affected by international crimes. On individuals having "moral value," see Thiam, "Fourth Report," 57.

154. Luban, "Theory of Crimes Against Humanity," 88; see also 124. See also Drumbl, *Atrocity, Punishment and International Law*, 3; Simpson, *Law, War and Crime*, 51.

155. On scale, see Delaney and Leitner, "Political Construction of Scale," 93.

156. For work emphasizing the lived experience of the global and the co-constitutive nature of global and local ideas and practices, see, for example, Autesserre, *Peaceland*; Feldman, "Ad Hoc Humanity"; Levy and Sznaider, *Holocaust and Memory*, chapter 1; Eslava, *Local Space, Global Life*.

157. Riles, "View from the International Plane," 40–41.

158. For an analysis of human rights discourse as a "regime of seeing" that produces hierarchies between those who are positioned as the agents (possessing the rights lacked by others) and others (who are depicted as suffering and rights-*less*), see Hesford, *Spectacular Rhetorics*, 21; see also 4. Hesford writes that "the history of human rights can be told as a history of selective and differential visibility, which has positioned certain bodies, populations, and nations as objects of recognition and granted others the power and means to look and to confer recognition" (ibid., 30). More generally, see ibid., introduction and chapter 1.

159. Hesford, *Spectacular Rhetorics*, 4.

160. Ndebele, "Rediscovery of the Ordinary," 152.

161. Ndebele, 144. See also Barthes, *Mythologies*, 16–17.

162. Ndebele, "Rediscovery of the Ordinary," 150.

163. See Drumbl, *Atrocity, Punishment and International Law*, 20–21.

164. Dorsett and McVeigh discuss the importance of understanding crimes against humanity as "particular wrongs associated with the lives lived in relation with others" (*Jurisdiction*, 128). See also the discussion toward the end of Chapter 4.

165. Ndebele, "Rediscovery of the Ordinary," 148.

166. Butler cautions against the danger of when "we take our moral horror to be a sign of our humanity" (*Frames of War*, 50), precisely because that horror is politically and discursively conditioned and not equally applied.

167. Butler, *Frames of War*, 6.

168. Regarding scale, see Delaney and Leitner, "Political Construction of Scale," 93; Marston, "Social Construction of Scale," 221; De Sousa Santos, "Law," 297.

169. Behrendt, "Genocide," 132. For a discussion of the nature of genocide in Australia (discussed next), see ibid., 140. I should also note that my intention in this discussion is not to suggest that settler-colonial injustice does not constitute genocide in a legal sense.

170. Behrendt, 142.

171. Woolford, "Canada's MMIWG Report Spurs Debate on the Shifting Definitions of Genocide." My discussion here is also informed by the rich discussions at the "Workshop

on Methodological and Theoretical Perspectives in International Criminal Justice" at the University of Oslo, April 24–25, 2014. Vernon also highlights the social and political life and affective force of notions of international crime ("What Is Crime Against Humanity?").

172. Butler, *Frames of War*, 11; see also 9–12. See also Green and Ward on the "crucial role" of civil society "in defining state actions as illegitimate where they violate legal rules or shared moral beliefs" (*State Crime*, 4).

173. See, for example, Clarke, "Rethinking Africa Through Its Exclusions"; Gardam and Jarvis, *Women, Armed Conflict, and International Law*; Buss, "Performing Legal Order"; Behrendt, "Genocide."

Chapter 4

1. High Court of Australia, "Court Etiquette."

2. The United Nations Diplomatic Conference of Plenipotentiaries on the Establishment of an International Criminal Court ("the Rome Conference") was the international conference in 1998 at which the treaty establishing the ICC (the Rome Statute of the International Criminal Court, or Rome Statute) was finalized and adopted. For the conference's records, see United Nations, "United Nations Diplomatic Conference of Plenipotentiaries on the Establishment of an International Criminal Court, Rome, 15 June–17 July, 1998: Official Records." For the most current version of the Rome Statute, see International Criminal Court, "Resource Library." See also International Criminal Court, home page.

3. See, for example, Cassese, "Is the ICC Still Having Teething Problems?," 434. See also Kirsch, "Role of the International Criminal Court in Enforcing International Criminal Law," 541 and 547; Boas, "What Is International Criminal Justice?," 2 and 6–7. See also Simpson, *Law, War and Crime*, 34.

4. For a similar argument about modern law per se, see Fitzpatrick, *Mythology of Modern Law*, 7, see also 5–6.

5. See Fitzpatrick, x and 1, and also 5–7.

6. Examples of such contextual relations around harm are provided later in the chapter, but the notion of "actually existing solidarities" that emerge from contextually grounded relations comes from Malkki, "Things to Come," 436.

7. Annan, "Secretary-General Says Establishment of International Criminal Court Is Gift of Hope to Future Generations" and "Secretary General's Statement to the Inaugural Meeting of Judges of the International Criminal Court." Annan's latter words are also quoted on the court's website and in court exhibitions (see International Criminal Court, "About").

8. United Nations, *United Nations Diplomatic Conference of Plenipotentiaries on the Establishment of an International Criminal Court, Rome, 15 June–17 July, 1998: Official Records: Volume 2* (hereafter, *UN Conference, volume 2*), 67, 62, and 66; see also 109.

9. United Nations, *UN Conference, volume 2*, 93 and 92. See also Schabas, *Introduction to the International Criminal Court*, xi.

10. International Criminal Court, "About."

11. Cassese, "Rationale for International Criminal Justice," 128; Fernández de Gurmendi, "15 Years of ICC."

12. United Nations, *UN Conference, volume 2*, 85; see also 92, 112, and 117.

13. United Nations, *UN Conference, volume 2*, 91, 95; 95, 85; 94, 88; 90, 85, 109; 87; and 89, respectively. See also United Nations Secretary-General, *Rule of Law and Transitional Justice in Conflict and Post-Conflict Societies*, 13; Schiff, *Building the International Criminal Court*, 1; Kendall, "Beyond the Restorative Turn."

14. See, for example, Damaška, "What Is the Point of International Criminal Justice?"; Tallgren, "Sensibility and Sense of International Criminal Law"; Akhavan, "Rise, and Fall, and Rise, of International Criminal Justice"; Clark, *Distant Justice*; Burgis-Kasthala, "Defining Justice During Transition?," 512–16.

15. See International Criminal Court, "Understanding the International Criminal Court," 1. However, the court notes that it is pursuing these goals in partnership.

16. Quoted in Clark, *Distant Justice*, 49.

17. See State of Victoria, "Neighbourhood Justice Centre." For a related discussion, see Mégret, "What Sort of Global Justice Is 'International Criminal Justice'?," 78–81. Tallgren and others have written about the lack of philosophical underpinning for current approaches to international criminal justice. See Tallgren, "Sensibility and Sense of International Criminal Law," and, for example, Drumbl, "Toward a Criminology of International Crime." On rehabilitation, see Holá and van Wijk, "Life After Conviction at International Criminal Tribunals."

18. Nouwen and Werner, "Monopolizing Global Justice," 163.

19. Clarke, *Fictions of Justice*; Nouwen and Werner, "Monopolizing Global Justice"; Kelsall, *Culture Under Cross-Examination*. Regarding victims, see Kendall and Nouwen, "Representational Practices at the International Criminal Court."

20. See, for example, Sands, *From Nuremberg to The Hague*. There are also alternative and earlier starting points for the project of international criminal justice. See Schabas, *Introduction to the International Criminal Court*, 1–8; Robertson, *Crimes Against Humanity*, chapter 1; Glasius, *International Criminal Court*, chapter 1; Heller and Simpson, *Hidden Histories of War Crimes Trials*. However, there is still a teleological sense to these narrations that led us to the supposedly humanitarian present (Simpson, *Law, War and Crime*, 33–34).

21. See, however, Craven, Pahuja, and Simpson, *International Law and the Cold War*. Their work is part of the Cold War International Law project. See Cold War International Law, home page.

22. See United Nations International Criminal Tribunal for the Former Yugoslavia, "Global Spread of International Criminal Justice."

23. See, for example, Boas, "What Is International Criminal Justice?," 12–17; Kelsall, *Culture Under Cross-Examination*, 6.

24. Burgis-Kasthala, "Defining Justice During Transition?," 516–17. On transitional justice, see, among an extensive body of work, United Nations Secretary-General, *Rule of Law and Transitional Justice in Conflict and Post-Conflict Societies*; Teitel, *Transitional Justice*; Kritz, *Transitional Justice*; Minow, *Between Vengeance and Forgiveness*; Leebaw, "Irreconcilable Goals of Transitional Justice"; Nagy, "Transitional Justice as Global Project."

25. Thank you to Barbora Holá for this reminder.

26. Some notable exceptions do exist. See, for example, Simpson, *Law, War and Crime*, chapter 2; O'Keefe, *International Criminal Law*, chapter 3. For some examples of recent work focusing on questions of the internationality or globality of the ICC and international law more broadly, see Tallgren, "Voice of the International"; Mégret, "What Sort of Global Justice Is 'International Criminal Justice'?"; Nouwen and Werner, "Monopolizing Global Justice"; and A. Roberts, *Is International Law International?* On the International Court of Justice, see Burgis, *Boundaries of Discourse in the International Court of Justice*, chapter 1.

27. Boas, "What Is International Criminal Justice?," 1. See also O'Keefe, *International Criminal Law*, 86.

28. International Criminal Court, "About."

29. For an excellent analytical overview of this field, see Nouwen, "'Hybrid Courts.'" For some of the broader literature, see, for example, D. Cohen, "'Hybrid' Justice in East Timor, Sierra Leone, and Cambodia"; Dickinson, "Promise of Hybrid Courts"; Williams, *Hybrid and Internationalised Criminal Tribunals*. On high standards in particular, see Elander and Hughes, "Internationalising Criminal Justice."

30. See Clarke, *Fictions of Justice*; Mamdani, *Beyond Nuremberg*; Nouwen and Werner, "Monopolizing Global Justice"; Drumbl, *Atrocity, Punishment and International Law*; Kelsall, *Culture Under Cross-Examination*.

31. See United Nations, *UN Conference, volume 2*.

32. United Nations, *UN Conference, volume 2*, 65; see also 100.

33. Fitzpatrick, *Mythology of Modern Law*, 2–6.

34. For example, O'Keefe states that the "juridical character of a criminal court as either international or municipal is a function of the legal order on which the court formally depends for its existence" (*International Criminal Law*, 87). See also author's interview with NGO representative 1, April 2014.

35. United Nations, *UN Conference, volume 2*, 112; see also 95 and 101.

36. United Nations, *UN Conference, volume 2*, 80, 95, and 85.

37. Sandström, "Report on the Question of International Criminal Jurisdiction," 20. See also United Nations, *UN Conference, volume 2*, 85, 87, 93, and 116; Cassese, "Rationale for International Criminal Justice," 127; Simpson, *Law, War and Crime*, 33 and 37.

38. Arendt, *Eichmann in Jerusalem*, 270.

39. Schiff, *Building the International Criminal Court*, 1. See also United Nations, *UN Conference, volume 2*, 108.

40. United Nations, *UN Conference, volume 2*, 85.

41. See Koller, "Faith of the International Criminal Lawyer," 1040–41 and 1043.

42. However, it should be noted that I have not exhaustively analyzed these debates. But see, for example, Alfaro, "Report on the Question of International Criminal Jurisdiction," 16, emphasis omitted, and whole report; International Law Commission, *Yearbook of the International Law Commission, 1950*, 1:10. See also Sandström, "Report on the Question of International Criminal Jurisdiction."

43. See, for example, Findlay and McLean, "Emerging International Criminal Justice," 463 and 457.

44. Author's interview with ICC representative 1, May 2014.

45. See International Criminal Court, "About." See also Simpson, *Law, War and Crime*, 30–34.

46. Coalition for the International Criminal Court, "Setting Justice Standards."

47. The quotes are from, in order, International Criminal Court, "Reporting on the International Criminal Court," 9; International Criminal Court, "About"; Rome Statute, Articles 36(3), 42(3), 43(3), and 44(2). More broadly, see Elander and Hughes, "Internationalising Criminal Justice."

48. International Criminal Court, "Understanding the International Criminal Court," 20.

49. United Nations, *UN Conference, volume 2*, 107 and 99; see also 92, 98, 100, and 119.

50. Fernández de Gurmendi, "15 Years of ICC."

51. Fitzpatrick, *Mythology of Modern Law*, 10.

52. For a related discussion, see Simpson, *Law, War and Crime*, chapter 2.

53. United Nations, *UN Conference, volume 2*, 76.

54. United Nations, *UN Conference, volume 2*, 80; see also 87, 91, 114, and 119. See also Cassese, "Rationale for International Criminal Justice," 124.

55. International Criminal Court, "Office of the Prosecutor." See also Clark, *Distant Justice*, chapter 2.

56. United Nations, "Central African Republic." Of course, this may be the case in this country at this point in time, but I am using this example to demonstrate how these broader claims regarding international criminal justice are made in practice.

57. See Nouwen, "'Hybrid Courts,'" 191; Byron, "International Criminal Tribunal for Rwanda," 147.

58. United Nations, *UN Conference, volume 2*, 90; Schabas, *Introduction to the International Criminal Court*, 1; Clark, *Distant Justice*, 37–38.

59. United Nations, *UN Conference, volume 2*, 75.

60. See Glasius, *International Criminal Court*, 13; International Criminal Court, "Understanding the International Criminal Court," 4. It is also a feature that was highlighted in tours of the court that I took in 2014 and 2017.

61. United Nations, *UN Conference, volume 2*, 77; see also 77–120.

62. United Nations, *UN Conference, volume 2*, 76 and 68.

63. Clark argues that in practice, the court has taken a restrictive and noncollaborative approach to complementarity that has involved the consistent prioritization of international justice over national justice (*Distant Justice*, chapter 2).

64. See, for example, Nouwen and Werner, "Doing Justice to the Political"; Koskenniemi, "Between Impunity and Show Trials"; de Lint, "Introduction"; Findlay, *International and Comparative Criminal Justice*; Chazal, "Beyond Borders?"; Burgis-Kasthala, "Defining Justice During Transition?"

65. Thus, it is noted in the International Law Commission debates about an international criminal jurisdiction that "proximity of the trial to the place where the crime was allegedly committed may cast a shadow over the proceedings, raising questions concerning respect for the defendant's right to a fair and impartial trial" (International Law Com-

mission, "Report of the International Law Commission on the Work of Its Forty-Sixth Session," 51).

66. United Nations, *UN Conference, volume 2*, III; see also 115–16 and 119.

67. See International Criminal Court, "Understanding the International Criminal Court," 4 and 5; Nouwen, "'Hybrid Courts,'" 191. See also Clark, *Distant Justice*, chapter 2.

68. United Nations, *UN Conference, volume 2*, 61. Court staff have explained that they "establish the law to people in power" Yates, *Reckoning*. Elsewhere Balint has framed international crimes as those undertaken "in the name of the state" (*Genocide, State Crime, and the Law: In the Name of the State*).

69. See also Glasius, *International Criminal Court*, 2. On the need to more adequately recognize state and institutional actors in national and international justice processes, see Balint, *Genocide, State Crime, and the Law*, 206.

70. Nouwen refers to the purpose of hybrids as bringing together "the best of two worlds," although she acknowledges that they also exist in relation to, on a spectrum with, each other ("'Hybrid Courts,'" 190; see also 192).

71. Fichtelberg, *Hybrid Tribunals*, ix.

72. International Criminal Court, "Witnesses."

73. International Criminal Court, "Interacting with Communities Affected by Crimes." The first quote now appears on the court's LinkedIn profile (International Criminal Court, "International Criminal Court").

74. International Criminal Court, Assembly of States Parties, "Strategic Plan for Outreach of the International Criminal Court."

75. International Criminal Court, "About." For a discussion of a center-periphery divide in international criminal justice, see De Vos, Kendall, and Stahn, introduction, 19. With respect to this divide in legal spaces generally, see de Sousa Santos, "Law," 292.

76. The local is figured in media on the ICC website, for example, as a place of destruction and displacement against which the court's mandate is defined. See International Criminal Court, "Understanding the International Criminal Court," 12 and 16. See also Werner, "Reckoning," 172.

77. International Criminal Court, "Interacting with Communities Affected by Crimes."

78. On the invocation of "the victims" as the motivating force for international justice, see Kendall and Nouwen, "Representational Practices at the International Criminal Court," 253–56. For more on the "figure" of the victim in international criminal justice, see Elander, *Figuring Victims in International Criminal Justice*.

79. International Criminal Court, "Victims' Participation Before the International Criminal Court (ICC)."

80. International Criminal Court, "Georgia."

81. See, for example, Anghie, *Imperialism, Sovereignty and the Making of International Law*, introduction and chapter 1; Ferguson and Gupta, "Spatializing States," 988. Malkki, "National Geographic," 29–30.

82. For alternative conceptualizations of the global and local that acknowledge their independence, see Sassen, "Introduction"; Autesserre, *Peaceland*; Feldman, "Ad Hoc Humanity."

83. International Criminal Court, "Interacting with Communities Affected by Crimes" and "How the Court Works."

84. International Criminal Court, "Interacting with Communities Affected by Crimes." On the international as "removed" in relation to hybrid tribunals, see Elander and Hughes, "Internationalising Criminal Justice."

85. International Criminal Court, "Registry" (emphasis added).

86. International Criminal Court, "Interacting with Communities Affected by Crimes."

87. It shares this characteristic with other global justice projects, such as transitional justice, which emerge from concrete historical circumstances and then become generalized and detached from their original sociohistorical contexts. See Arthur, "How 'Transitions' Reshaped Human Rights"; Nagy, "Transitional Justice as Global Project."

88. Fitzpatrick, *Mythology of Modern Law*, 10.

89. Anghie, *Imperialism, Sovereignty and the Making of International Law*, introduction, 22, and 161. For related discussions, see Said, *Orientalism*, and Ferguson and Gupta, "Spatializing States," 988.

90. See Fitzpatrick and Darian-Smith, "Laws of the Postcolonial," 10; R. Young, *White Mythologies*, chapter 1. Indeed, Fitzpatrick's *Mythology of Modern Law* is centrally directed toward revealing the racial and cultural discrimination at the heart of this mythology.

91. In this sense Nouwen notes that location inside or outside an affected country does not affect whether a court is national or international ("'Hybrid Courts,'" 209).

92. See Bevers, Blokker, and Roording, "Netherlands and the International Criminal Court," 148–49. This contradiction between the ICC's geographical and jurisdictional separateness from and yet coexistence with the Dutch state has had concrete implications for witnesses who have appeared before the ICC and then tried to seek asylum in the Netherlands. See International Bar Association, "Witnesses Before the International Criminal Court," 52–54.

93. Headquarters Agreement Between the International Criminal Court and the Host State, Article 6.

94. See, for example, Headquarters Agreement Between the International Criminal Court and the Host State, Articles 13 and 17–18.

95. International Criminal Court, "How the Court Works."

96. The court "may sit elsewhere, whenever it considers it desirable" (Rome Statute, Article 3). See also International Criminal Court, "Understanding the International Criminal Court," 27.

97. International Criminal Court, "How the Court Works."

98. Rome Statute, Article 107; see also Articles 105 and 106. For an excellent discussion of the imprisonment conditions of detainees sentenced by previous international criminal tribunals, see Holá and van Wijk, "Life After Conviction at International Criminal Tribunals."

99. International Criminal Court, "Understanding the International Criminal Court," 4–5.

100. United Nations, *UN Conference, volume 2*, 66; see also 67–68, 84–86, 90, and 92.

101. International Criminal Court, "Office of the Prosecutor."

102. This may represent a departure from previous configurations of internationality that characterized the ad hoc and hybrid tribunals, whose international staff members were

not nationals of the country where the conflict at issue occurred. In the establishment of a permanent ICC whose existence is not related to one specific site of harm, internationality becomes defined as multiculturalism.

103. International Criminal Court, "Court Today," 1. For updates on these figures, see International Criminal Court, "About."

104. International Criminal Court, "Court Today." In terms of geopolitical groupings, Western Europe and North America are grouped together with Australia (which is not included in the Asia Pacific region). See International Criminal Court, "States Parties to the Rome Statute."

105. Quoted in Jaulmes, "Model Prison for Those Accused of the Most Heinous Crimes."

106. Jaulmes.

107. See, for example, author's interview with NGO representative 1. An emphasis on staff diversity and representativeness was also a feature of the Rome Conference. See United Nations, *UN Conference, volume 2*, 96, 107, 109, and 111–13. See also Winter, "Special Court for Sierra Leone."

108. Rome Statute, Articles 36(8) and 44(2). See also International Criminal Court, "Understanding the International Criminal Court," 9. These factors are considered along with professional qualifications. See, for example, International Criminal Court, "Judicial Divisions."

109. International Criminal Court, "Presidency," "Office of the Prosecutor," and "Who's Who."

110. Rome Statute, Articles 42(2), 36(7) and (8). The Bureau of the Assembly of States Parties (the oversight and management body of states monitoring the ICC) is also meant to have "a representative character, taking into account, in particular, equitable geographical distribution and the adequate representation of the principal legal systems of the world" (ibid., Article 112(3)). See also International Criminal Court, "ICC at a Glance."

111. Rome Statute, Article 103(3).

112. International Criminal Court, "Understanding the International Criminal Court," 37 and 43.

113. International Criminal Court, "How the Court Works."

114. International Criminal Court, *ICC in 3 Minutes*. In practice, judges also acknowledge the broader audience to their work, as I have experienced in the courtroom and witnessed in the court's live streaming and transcripts.

115. International Criminal Court, "Understanding the International Criminal Court," 43. For other accessibility initiatives, see International Criminal Court Forum, home page. The forum is a collaboration between the Office of the Prosecutor and the University of California, Los Angeles, and provides a space for debating key issues related to the court's operations.

116. International Criminal Court, "Registry."

117. International Criminal Court, "Staff Regulations," Article I, 1.1(a).

118. International Criminal Court, "About" and *ICC in 3 Minutes*.

119. International Criminal Court, "Get Involved." On the ICC and "we-talk," see Tallgren, "Voice of the International."

120. International Criminal Court, "Get Involved" (emphasis added).

121. International Criminal Court, "Get Involved."

122. Fitzpatrick, *Mythology of Modern Law*, 9.

123. Lohne, "Penal Humanitarianism Beyond the Nation State," 10.

124. Clark, *Distant Justice*, 35; see also 17. See also Elander and Hughes, "Internationalising Criminal Justice."

125. Clark, *Distant Justice*, introduction, chapter 2, and 17, 35, 13, and 40–41.

126. Clark, 303.

127. Clark, 303–4 and chapters 6 and 7.

128. Clark, 37.

129. Fitzpatrick, *Mythology of Modern Law*, 1; see also 1–3.

130. Chakrabarty, *Provincializing Europe*, 3–4. See also Wolfe, "History and Imperialism," 414; Shohat and Stam, *Unthinking Eurocentrism*, chapter 1; Anghie, *Imperialism, Sovereignty and the Making of International Law*.

131. Resnik and Curtis, *Representing Justice*, 278. This discussion is also informed by a tour I took of the International Criminal Court in 2014.

132. Coalition for the International Criminal Court, "Five Facts About the ICC's New Home."

133. The ICC website describes it as "close to the North Sea . . . in an area between nature and city, set in the rolling dune landscape on the edge of The Hague" (International Criminal Court, "How the Court Works").

134. Indeed, Clark argues that the ICC has "paradoxically failed to insulate itself from interference and politicisation because of its weak grasp of the domestic terrain" (*Distant Justice*, 23).

135. Author's interview with NGO representative 1.

136. See Clarke, *Fictions of Justice*, chapter 1; Clark, *Distant Justice*, 305.

137. International Criminal Court, Assembly of States Parties, "Report of the Bureau on Equitable Geographical Representation and Gender Balance in the Recruitment of Staff of the International Criminal Court," 3. A need to focus on more equitable gender representation at the court is also highlighted (ibid., 4).

138. See, for example, Hoffman, "Dusan Tadic Trial and Due Process Issues"; Stromseth, "International Criminal Court and Justice on the Ground," 436; Kelsall, *Culture Under Cross-Examination*, 8; Schabas, *Introduction to the International Criminal Court*, 59–61; Schiff, *Building the International Criminal Court*, 1; Elander and Hughes, "Internationalising Criminal Justice."

139. Sandström, "Report on the Question of International Criminal Jurisdiction," 20–21; Tallgren, "Sensibility and Sense of International Criminal Law," 565. See also author's interview with ICC representative 2, May 2014. And for a related discussion, see Simpson, *Law, War and Crime*, 34–35.

140. Author's interviews with international criminal justice practitioner 1, April 2014, and ICC representative 1; Drumbl, "International Criminal Law," 44–45; Simpson, *Law, War and Crime*, 35–40 and 30; author's interview with ICC representative 2. See also Cryer,

"International Criminal Law vs State Sovereignty." For the broader relation between the global and the local in the history of war crimes trials, see Simpson, *Law, War and Crime*, chapter 2. On the role of civil society, see Glasius, *International Criminal Court*, chapter 1.

141. On the creation of a "shareholder" economy through the state funding of the ICC and the uneven dynamics of "resource allocation" at the ICC, see Kendall, "Commodifying Global Justice" (the quotes are on 113 and 131).

142. For the court's "international legal personality," see Rome Statute, Article 4(1). Regarding complementarity and state consent, see, for example, ibid., Articles 1, 17, and 52. See also author's interview with ICC representative 2.

143. Rome Statute, preamble.

144. International Criminal Court, "How the Court Works" and "ICC at a Glance." See also United Nations, *UN Conference, volume 2*, 103 and 111.

145. International Criminal Court, "Understanding the International Criminal Court," 19.

146. For a discussion of culture and international criminal justice, see Kelsall, *Culture Under Cross-Examination*, 18–19.

147. Nouwen and Werner, "Monopolizing Global Justice," 173. Drumbl, "International Criminal Law," 41; Dixon and Tenove, "International Criminal Justice as a Transnational Field"; Tallgren, "Voice of the International," 137.

148. International Criminal Court, "About."

149. Nouwen, "'Hybrid Courts,'" 191.

150. Baker, "100 Most Influential People."

151. Rome Statute, Article 48.

152. See International Criminal Court, twitter feed. My argument here is inspired by Abu-Lughod's work on the "modern infrastructures of honor crimes" ("Seductions of the 'Honor Crime,'" 40). On networks of legal humanitarianism, see also Kendall, "Beyond the Restorative Turn."

153. Coalition for the International Criminal Court, "The Fight for Global Justice"; International Criminal Court, "About"; Christine Chung quoted in Yates, *Reckoning*. For a discussion of this film, see also Werner, "Reckoning."

154. Although the court is accountable to the Assembly of States Parties, staff members enjoy significant immunities and protections regarding the impact of their actions on others.

155. Mégret, "What Sort of Global Justice Is 'International Criminal Justice'?," 88. See also Branch, "International Justice, Local Injustice," 25–26.

156. Tallgren, "Voice of the International," 137; see also 142–43 and 154.

157. Shohat and Stam, *Unthinking Eurocentrism*, introduction and chapter 1; Said, *Orientalism*; Chakrabarty, *Provincializing Europe*; Anghie, *Imperialism, Sovereignty and the Making of International Law*. See also Tallgren, "Voice of the International," 135.

158. On remnants of colonialism, see Stoler, "Imperial Debris," 195–96. On the endurance of colonial forms in international law specifically, see Anghie, *Imperialism, Sovereignty and the Making of International Law*, introduction and chapter 3. See also Fitzpatrick, *Mythology of Modern Law*; Pupavac, "Misanthropy Without Borders," 101.

159. See Featherstone, *Solidarity*; Kennedy, "Reparative Transnationalism."

160. Svirsky, "Local Coalitions, Global Partners," 546–47. See also the collaborative work of the Movement of Mothers of Srebrenica and Žepa Enclaves ("About Us").

161. Quoted in Smith, "Aboriginal Groups Welcome Refugees."

162. Dorsett and McVeigh, *Jurisdiction*, 128.

163. RISE, "Stolenwealth Games Boycott."

164. Kwon, "Remarks at Solemn Hearing in Commemoration of the 20th Anniversary of the Adoption of the Rome Statute of the International Criminal Court."

165. Bensouda, "Commemoration of the 20th Anniversary of the Adoption of the Rome Statute of the International Criminal Court."

166. Ra'ad Al Hussein, "Keynote Speech by Zeid Ra'ad Al Hussein." On the emphasis on growth in the "market culture" of the ICC and its related "simple" messaging, see Schwöbel, "Market and Marketing Culture of International Criminal Law," 265–71. See also Nouwen and Werner, "Monopolizing Global Justice," 162.

167. See Kamatali, "Challenge of Linking International Criminal Justice and National Reconciliation," 127; Schabas, *Introduction to the International Criminal Court*, 51; Nouwen, "'Hybrid Courts,'" 194; Cassese, "Rationale for International Criminal Justice," 124–25 and 127. This rationale for international engagement also seems more tethered to a sense of global interrelation as an already existing practice (in the spread of diasporas around the world) than to the figuring internationality as a new global project to be pursued.

168. Nouwen and Werner, "Monopolizing Global Justice," 170–71.

169. Malkki, "Things to Come," 436.

170. Kothari, "Visualising Solidarity" (this is an approximation of Kothari's words during this presentation).

171. See I. Young, *Responsibility for Justice*, chapter 2 and 4; Orford, *Reading Humanitarian Intervention*, 14–18; Butler, *Frames of War*, chapters 1 and 2.

Conclusion

Epigraph: The full Thiam quote involves the Inernational Law Commission member expressing skepticism about the imagined claims of others that this legal system exists. Yet despite its lack of empirical reality, the way the statement is framed still positions such a system as an ideal. For another example see Cassese, "Rationale for International Criminal Justice," 130.

1. United Nations, *United Nations Diplomatic Conference of Plenipotentiaries on the Establishment of an International Criminal Court, Rome, 15 June–17 July, 1998: Official Records: Volume 2*, 85.

2. Annan, "Secretary General's Statement to the Inaugural Meeting of Judges of the International Criminal Court."

3. See, for example, Agamben, *Remnants of Auschwitz*, chapter 1, and the common designation of the Holocaust as unimaginable.

4. Darby notes the cultural dynamic of understandings of the international more generally (introduction, 1–2).

5. This line of critique, as noted throughout the book, is inspired by previous excellent postcolonial and settler-colonial work. See J. Evans, "Ethos of the Historian"; Dorsett and McVeigh, *Jurisdiction*.

6. Instead, as Liisa Malkki has charted in relation to representations of refugees, this becomes another "privileged site . . . through which 'the international community' constitutes itself" ("Speechless Emissaries," 378).

7. See also Hesford, *Spectacular Rhetorics*, 121–22 and 57.

8. International Panel of Eminent Personalities to Investigate the 1994 Genocide in Rwanda and the Surrounding Events, *Rwanda*, paragraph 4.

9. As reflected in Chapter 3, this policing occurs in various ways, both through legal judgments that reject claims of genocide and through the delegitimation of the use of that label by social and political commentators when it is applied to particular events of harm.

10. See, for example, Massey, *For Space*, 61; Riles, "View from the International Plane"; Malkki, "Things to Come," 439–41, and "Citizens of Humanity"; Featherstone, *Solidarity*, 46 and 53.

11. Riles, "View from the International Plane," 48.

12. Douzinas and Warrington, *Justice Miscarried*, chapter 6.

13. Thank you to Ilana Feldman for highlighting this point. See Luban, "Theory of Crimes Against Humanity," 88 and 124.

14. See, for example, Hesford, *Spectacular Rhetorics*; Fassin, "Humanitarianism as a Politics of Life"; Orford, *Reading Humanitarian Intervention*. See also Tallgren, "Voice of the International," 154.

15. Anghie, *Imperialism, Sovereignty and the Making of International Law*, 4.

16. See Césaire, *Discourse on Colonialism*.

17. Regarding the centrality of notions of property and practices of appropriation to the colonial enterprise, see Moreton-Robinson, *White Possessive*.

18. Stoler, "Imperial Debris," 195; Anghie, *Imperialism, Sovereignty and the Making of International Law*, 117. See also Mertens, "Frames of Empire."

19. Stoler, "Imperial Debris," 193.

20. International Criminal Court, home page.

21. Said, *Orientalism*; Shohat and Stam, *Unthinking Eurocentrism*, 146–47; Wolfe, "History and Imperialism," 410.

22. Dorsett and McVeigh, *Jurisdiction*, 117; Fitzpatrick, *Mythology of Modern Law*, 65; Nouwen and Werner, "Monopolizing Global Justice," 160. On the importance of a "global sociolegal perspective," see Darian-Smith, *Laws and Societies in Global Contexts*, 378 (see also her conclusion).

23. International Criminal Court, "How the Court Works."

24. Coalition for the International Criminal Court, "Global Justice for Atrocities." See also International Criminal Court, Assembly of States Parties, "Reports of the Bureau on the Plan of Action of the Assembly of States Parties for Achieving Universality and Full Implementation of the Rome Statute of the International Criminal Court," 2013, 2017, and 2018.

25. Anghie, *Imperialism, Sovereignty and the Making of International Law*, 179, chapter 3, and more generally.

26. See Darby, introduction, 1.

27. On this point, Clarke demonstrates how the cultural bias of the court's operations is a function of the particular crimes it focuses on, among other matters ("Rethinking Africa Through Its Exclusions"). See also the related work of Orford, *Reading Humanitarian Intervention*.

28. For a related discussion of the world that is productively imagined through criminological theory, see Aas, "'Earth Is One but the World Is Not.'"

29. Butler, *Frames of War*, 37.

30. Anghie, *Imperialism, Sovereignty and the Making of International Law*, chapter 3 and 179.

31. On the significance of an engagement with the colonial past as a necessary ground for just relations in the present and future, see Balint et al., *Keeping Hold of Justice*, in particular the introduction, conclusion, and chapter 3.

32. See, in order, Nouwen, "'Hybrid Courts'"; Kamatali, "Challenge of Linking International Criminal Justice and National Reconciliation"; "Call for International Tribunal to Try Killers"; East Timor and Indonesia Action Network, "Lawyers and Law Professors Call for East Timor Justice." See also the country self-referrals to the ICC in the case of the Democratic Republic of Congo, Uganda, the Central African Republic, and Mali (International Criminal Court, "Situations Under Investigation").

33. Glasius, *International Criminal Court*, especially chapter 1.

34. International Criminal Court, "Office of the Prosecutor."

35. This includes developing new iconographies of internationality that may not depend on the visualization of the international as a separate site and an attribute defined by scalar height and that may enable something to be both international and proximate or knowable.

36. See, respectively, Halilovich, "Trans-Local Communities in the Age of Transnationalism"; Kennedy, "Reparative Transnationalism"; Featherstone, *Solidarity*, 52.

37. Angela Davis spoke of the importance of situating justice struggles as long-term projects at the Justice Through Conflict; Conflict Through Justice Symposium, October 24–25, 2016, University of Melbourne. This contrasts with the tendency discussed in Chapter 4 to affirm the existence of international criminal justice and call for the rapid expansion of its jurisdiction. Another important intervention would be to ask people experiencing international crime and justice about their views on how these concepts are currently defined (thank you to Nicola Henry).

38. Others have also questioned the utility of the notion of crime. More generally, Christie notes that "crime is one, but only one, among the numerous ways of classifying deplorable acts" (*Suitable Amount of Crime*, 7). And in relation to crimes against humanity specifically, Vernon pertinently implores his readers to "think about exactly why 'crime' is the right figure to employ" ("What Is Crime Against Humanity?," 249).

Works Cited

Statutes, Cases, and Conventions

Convention on the Prevention and Punishment of the Crime of Genocide. December 9, 1948. S. Exec. Doc. O, 81–1 (1949), 78 UNTS 277 (entered into force January 12, 1951).

"Draft Code of Crimes Against the Peace and Security of Mankind." Text adopted by the International Law Commission at its 48th session, 1996. http://legal.un.org/docs/?path=../ilc/texts/instruments/english/draft_articles/7_4_1996.pdf&lang=EF.

Headquarters Agreement Between the International Criminal Court and the Host State. July 7, 2007, ICC-BD/04-01-08 (entered into force March 1, 2008). https://www.icc-cpi.int/NR/rdonlyres/99A82721-ED93-4088-B84D-7B8ADA4DD062/280775/ICCBD040108ENG1.pdf.

International Criminal Court. Regulations of the Registry, March 6, 2006, ICC-BD/03-03–13 (as amended on 1 August 2018). https://www.icc-cpi.int/resource-library/Documents/RegulationsRegistryEng.pdf.

———. Rome Statute of the International Criminal Court. July 17, 1998. UN Doc. A/CONF.183/9. https://www.icc-cpi.int/resource-library/Documents/RS-Eng.pdf.

———. Staff Regulations. September 12, 2003, ICC-ASP/2/10. https://www.icc-cpi.int/NR/rdonlyres/3119BD70-DFB6-4B8C-BC17-3019CC1D0E21/140182/Staff_Regulations_120704EN.pdf.

International Military Tribunal (Nuremberg). *Trial of the Major War Criminals Before the International Military Tribunal.* Vol. 2. Nuremberg, Germany: International Military Tribunal, 1947.

UN General Assembly, Resolution 174 (II) (November 21, 1947).

UN General Assembly, Resolution 177 (II) (November 21, 1947).

UN Security Council, Resolution 1757, S/Res/1757 (May 30, 2007).

Academic References and Other Sources

Aas, Katja Franko. "'The Earth Is One but the World Is Not': Criminological Theory and Its Geopolitical Divisions." *Theoretical Criminology* 16, no. 1 (2012): 5–20.

———. *Globalization and Crime.* London: SAGE Publications, 2013.

Abu-Lughod, Lila. "Seductions of the 'Honor Crime.'" *Differences* 22, no. 1 (2011): 17–63.

Addis, Adeno. "Imagining the International Community: The Constitutive Dimension of Universal Jurisdiction." *Human Rights Quarterly* 31, no. 1 (2009): 129–62.

AFP/Reuters. "Michael Kirby Recommends UN Refer North Korea to International Criminal Court over Rights Abuses." ABC [Australian Broadcasting Corporation] News, April 18, 2014. https://www.abc.net.au/news/2014-04-18/an-michael-kirby-recommends-un-refer-north-korea-to-internation/5398998.

African Rights. *Rwanda: Death, Despair and Defiance.* London: African Rights, 1995.

Agamben, Giorgio. *Remnants of Auschwitz: The Witness and the Archive.* Translated by Daniel Heller-Roazen. New York: Zone Books, 1999.

Ahluwalia, Pal. "Fanon's Nausea: The Hegemony of the White Nation." *Social Identities* 9, no. 3 (2003): 341–56.

Akhavan, Payam. "Beyond Impunity: Can International Criminal Justice Prevent Future Atrocities?" *American Journal of International Law* 95, no. 1 (2001): 7–31.

———. "The Rise, and Fall, and Rise, of International Criminal Justice." *Journal of International Criminal Justice* 11, no. 3 (2013): 527–36.

Alayarian, Aida. *Consequences of Denial: The Armenian Genocide.* London: Karnac, 2008.

Alexander, Jeffrey C. "On the Social Construction of Moral Universals: The 'Holocaust' from War Crime to Trauma Drama." *European Journal of Social Theory* 5, no. 1 (2002): 5–85.

Alfaro, Ricardo J. "Report on the Question of International Criminal Jurisdiction." UN Doc. A/CN.4/15. In *Yearbook of the International Law Commission, 1950,* 2:1–18. New York: United Nations, 1957.

Amnesty International. "Dozens of Countries Call on UN to Refer Syria to International Criminal Court." Amnesty International. January 14, 2013. https://www.amnesty.org.uk/press-releases/dozens-countries-call-un-refer-syria-international-criminal-court.

———. "'We Are at Breaking Point'—Rohingya: Persecuted in Myanmar, Neglected in Bangladesh." London: Amnesty International, 2016.

Anghie, Antony. *Imperialism, Sovereignty and the Making of International Law.* Cambridge: Cambridge University Press, 2004.

Annan, Kofi. "Advocating for an International Criminal Court." *Fordham International Law Journal* 21, no. 2 (1997): 363–66.

———. "Rwanda Genocide 'Must Leave Us Always with a Sense of Bitter Regret and Abiding Sorrow', Says Secretary-General to New York Memorial Conference." UN Doc. SG/SM/9223-AFR/870-HQ/631. March 26, 2004. https://www.un.org/press/en/2004/sgsm9223.doc.htm.

———. "Secretary-General, in 'Mission of Healing' to Rwanda, Pledges Support of United Nations for Country's Search for Peace and Progress." UN Doc. SG/SM/6552 AFR/56. May 6, 1998. https://www.un.org/press/en/1998/19980506.SGSM6552.html.

———. "Secretary-General Says Establishment of International Criminal Court Is Gift of Hope to Future Generations." UN Doc. SG/SM/6643 L/2891. July 20, 1998. https://www.un.org/press/en/1998/19980720.sgsm6643.html.

———. "Secretary General's Statement to the Inaugural Meeting of Judges of the International Criminal Court." March 11, 2003. https://www.un.org/sg/en/content/sg/statement/2003-03-11/secretary-generals-statement-inaugural-meeting-judges-international.

———. "Srebrenica Tragedy Will Forever Haunt United Nations History, Says Secretary-General on Fifth Anniversary of City's Fall." UN Doc. SG/SM/7489. July 10, 2000. https://www.un.org/press/en/2000/20000710.sgsm7489.doc.html.

Arendt, Hannah. *Eichmann in Jerusalem: A Report on the Banality of Evil*. New York: Penguin Books, 1977.

Arthur, Paige. "How 'Transitions' Reshaped Human Rights: A Conceptual History of Transitional Justice." *Human Rights Quarterly* 31, no. 2 (2009): 321–67.

Asquith, Christina, and Audrey Pence. "Why Turkey Won't Say the G-Word When It Comes to the Armenians." CNN, April 24, 2015. https://edition.cnn.com/2015/04/24/europe/armenia-turkey-massacre/index.html.

Assemblée Nationale. *Mission d'information sur le Rwanda: Rapport d'information*. December 15, 1998. http://www.assemblee-nationale.fr/11/dossiers/rwanda/r1271.asp.

Associated Press. "'We Will Not Let Aleppo Become Another Rwanda': UN Envoy Likens Syrian Civil War to Genocide." *South China Morning Post*, October 7, 2016. https://www.scmp.com/news/world/middle-east/article/2025957/we-will-not-let-aleppo-become-another-rwanda-un-envoy-likens.

Autesserre, Séverine. *Peaceland: Conflict Resolution and the Everyday Politics of International Intervention*. Cambridge: Cambridge University Press, 2014.

Baker, Aryn. "The 100 Most Influential People: Fatou Bensouda." *Time*, 2017. http://time.com/collection/2017-time-100/4736260/fatou-bensouda/.

Balint, Jennifer. *Genocide, State Crime, and the Law: In the Name of the State*. New York: Routledge, 2012.

———. "Stating Genocide in Law: The Aboriginal Embassy and the ACT Supreme Court." In *The Aboriginal Tent Embassy: Sovereignty, Black Power, Land Rights and the State*, edited by Gary Foley, Andrew Schaap, and Edwina Howell, 235–50. New York: Routledge, 2014.

Balint, Jennifer, Julie Evans, and Nesam McMillan. "Justice Claims in Colonial Contexts: Commissions of Inquiry in Historical Perspective." *Australian Feminist Law Journal* 42, no. 1 (2016): 75–96.

———. "Rethinking Transitional Justice, Redressing Indigenous Harm: A New Conceptual Approach." *International Journal of Transitional Justice* 8, no. 2 (2014): 194–216.

Balint, Jennifer, Julie Evans, Mark McMillan, and Nesam McMillan. *Keeping Hold of Justice: Encounters Between Law and Colonialism*. Ann Arbor: University of Michigan Press, 2020.

Balint, Jennifer, Kristian Lasslett, and Kate MacDonald. "'Post-Conflict' Reconstruction, the Crimes of the Powerful and Transitional Justice." *State Crime* 6, no. 1 (2017): 4–12.

Barker, Greg, dir. "Ghosts of Rwanda." *Frontline*. PBS, April 1, 2004. https://www.pbs.org/wgbh/pages/frontline/shows/ghosts/.

Barnett, Michael. *Eyewitness to a Genocide: The United Nations and Rwanda*. Ithaca, NY: Cornell University Press, 2002.

Barrera, Jorge. "Former Harper-Era Minister Doubles Down on Calling MMIWG Inquiry Report 'Propagandist.'" CBC News, June 2, 2019. https://www.cbc.ca/news/indigenous/valcourt-mmiwg-report-1.5159437.

Barthes, Roland. *Mythologies*. Translated by Annette Lavers. New York: Noonday Press, 1972.

Bassiouni, Mahmoud Cherif. *Crimes Against Humanity: Historical Evolution and Contemporary Application*. New York: Cambridge University Press, 2011.

———. "The Establishment of the International Criminal Court (ICC)." In *Genocide at the Millennium—Genocide: A Critical Bibliographic Review*, edited by Samuel Totten, 5: 241–85. New Brunswick, NJ: Transaction Publishers, 2005.

———. *Introduction to International Criminal Law*. 2nd ed. Leiden, the Netherlands: Martinus Nijhoff, 2013.

Bazambanza, Rupert. *Sourire malgré tout: L'histoire du génocide au Rwanda*. Montreal, QC: Éditions Images Interculturelles, 2004.

BBC News. "Downing of MH17 Jet in Ukraine 'May Be War Crime'—UN." BBC News, July 28, 2014. https://www.bbc.com/news/world-europe-28520813.

Behrendt, Larissa. "Genocide: The Distance Between Law and Life." *Aboriginal History* 25 (2001): 132–47.

Beirne, Piers, and Nigel South, eds. *Issues in Green Criminology: Confronting Harms Against Environments, Humanity and Other Animals*. Abingdon, UK: Routledge, 2013.

Belgian Senate. *Parliamentary Commission of Inquiry Regarding the Events in Rwanda*. December 6, 1997. http://www.senate.be/english/rwanda.html.

Benaron, Naomi. *Running the Rift*. Chapel Hill, NC: Algonquin Books, 2012.

Bennett, Jill, and Rosanne Kennedy. Introduction to *World Memory: Personal Trajectories in Global Time*, edited by Jill Bennett and Rosanne Kennedy, 1–15. New York: Palgrave Macmillan, 2002.

———, eds. *World Memory: Personal Trajectories in Global Time*. New York: Palgrave MacMillan, 2002.

Bensouda, Fatou. "Commemoration of the 20th Anniversary of the Adoption of the Rome Statute of the International Criminal Court." July 17, 2018. https://www.icc-cpi.int/itemsDocuments/20180717-otp-speech.pdf.

Bevers, Hans, Niels Blokker, and Jaap Roording. "The Netherlands and the International Criminal Court: On Statute Obligations and Hospitality." *Leiden Journal of International Law* 16, no. 1 (2003): 134–56.

Bhabha, Homi K. *The Location of Culture*. London: Routledge, 1994.

Black, Ian. "Russia and China Veto UN Move to Refer Syria to International Criminal Court." *Guardian*, May 22, 2014. https://www.theguardian.com/world/2014/may/22/russia-china-veto-un-draft-resolution-refer-syria-international-criminal-court.

Blair, Tony. "If Darfur Is Not to Be Another Rwanda, We Must Act, and Now, to Avert Catastrophe." *Independent*, September 17, 2006. https://www.independent.co.uk/voices/commentators/tony-blair-if-darfur-is-not-to-be-another-rwanda-we-must-act-and-now-to-avert-catastrophe-416305.html.

Boas, Gideon. "What Is International Criminal Justice?" In *International Criminal Justice: Legitimacy and Coherence*, edited by Gideon Boas, William A. Schabas, and Michael P. Scharf, 1–24. Northampton, MA: Edward Elgar Publishing, 2012.

Boeston, Jelke. "Of Exceptions and Continuities: Theory and Methodology in Research on Conflict-Related Sexual Violence." *International Feminist Journal of Politics* 19, no. 4 (2017): 506–19.

Boltanski, Luc. *Distant Suffering: Morality, Media and Politics*. Cambridge: Cambridge University Press, 1999.

Borton, John, and John Eriksson. *Lessons from Rwanda—Lessons for Today: Assessment of the Impact and Influence of the Joint Evaluation of Emergency Assistance to Rwanda*. Copenhagen: Denmark Ministry of Foreign Affairs, 2004.

Braeckman, Colette. *Rwanda, histoire d'un génocide*. Paris: Fayard, 1994.

Branch, Adam. "International Justice, Local Injustice: The International Criminal Court in Northern Uganda." *Dissent*, 51, no. 3 (2004): 22–26.

Buchanan, Ruth, and Rebecca Johnson. "Strange Encounters: Exploring Law and Film in the Affective Register." *Studies in Law, Politics, and Society* 46 (2008): 33–60.

Buchanan, Ruth, and Sundhya Pahuja. "Law, Nation and (Imagined) International Communities." *Law Text Culture* 8 (2004): 137–66.

Buncombe, Andrew. "UN Chief Wants Syria Crisis Referred to International Criminal Court." *Independent*, September 28, 2015. https://www.independent.co.uk/news/world/middle-east/un-chief-wants-syria-crisis-referred-to-international-criminal-court-a6670361.html.

Burgis, Michelle L. *Boundaries of Discourse in the International Court of Justice: Mapping Arguments in Arab Territorial Disputes*. Leiden, the Netherlands: Martinus Nijhoff Publishers, 2009.

Burgis-Kasthala, Michelle. "Defining Justice During Transition? International and Domestic Contestations over the Special Tribunal for Lebanon." *International Journal of Transitional Justice* 7, no. 3 (2013): 497–517.

Buss, Doris. "Performing Legal Order: Some Feminist Thoughts on International Criminal Law." *International Criminal Law Review* 11, no. 3 (2011): 409–23.

Butler, Judith. *Frames of War: When Is Life Grievable?* New York: Verso, 2009.

———. *Precarious Life: The Powers of Mourning and Violence*. London: Verso, 2004.

———. "Rethinking Vulnerability and Resistance." In *Vulnerability in Resistance*, edited by Judith Butler, Zeynep Gambetti, and Leticia Sabsay, 12–27. Durham, NC: Duke University Press, 2016.

Butler, Judith, Zeynep Gambetti, and Leticia Sabsay. Introduction to *Vulnerability in Resistance*, edited by Judith Butler, Zeynep Gambetti, and Leticia Sabsay, 1–11. Durham, NC: Duke University Press, 2016.

Byron, Charles Michael Dennis. "The International Criminal Tribunal for Rwanda, President." In *The Pursuit of International Criminal Justice: A World Study on Conflicts, Victimization, and Post-Conflict Justice*, edited by Mahmoud Cherif Bassiouni, 1:146–49. Antwerp, Belgium: Intersentia, 2010.

Calabresi, Massimo. "Susan Rice: A Voice for Intervention." *Time*, March 24, 2011. http://content.time.com/time/magazine/article/0,9171,2061224,00.html.

"Call for International Tribunal to Try Killers." *Age*, October 25, 2005. https://www.theage.com.au/world/call-for-international-tribunal-to-try-killers-20051025-ge1428.html.

Cameron, Colin. "'The Second Betrayal?' Commemorating the 10th Anniversary of the Rwandan Genocide." In *African Studies Association of Australasia and the Pacific 2003*

Conference Proceedings: African on a Global Stage. Accessed February 28, 2020. http://afsaap.org.au/assets/Cameron.pdf.

Cassese, Antonio. *International Criminal Law.* 2nd ed. Oxford: Oxford University Press, 2008.

———. "Is the ICC Still Having Teething Problems?" *Journal of International Criminal Justice* 4, no. 3 (2006): 434–441.

———. "The Rationale for International Criminal Justice." In *The Oxford Companion to International Criminal Justice,* edited by Antonio Cassese, 123–30. Oxford: Oxford University Press, 2009.

Caton-Jones, Michael, dir. *Shooting Dogs.* London: BBC Films, 2005.

CBS News. "The Shame of Srebrenica." *60 Minutes.* New York: CBS News, 1999.

Center for Constitutional Rights. "The Genocide of the Palestinian People: An International Law and Human Rights Perspective." August 25, 2016. https://ccrjustice.org/genocide-palestinian-people-international-law-and-human-rights-perspective.

Center for Human Rights and Humanitarian Law. "The Rwanda Commemoration Project: Genocide in Our Time." Washington: American University Washington College of Law. Accessed December 15, 2019. https://www.wcl.american.edu/impact/initiatives-programs/center/programs/past-initiatives/genocide/resource-booklet/.

Césaire, Aimé. *Discourse on Colonialism.* Translated by Joan Pinkham. New York: Monthly Review Press, 1972.

Chakrabarty, Dipesh. *Provincializing Europe: Postcolonial Thought and Historical Difference.* Princeton, NJ: Princeton University Press, 2007.

Chazal, Nerida. "Beyond Borders? The International Criminal Court and the Geopolitics of International Criminal Justice." *Griffith Law Review* 22, no. 3 (2013): 707–28.

Cheah, Pheng, and Bruce Robbins, eds. *Cosmopolitics: Thinking and Feeling Beyond the Nation.* Minneapolis: University of Minnesota Press, 1998.

Chishugi, Leah. *A Long Way from Paradise: Surviving the Rwandan Genocide.* London: Virago, 2010.

Chouliaraki, Lilie. *The Spectatorship of Suffering.* London: SAGE Publications, 2006.

Chrisafis, Angelique. "Macron Asks Experts to Investigate French Role in Rwandan Genocide." *Guardian,* April 5, 2019. https://www.theguardian.com/world/2019/apr/05/macron-asks-experts-investigate-french-role-rwandan-genocide.

Christie, Nils. *A Suitable Amount of Crime.* London: Routledge, 2004.

Churchill, Ward. "Genocide: Toward a Functional Definition." *Alternatives* 11, no. 3 (1986): 403–30.

Clark, Phil. *Distant Justice: The Impact of the International Criminal Court on African Politics.* Cambridge: Cambridge University Press, 2018.

Clarke, Kamari M. *Fictions of Justice: The International Criminal Court and the Challenge of Legal Pluralism in Sub-Saharan Africa.* New York: Cambridge University Press, 2009.

———. "Rethinking Africa Through Its Exclusions: The Politics of Naming Criminal Responsibility." *Anthropological Quarterly* 83, no. 3 (2010): 625–51.

Clarke, Kamari M., Abel S. Knottnerus, and Eefje de Volder. "Africa and the ICC: An Introduction." In *Africa and the ICC: Perceptions of Justice,* edited by Kamari M. Clarke, Abel S. Knottnerus, and Eefje de Volder, 1–35. Cambridge: Cambridge University Press, 2016.

Clinard, Marshall B., and Peter C. Yeager. *Corporate Crime*. New York: Free Press, 1980.

Clinton, Bill. "Remarks by the President to Genocide Survivors, Assistance Workers, and U.S. and Rwandan Government Officials." March 25, 1998. https://clintonwhitehouse4 .archives.gov/Africa/19980325-16872.html.

Coalition for the International Criminal Court. "Explore the International Criminal Court System." Accessed January 11, 2020. http://www.coalitionfortheicc.org/explore-icc -system-0.

———. "The Fight for Global Justice." Accessed May 22, 2018. http://www.coalitionfortheicc .org/fight-global-justice.

———. "Five Facts About the ICC's New Home." #GlobalJUSTICE. December 16, 2005. https://ciccglobaljustice.wordpress.com/2015/12/16/five-facts-about-the-iccs-new-home/.

———. "Global Justice for Atrocities." Accessed December 17, 2018. http://www .coalitionfortheicc.org/fight/global-justice-atrocities.

———. "Setting Justice Standards." Accessed December 17, 2018. http://www .coalitionfortheicc.org/fight/strong-icc/setting-justice-standards.

Cohen, David. "'Hybrid' Justice in East Timor, Sierra Leone, and Cambodia: 'Lessons Learned' and Prospects for the Future." *Stanford Journal of International Law* 43, no. 1 (2007): 1–38.

Cohen, Stanley. *Against Criminology*. New Brunswick, NJ: Transaction Publishers, 1998.

Cold War International Law. Home page. Accessed December 17, 2018. http://www .coldwarinternationallaw.org/.

Cole, Ethan. "Church Council: Don't Let Zimbabwe Be Another Rwanda." *Christian Post*, June 28, 2008. https://www.christianpost.com/news/church-council-dont-let-zimbabwe -be-another-rwanda-33017/.

Combres, Élisabeth. *Broken Memory: A Novel of Rwanda*. Toronto, ON: Groundwood Books, 2009.

Courtemanche, Gil. *A Sunday by the Pool in Kigali*. Translated by Patricia Claxton. Melbourne, Australia: Text Publishing, 2000.

Craven, Matt, Sundhya Pahuja, and Gerry Simpson, eds. *International Law and the Cold War*. Cambridge: Cambridge University Press, 2019.

Crawley, Karen, and Olivera Simić. "Unintended Consequences: Representations of Rwandan Women and Their Children Born from Rape." *Australian Feminist Law Journal* 36, no. 1 (2012): 87–106.

Cryer, Robert. "International Criminal Law vs State Sovereignty: Another Round?" *European Journal of International Law* 16, no. 5 (2006): 979–1000.

Cryer, Robert, Håkan Friman, Darryl Robinson, and Elizabeth Wilmshurst. *An Introduction to International Criminal Law and Procedure*. 2nd ed. New York: Cambridge University Press, 2010.

Cunneen, Chris. "Criminology, Genocide and the Forced Removal of Indigenous Children from Their Families." *Australian and New Zealand Journal of Criminology* 32, no. 2 (1999): 124–38.

Curthoys, Ann, and John Docker. "Defining Genocide." In *The Historiography of Genocide*, edited by Dan Stone, 9–41. New York: Palgrave Macmillan, 2008.

Da Silva, Denise Ferreira. "Many Hundred Thousand Bodies Later: An Analysis of the 'Legacy' of the International Criminal Tribunal for Rwanda." In *Events: The Force of International Law*, edited by Fleur Johns, Richard Joyce, and Sundhya Pahuja, 165–76. New York: Routledge, 2011.

Dallaire, Roméo. "Looking at Darfur, Seeing Rwanda." *New York Times*, October 4, 2004. https://www.nytimes.com/2004/10/04/opinion/looking-at-darfur-seeing-rwanda.html

Dallaire, Roméo, with Brent Beardsley. *Shake Hands with the Devil: The Failure of Humanity in Rwanda*. Toronto, ON: Random House, 2003.

Damaška, Mirjan. "What Is the Point of International Criminal Justice?" *Chicago-Kent Law Review* 83, no. 1 (2008): 329–65.

Darby, Phillip. Introduction to *Postcolonizing the International: Working to Change the Way We Are*, edited by Phillip Darby, 1–10. Honolulu: University of Hawaii Press, 2006.

Darian-Smith, Eve. *Laws and Societies in Global Contexts: Contemporary Approaches*. New York: Cambridge University Press, 2013.

———. "Laws & Societies in Global Contexts: Contemporary Approaches." Paper presented at Melbourne Law School, Melbourne, Australia, September 8, 2015.

Darian-Smith, Eve, and Philip McCarty. "Beyond Interdisciplinarity: Developing a Global Transdisciplinary Framework." *Transcience* 7, no. 2 (2016): 1–26.

Dauge-Roth, Alexandre. *Writing and Filming the Genocide of the Tutsis in Rwanda: Dismembering and Remembering Traumatic History*. Lanham, MD: Lexington Books, 2010.

Dawes, James. *That the World May Know: Bearing Witness to Atrocity*. Cambridge, MA: Harvard University Press, 2007.

De Geouffre de la Pradelle, Géraud. "Introducing the Ongoing Citizen Inquiry Commission." *Survie*, February 15, 2006. https://survie.org/themes/genocide-des-tutsis-au-rwanda/article/introducing-the-ongoing-citizen.

De Lint, Willem. "Introduction: What Crime? Which Justice? What International Society?" In *Criminal Justice in International Society*, edited by Willem de Lint, Marinella Marmo, and Nerida Chazal, 1–13. New York: Routledge, 2014.

De Sousa Santos, Boaventura. "Law: A Map of Misreading. Toward a Postmodern Conception of Law." *Journal of Law and Society* 14, no. 3 (1987): 279–302.

De Vos, Christian, Sara Kendall, and Carsten Stahn, eds. *Contested Justice: The Politics and Practice of International Criminal Court Interventions*. Cambridge: Cambridge University Press, 2015.

———. Introduction to *Contested Justice: The Politics and Practice of International Criminal Court Interventions*, edited by Christian De Vos, Sara Kendall, and Carsten Stahn, 1–20. Cambridge: Cambridge University Press, 2015.

De Waal, Alex. "Writing Human Rights and Getting It Wrong." *Boston Review*, June 6, 2016. https://bostonreview.net/world/alex-de-waal-writing-human-rights.

Dean, Carolyn J. "Empathy, Pornography, and Suffering." *Differences* 14, no. 1 (2003): 88–124.

Debrix, François. "Deterritorialised Territories, Borderless Borders: The New Geography of International Medical Assistance." *Third World Quarterly* 19, no. 5 (1998): 827–46.

DeChaine, Robert D. "Humanitarian Space and the Social Imaginary: Médecins Sans Frontières / Doctors Without Borders and the Rhetoric of Global Community." *Journal of Communication Inquiry* 26, no. 4 (2002): 354–69.

DeGuzman, Margaret M. "What Is the Gravity Threshold for an ICC Investigation? Lessons from the Pre-Trial Chamber Decision in the Comoros Situation." *ASIL Insights*, August 11, 2015. https://www.asil.org/insights/volume/19/issue/19/what-gravity-threshold -icc-investigation-lessons-pre-trial-chamber.

Delaney, David, Richard Thompson Ford, and Nicholas K. Blomley. "Preface: Where Is Law?" In *The Legal Geographies Reader: Law, Power, and Space*, edited by Nicholas K. Blomley, David Delaney, and Richard Thompson Ford, xiii–xxii. Oxford: Wiley-Blackwell, 2001.

Delaney, David, and Helga Leitner. "The Political Construction of Scale." *Political Geography* 16, no. 2 (1997): 93–97.

Des Forges, Alison. *Leave None to Tell the Story: Genocide in Rwanda*. New York: Human Rights Watch, 1999.

Destexhe, Alain. *Rwanda and Genocide in the Twentieth Century*. Translated by Alison Marschner. London: Pluto Press, 1995.

Dickinson, Laura A. "The Promise of Hybrid Courts." *American Journal of International Law* 97, no. 2 (2003): 295–310.

Diop, Boubacar Boris, and Fiona McLaughlin. *Murambi, The Book of Bones*. Bloomington: Indiana University Press, 2006.

Dirlik, Arif. "Is There History After Eurocentrism? Globalism, Postcolonialism, and the Disavowal of History." *Cultural Critique* 42 (1999): 1–34.

Dixon, Peter, and Chris Tenove. "International Criminal Justice as a Transnational Field: Rules, Authority and Victims." *International Journal of Transitional Justice* 7, no. 3 (2013): 393–412.

Dorsett, Shaunnagh, and Shaun McVeigh. *Jurisdiction*. Abingdon, UK: Routledge, 2012.

Doty, Roxanne Lynn. *Imperial Encounters: The Politics of Representation in North-South Relations*. Minneapolis: University of Minnesota Press, 1996.

Douzinas, Costas. *Human Rights and Empire: The Political Philosophy of Cosmopolitanism*. London: Routledge-Cavendish, 2007.

Douzinas, Costas, and Ronnie Warrington. *Justice Miscarried: Ethics and Aesthetics in Law*. London: Harvester Wheatsheaf, 1994.

Drumbl, Mark A. *Atrocity, Punishment and International Law*. Cambridge: Cambridge University Press, 2007.

———. "International Criminal Law: Taking Stock of a Busy Decade." *Melbourne Journal of International Law* 10, no. 1 (2009): 38–45.

———. *Reimagining Child Soldiers in International Law and Policy*. New York: Oxford University Press, 2012.

———. "Toward a Criminology of International Crime." *Ohio State Journal on Dispute Resolution* 19, no. 1 (2003): 263–82.

———. "Tragic Perpetrators and Imperfect Victims." Paper presented at the Asser Institute, The Hague, October 4, 2017. http://www.asser.nl/about-the-institute/asser-today/tragic -perpetrators-and-imperfect-victims/.

East Timor and Indonesia Action Network. "Lawyers and Law Professors Call for East Timor Justice." February 24, 2002. http://www.etan.org/news/2002a/01law.htm.

Einarsen, Terje. *The Concept of Universal Crimes in International Law.* Oslo: Torkel Opsahl Academic EPublisher, 2012.

Elander, Maria. *Figuring Victims in International Criminal Justice: The Case of the Khmer Rouge Tribunal.* New York: Routledge, 2018.

Elander, Maria, and Rachel Hughes. "Internationalising Criminal Justice—'The National' and 'the International' at the ECCC." Paper presented at the Redress and the Ethics of the International Conference, Australian National University, Canberra, March 22–23, 2018.

Eliasson, Jan. "UN 'Failed to Protect' People of Srebrenica, Deputy Secretary-General Says at Genocide Commemoration, 'There Will Be Justice for Crimes Committed.'" UN Doc. DSG/SM/887. July 11, 2015. https://www.un.org/press/en/2015/dsgsm887.doc.htm.

Eriksson, John, Howard Adelman, John Borton, Hanne Christensen, Krishna Kumar, Astri Suhrke, David Tardif-Douglin, Stein Villumstad, and Lennart Wohlgemuth. *The International Response to Conflict and Genocide: Lessons from the Rwanda Experience (Synthesis Report).* Copenhagen: Danish Ministry of Foreign Affairs, 1996.

Escobar, Arturo. "Beyond the Third World: Imperial Globality, Global Coloniality and Anti-Globalisation Social Movements." *Third World Quarterly* 25, no. 1 (2004): 207–30.

Eslava, Luis. *Local Space, Global Life: The Everyday Operation of International Law and Development.* Cambridge: Cambridge University Press, 2015.

Evans, Gareth, and Mohamed Sahnoun. "The Responsibility to Protect." *Foreign Affairs* 81, no. 6 (2002): 99–110.

Evans, Julie. "The Ethos of the Historian: The Minutes of Evidence Project, and Lives Lived with Law on the Ground." *Law Text Culture* 20 (2016): 136–64.

Fassin, Didier. "Humanitarianism as a Politics of Life." *Public Culture* 19, no. 3 (2007): 499–520.

Favreau, Robert, dir. *A Sunday in Kigali.* Montreal, QC: Equinoxe Productions, 2006.

Featherstone, David. *Solidarity: Hidden Histories and Geographies of Internationalism.* London: Zed Books, 2012.

Feldman, Ilana. "Ad Hoc Humanity: UN Peacekeeping and the Limits of International Community in Gaza." *American Anthropologist* 112, no. 3 (2010): 416–29.

Feldman, Ilana, and Miriam Ticktin, eds. *In the Name of Humanity: The Government of Threat and Care.* Durham, NC: Duke University Press, 2010.

Ferencz, Benjamin. "Ferencz Closes Lubanga Case for ICC Prosecution." August 2011. http://benferencz.org/lectures.html#lubanga.

Ferguson, James, and Akhil Gupta. "Spatializing States: Toward an Ethnography of Neoliberal Governmentality." *American Ethnologist* 29, no. 4 (2002): 981–1002.

Fernández de Gurmendi, Silvia. "15 Years of ICC: International Criminal Justice Is Working and Needs Strong Support." HuffPost, June 30, 2017. https://www.huffingtonpost.com /entry/15-years-of-icc-international-criminal-justice-is_us_59567058e4b0326c0a8d0fbb.

Ferroggiaro, William. *The U.S. and the Genocide in Rwanda: Information, Intelligence and the U.S. Response.* Washington: National Security Archive, 2004.

Fichtelberg, Aaron. *Hybrid Tribunals: A Comparative Examination*. New York: Springer, 2015.

Findlay, Mark. *International and Comparative Criminal Justice: A Critical Introduction*. Abingdon, UK: Routledge, 2013.

Findlay, Mark, and Ralph Henham. *Beyond Punishment: Achieving International Criminal Justice*. Basingstoke, UK: Palgrave Macmillan, 2010.

Findlay, Mark, and Clare McLean. "Emerging International Criminal Justice." *Current Issues in Criminal Justice* 18, no. 3 (2007): 457–80

Fitzpatrick, Peter. *The Mythology of Modern Law*. New York: Routledge, 1992.

Fitzpatrick, Peter, and Eve Darian-Smith. "Laws of the Postcolonial: An Insistent Introduction." In *Laws of the Postcolonial*, edited by Eve Darian-Smith and Peter Fitzpatrick, 1–15. Ann Arbor: University of Michigan Press, 1999.

Fletcher, Laurel E. "Refracted Justice: The Imagined Victim and the International Criminal Court." In *Contested Justice: The Politics and Practice of International Criminal Court Interventions*, edited by Christian De Vos, Sara Kendall, and Carsten Stahn, 302–25. Cambridge: Cambridge University Press, 2015.

Fletcher, Laurel E., and Harvey M. Weinstein. "A World unto Itself? The Application of International Justice in the Former Yugoslavia." In *My Neighbor, My Enemy: Justice and Community in the Aftermath of Mass Atrocity*, edited by Eric Stover and Harvey M. Weinstein, 29–48. Cambridge: Cambridge University Press, 2004.

Foundation Rwanda. Home page. Accessed May 22, 2018. http://www.foundationrwanda .org.

Fournet, Caroline. *The Crime of Destruction and the Law of Genocide: Their Impact on Collective Memory*. Aldershot, UK: Ashgate, 2007.

Friedrichs, David O. "Transnational Crime and Global Criminology: Definitional, Typological, and Contextual Conundrums." *Social Justice* 34, no. 2 (2007): 4–18.

Fry, Elinor. "The Nature of International Crimes and Evidentiary Challenges: Preserving Quality While Managing Quantity." In *Pluralism in International Criminal Law*, edited by Elies Van Sliedregt and Sergey Vasiliev, 251–72. Oxford: Oxford University Press, 2014.

Gardam, Judith G., and Michelle J. Jarvis. *Women, Armed Conflict, and International Law*. Boston: Kluwer Law International, 2001.

Gearin, Mary, and Matt Brown. "Rudd Says Australia Condemns Syrian Regime's Chemical Weapons Attack in Damascus." ABC [Australian Broadcasting Corporation] News, August 29, 2013. https://www.abc.net.au/news/2013-08-29/us-concludes-syrian-regime -behind-chemical-attack/4920332.

Genocide Archive of Rwanda. "Welcome to the Genocide Archive of Rwanda." Accessed May 22, 2018. http://www.genocidearchiverwanda.org.rw/index.php/Welcome_to _Genocide_Archive_Rwanda.

George, Terry, dir. *Hotel Rwanda*. Santa Monica, CA: Lionsgate Films, 2004.

Geras, Norman. *Crimes Against Humanity: The Birth of a Concept*. Manchester, UK: Manchester University Press, 2011.

Glasius, Marlies. *The International Criminal Court: A Global Civil Society Achievement*. London: Routledge, 2006.

Glucksmann, Raphaël, and David Hazan. *Tuez-les tous! Rwanda: Histoire d'un génocide "sans importance."* Paris: Dum Dum Films, 2005.

Gourevitch, Philip. "The Genocide Fax." *New Yorker*, May 3, 1998. https://www.newyorker.com/magazine/1998/05/11/the-genocide-fax.

———. *We Wish to Inform You That Tomorrow We Will Be Killed with Our Families: Stories from Rwanda.* New York: Picador, 1998.

Green, Penny, and Tony Ward. *State Crime: Governments, Violence and Corruption.* London: Pluto Press, 2004.

Grewal, San. "Somalia 'Is Not a Human Place.'" *Star*, May 12, 2007. http://www.thestar.com/News/article/213112.

Grünfeld, Fred, and Anke Huijboom. *The Failure to Prevent Genocide in Rwanda: The Role of Bystanders.* Leiden, the Netherlands: Martinus Nijhoff, 2007.

Hagan, John, and Ron Levi. "Justiciability as Field Effect: When Sociology Meets Human Rights." *Sociological Forum* 22, no. 3 (2007): 372–80.

Hagan, John, and Wenona Rymond-Richmond. *Darfur and the Crime of Genocide.* New York: Cambridge University Press, 2009.

Halilovich, Hariz. "Trans-Local Communities in the Age of Transnationalism: Bosnians in Diaspora." *International Migration* 50, no. 1 (2012): 162–78.

Hall, Stuart. "The West and the Rest: Discourse and Power." In *Formations of Modernity*, edited by Stuart Hall and Bram Gieben, 275–331. Cambridge: Polity Press, 1992.

Haltiwanger, John. "Is Genocide Occurring Against the Rohingya in Myanmar?" *Newsweek*, September 5, 2017. https://www.newsweek.com/genocide-occurring-against-rohingya-myanmar-experts-weigh-659841.

Harris, Evan. "Clinton Cites Rwanda, Bosnia in Rationale for Libya Intervention." ABC News, March 27, 2011. https://abcnews.go.com/blogs/politics/2011/03/clinton-cites-rwanda-bosnia-in-rationale-for-libya-intervention/.

Harrison, David, prod. "Rwanda: The Bloody Tricolor." *Panorama.* BBC One, August 20, 1995.

Hatzfeld, Jean. *Life Laid Bare: The Survivors in Rwanda Speak.* Translated by Linda Coverdale. New York: Other Press, 2006.

Haveman, Roelof, Olga Kavran, and Julian Nicholls, eds. *Supranational Criminal Law: A System Sui Generis.* Antwerp, Belgium: Intersentia, 2003.

Haveman, Roelof, and Alette Smeulers. "Criminology in a State of Denial—Towards a Criminology of International Crimes: Supranational Criminology." In *Supranational Criminology: Towards a Criminology of International Crimes*, edited by Alette Smeulers and Roelof Haveman, 3–26. Antwerp, Belgium: Intersentia, 2008.

Heller, Kevin Jon. "What Is an International Crime? (A Revisionist History)." *Harvard International Law Journal* 58, no. 2 (2016): 353–420

Heller, Kevin Jon, and Gerry Simpson, eds. *The Hidden Histories of War Crimes Trials.* Oxford: Oxford University Press, 2013.

Henry, Nicola. *War and Rape: Law, Memory, and Justice.* New York: Routledge, 2011.

Hesford, Wendy S. *Spectacular Rhetorics: Human Rights Visions, Recognitions, Feminisms.* Durham, NC: Duke University Press, 2011.

High Court of Australia. "Court Etiquette." Accessed December 17, 2018. http://www.hcourt.gov.au/about/court-etiquette.

Hoffman, Paul. "The Dusan Tadic Trial and Due Process Issues." *Whittier Law Review* 19, no. 2 (1997): 313–16.

Holá, Barbora, and Joris van Wijk. "Life After Conviction at International Criminal Tribunals: An Empirical Overview." *Journal of International Criminal Justice* 12, no. 1 (2014): 109–32.

hooks, bell. *Talking Back: Thinking Feminist, Thinking Black.* Boston: South End Press, 1989.

Hovannisian, Richard G., ed. *The Armenian Genocide in Perspective.* New Brunswick, NJ: Transaction Books, 1986.

Howard-Hassmann, Rhoda E. "Genocide and State-Induced Famine: Global Ethics and Western Responsibility for Mass Atrocities in Africa." *Perspectives on Global Development and Technology* 4, nos. 3–4 (2005): 487–516.

Hughes, Nick, dir. *100 Days.* Nairobi, Kenya: Vivid Features, 2001.

Hughes, Rachel. "The Abject Artefacts of Memory: Photographs from Cambodia's Genocide." *Media, Culture and Society* 25, no. 1 (2003): 23–44.

———. "Ordinary Theatre and Extraordinary Law at the Khmer Rouge Tribunal." *Environment and Planning D* 33, no. 4 (2015): 714–31.

Human Rights Center. *The Victim's Court? A Study of 622 Victim Participants at the International Criminal Court.* Berkeley, CA: Human Rights Center, 2015.

Human Rights Watch. "UN Security Council Should Seek Justice for Myanmar Atrocities." August 27, 2018. https://www.hrw.org/news/2018/08/27/un-security-council-should-seek-justice-myanmar-atrocities.

Huyssen, Andreas. *Present Pasts: Urban Palimpsests and the Politics of Memory.* Stanford, CA: Stanford University Press, 2003.

Ibrahim, Azeem. "There's Only One Conclusion on the Rohingya in Myanmar: It's Genocide." CNN, October 23, 2017. https://edition.cnn.com/2017/10/23/opinions/myanmar-rohingya-genocide/index.html.

Ibuka. *The Rwandan Genocide.* Kigali, Rwanda: Ibuka, 2001.

Ignatieff, Michael. *The Warrior's Honor: Ethnic War and the Modern Conscience.* London: Chatto and Windus, 1998.

Ilibagiza, Immaculée, and Steve Erwin. *Left to Tell: Discovering God Amidst the Rwandan Holocaust.* Carlsbad, CA: Hay House, 2006.

Imperial War Museums. Home page. Accessed May 22, 2018. https://www.iwm.org.uk/.

International Bar Association. "Witnesses Before the International Criminal Court." London: International Bar Association, 2013.

International Commission on Intervention and State Sovereignty. "The Responsibility to Protect: Report of the International Commission on Intervention and State Sovereignty." Ottawa, ON: International Development Research Centre, 2001.

International Criminal Court. "About." Accessed May 22, 2018. https://www.icc-cpi.int/about.

———. "The Court Today." Accessed January 16, 2020. https://www.icc-cpi.int/iccdocs/PIDS/publications/TheCourtTodayEng.pdf.

———. "Georgia: Situation in Georgia." Accessed December 17, 2018. https://www.icc
-cpi.int/georgia.

———. "Get Involved." Accessed December 17, 2018. https://www.icc-cpi.int/get-involved
/Pages/default.aspx.

———. Home page. Accessed December 17, 2018. https://www.icc-cpi.int/.

———. "How the Court Works." Accessed May 22, 2018. https://www.icc-cpi.int/about
/how-the-court-works.

———. "The ICC at a Glance." ICC Doc. ICC-PIOS-FS-01-006/18_Eng. https://www.icc
-cpi.int/iccdocs/PIDS/docs/ICCAtAGlanceEng.pdf.

———. *The ICC in 3 Minutes* [video]. May 6, 2016. https://www.youtube.com/watch?v
=Jw_cQrGwMJo.

———. "ICC Rules of Decorum." ICC Doc. ICC-PIDS-RD-001-09_ENG. Accessed December 14, 2019. https://www.icc-cpi.int/iccdocs/PIDS/publications/ICCRODEngLR
.pdf.

———. "Interacting with Communities Affected by Crimes." Accessed December 17, 2018.
https://www.icc-cpi.int/about/interacting-with-communities.

———. "International Criminal Court." Accessed February 3, 2020. https://au.linkedin
.com/company/international-criminal-court---cour-p-nale-internationale.

———. "Judicial Divisions." Accessed December 17, 2018. https://www.icc-cpi.int/about
/judicial-divisions.

———. "Justice Matters." Accessed September 17, 2019. http://www.icc-cpi.int/iccdocs
/PIDS/other/JusticeMattersSlideshow-ENG.pdf.

———. "Office of the Prosecutor." Accessed December 17, 2018. https://www.icc-cpi.int
/about/otp.

———. "Permanent Premises of the ICC." Accessed September 13, 2019. https://www.icc
-cpi.int/itemsDocuments/pr898/Permanent-Premises-factsheet-for-groundbreaking
-ceremony.pdf.

———. "The Presidency." Accessed December 21, 2018. https://www.icc-cpi.int/about
/presidency.

———. "Registry." Accessed December 17, 2018. https://www.icc-cpi.int/about/registry.

———. "Reporting on the International Criminal Court: A Practical Guide for the Media."
The Hague: International Criminal Court. Accessed December 21, 2019. https://www
.icc-cpi.int/iccdocs/PIDS/docs/2017_Journalist_Guide_ENG.pdf.

———. "Resource Library: Core ICC Texts." Accessed December 17, 2018. https://www.icc
-cpi.int/resource-library#coreICCtexts.

———. "Situations Under Investigation." Accessed August 26, 2019. https://www.icc-cpi
.int/pages/situation.aspx.

———. "The States Parties to the Rome Statute." Accessed December 17, 2018. https://asp
.icc-cpi.int/en_menus/asp/states parties/pages/the states parties to the rome statute.aspx.

———. Twitter feed. Accessed December 22, 2019. https://twitter.com/intlcrimcourt.

———. "Understanding the International Criminal Court." Accessed December 14, 2019.
http://www.icc-cpi.int/iccdocs/PIDS/publications/UICCEng.pdf.

———. "Victims." Accessed December 17, 2018. https://www.icc-cpi.int/about/victims.

———. "Victims' Participation Before the International Criminal Court (ICC)" [video]. Accessed January 16, 2020. https://www.icc-cpi.int/about/victims.

———. "Visit Us." Accessed December 17, 2018. https://www.icc-cpi.int/visit.

———. "Who's Who." Accessed December 17, 2018. https://www.icc-cpi.int/about/registry /whos-who.

———. "Witnesses." Accessed December 17, 2018. https://www.icc-cpi.int/about/witnesses.

International Criminal Court, Assembly of States Parties. "Report of the Bureau on Equitable Geographical Representation and Gender Balance in the Recruitment of Staff of the International Criminal Court." November 14, 2016. https://asp.icc-cpi.int/iccdocs /asp_docs/ASP15/ICC-ASP-15-32-ENG.pdf.

———. "Report of the Bureau on the Plan of Action for Achieving Universality and Full Implementation of the Rome Statute of the International Criminal Court." November 15, 2013. https://asp.icc-cpi.int/iccdocs/asp_docs/ASP12/ICC-ASP-12-26-ENG.pdf.

———. "Report of the Bureau on the Plan of Action of the Assembly of States Parties for Achieving Universality and Full Implementation of the Rome Statute of the International Criminal Court." December 14, 2017. https://asp.icc-cpi.int/iccdocs/asp_docs/ASP16 /ICC-ASP-16-18-ENG.pdf.

———. "Report of the Bureau on the Plan of Action of the Assembly of States Parties for Achieving Universality and Full Implementation of the Rome Statute of the International Criminal Court." November 23, 2018. https://asp.icc-cpi.int/iccdocs/asp_docs/ASP17 /ICC-ASP-17-32-ENG.pdf.

———. "Strategic Plan for Outreach of the International Criminal Court." September 29, 2006. https://www.icc-cpi.int/NR/rdonlyres/FB4C75CF-FD15-4B06-B1E3 -E22618FB404C/185051/ICCASP512_English1.pdf.

International Criminal Court, Office of the Prosecutor. "Policy Paper on Case Selection and Prioritisation." September 15, 2016. https://www.icc-cpi.int/itemsDocuments/20160915 _OTP-Policy_Case-Selection_Eng.pdf.

International Criminal Court Forum. Home page. Accessed September 13, 2019. https:// iccforum.com.

International Law Commission. "Analytical Guide to the Work of the International Law Commission: Draft Code of Crimes Against the Peace and Security of Mankind (Part I)." Accessed September 17, 2019. http://legal.un.org/ilc/guide/7_3.shtml.

———. "Analytical Guide to the Work of the International Law Commission: Draft Code of Crimes Against the Peace and Security of Mankind (Part II)—Including the Draft Statute for an International Criminal Court." Accessed September 17, 2019. http://legal .un.org/ilc/guide/7_4.shtml.

———. "Comments and Observations Received Pursuant to General Assembly Resolution 36/106," In *Yearbook of the International Law Commission, 1982*, Vol. 2, part 1: 273–80. New York: United Nations, 1984.

———. "Membership." Accessed December 17, 2019. https://legal.un.org/ilc/ilcmembe .shtml.

———. "Report of the International Law Commission on the Work of Its Thirty-Fifth Session, 3 May–22 July 1983, Official Records of the General Assembly, Thirty-Eighth Session, Supplement No. 10." UN Doc. A/38/10. In *Yearbook of the International Law Commission, 1983*, Vol. 2, part 2: 1–91. New York: United Nations, 1985.

———. "Report of the International Law Commission on the Work of Its Thirty-Sixth Session, 7 May–27 July 1984, Official Records of the General Assembly, Thirty-Ninth Session, Supplement No.10." UN Doc. A/39/10. In *Yearbook of the International Law Commission, 1984*, Vol. 2, part 2: 1–109. New York: United Nations, 1985.

———. "Report of the International Law Commission on the Work of Its Thirty-Seventh Session, 6 May–26 July 1985, Official Records of the General Assembly, Fortieth Session, Supplement No. 10." UN Doc. A/40/10. In *Yearbook of the International Law Commission, 1985*, Vol. 2, part 2: 1–76. New York: United Nations, 1986.

———. "Report of the International Law Commission on the Work of Its Thirty-Eighth Session, 5 May–11 July 1986, Official Records of the General Assembly, Forty-First Session, Supplement No. 10." UN Doc. A/41/10. In *Yearbook of the International Law Commission, 1986*, Vol. 2, part 2: 1–67. New York: United Nations, 1987.

———. "Report of the International Law Commission on the Work of Its Thirty-Ninth Session, 4 May–17 July 1987, Official Records of the General Assembly, Forty-Second Session, Supplement No. 10." UN Doc. A/42/10. In *Yearbook of the International Law Commission, 1987*, Vol. 2, part 2: 1–58. New York: United Nations, 1989.

———. "Report of the International Law Commission on the Work of Its Forty-First session, 2 May–21 July 1989, Official Records of the General Assembly, Forty-Fourth Session, Supplement No. 10." UN Doc. A/44/10. In *Yearbook of the International Law Commission, 1989*, Vol. 2, part 2: 1–140. New York: United Nations, 1992.

———. "Report of the International Law Commission on the Work of Its Forty-Second Session, 1 May–20 July 1990, Official Records of the General Assembly, Forty-Fifth Session, Supplement No. 10." UN Doc. A/45/10. In *Yearbook of the International Law Commission, 1990*, Vol. 2, part 2: 1–110. New York: United Nations, 1993.

———. "Report of the International Law Commission on the Work of Its Forty-Third Session, 29 April–19 July 1991, Official Records of the General Assembly, Forty-Sixth Session, Supplement No. 10." UN Doc. A/46/10. In *Yearbook of the International Law Commission, 1991*, Vol. 2, part 2: 1–134. New York: United Nations, 1994.

———. "Report of the International Law Commission on the Work of Its Forty-Sixth Session, 2 May–22 July 1994, Official Records of the General Assembly, Forty-Ninth Session, Supplement No. 10." UN Doc. A/49/10. In *Yearbook of the International Law Commission, 1994*, Vol. 2, part 2: 1–182. New York: United Nations, 1997.

———. *Yearbook of the International Law Commission, 1949*. New York: United Nations, 1956.

———. *Yearbook of the International Law Commission, 1950*. Vol. 1. New York: United Nations, 1958.

———. *Yearbook of the International Law Commission, 1991*. Vol. 2, part 2. New York: United Nations, 1994.

———. *Yearbook of the International Law Commission, 1995*. Vol. 1. New York: United Nations, 1997.

International Panel of Eminent Personalities to Investigate the 1994 Genocide in Rwanda and the Surrounding Events. *Rwanda: The Preventable Genocide*. Addis Ababa, Ethiopia: Organization of African Unity, 2000.

Jaar, Alfredo. *Let There Be Light: The Rwanda Project 1994–1998*. Barcelona, Spain: Actar, 1998.

Jackson, David. "One Reason for Obama's Decision on Libya: Rwanda." *USA Today*, March 24, 2011. http://content.usatoday.com/communities/theoval/post/2011/03/one-reason-for-obamas-decision-on-libya-rwanda/1#.To_j8ZiXtlI.

Jallow, Hassan Bubacar. "International Criminal Tribunal for Rwanda, Prosecutor." In *The Pursuit of International Criminal Justice: A World Study on Conflicts, Victimization, and Post-Conflict Justice*, edited by Mahmoud Cherif Bassiouni, 1:149–54. Antwerp, Belgium: Intersentia, 2010.

Jansen, Hanna. *Over a Thousand Hills I Walk with You*. Minneapolis, MN: Carolrhoda Books, 2006.

Jaulmes, Adrien. "A Model Prison for Those Accused of the Most Heinous Crimes." Translated by Sophie Ashkinaze-Collender. *Worldcrunch*, April 7, 2017. https://worldcrunch.com/world-affairs/a-model-prison-for-those-accused-of-the-most-heinous-crimes.

Kabera, Eric, dir. *Keepers of Memory: Survivors' Accounts of the Rwandan Genocide*. Beverly Hills, CA: Choices, 2005.

Kagame, Paul. "Africa: Rwandans Know Why Gaddafi Must Be Stopped." *AllAfrica*, March 24, 2011. http://allafrica.com/stories/201103240033.html.

———. "Commemoration of the 14th Anniversary of Tutsi Genocide." Kigali, Rwanda, April 7, 2008. On file with author.

———. "Remarks by His Excellency Paul Kagame at the 13th Commemoration of Genocide of 1994." Murambi, Rwanda, April 7, 2007. On file with author.

———. "Speech by His Excellency Paul Kagame at the 10th Anniversary of the Genocide in Rwanda." Kigali, Rwanda, April 7, 2004. On file with author.

———. "Speech by President Kagame at the 15th Commemoration of the Genocide Against the Tutsi at the Nyanza Memorial Site in Kicukiro, Kigali." Kigali, Rwanda, April 7, 2009. On file with author.

———. "Speech by President Kagame at the 17th Genocide Commemoration Ceremony." Kigali, Rwanda, April 7, 2011. On file with author.

Kalisa, Chantal. "Theatre and the Rwandan Genocide." *Peace Review* 18, no. 4 (2006): 515–21.

Kamatali, Jean Marie. "The Challenge of Linking International Criminal Justice and National Reconciliation: The Case of the ICTR." *Leiden Journal of International Law* 16, no. 1 (2003): 115–33.

Kaul, Hans-Peter. "The International Criminal Court: Current Challenges and Perspectives." *Washington University Global Studies Law Review* 6, no. 3 (2007): 575–82.

Kayimahe, Vénuste. *France-Rwanda: Les coulisses du génocide: Témoignage d'un rescapé*. Paris: Dagarno, 2001.

Keane, Fergal. *Season of Blood: A Rwandan Journey*. London: Penguin Books, 1995.

Kelsall, Tim. *Culture Under Cross-Examination: International Justice and the Special Court for Sierra Leone*. Cambridge: Cambridge University Press, 2013.

Kendall, Sara. "Beyond the Restorative Turn: The Limits of Legal Humanitarianism." In *Contested Justice: The Politics and Practice of International Criminal Court Interventions*, edited by Christian De Vos, Sara Kendall, and Carsten Stahn, 352–76. Cambridge University Press, 2015.

———. "Commodifying Global Justice: Economies of Accountability at the International Criminal Court." *Journal of International Criminal Justice* 13, no. 1 (2015): 113–34.

———. "'Hybrid' Justice at the Special Court for Sierra Leone." In *Interdisciplinary Legal Studies: The Next Generation*, Studies in Law, Politics and Society, edited by Austin Sarat, 1–27. Bingley, UK: Emerald Group Publishing, 2010.

Kendall, Sara, and Sarah M. H. Nouwen. "Representational Practices at the International Criminal Court: The Gap Between Juridified and Abstract Victimhood." *Law and Contemporary Problems* 76, nos. 3–4 (2014): 235–62.

Kennedy, Rosanne. "Moving Testimony: Human Rights, Palestinian Memory, and the Transnational Public Sphere." In *Transnational Memory: Circulation, Articulation, Scales*, edited by Chiara De Cesari and Ann Rigney, 51–78. Berlin: De Gruyter, 2014.

———. "Reparative Transnationalism: The Friction and Fiction of Remembering in Sierra Leone." *Memory Studies* 11, no. 3 (2018): 342–54.

Kent, Lia. *The Dynamics of Transitional Justice: International Models and Local Realities in East Timor*. London: Routledge, 2012.

Kigali Genocide Memorial. "A Place for Remembrance and Learning." Accessed May 22, 2018. http://www.kgm.rw/.

Kigali Memorial Centre. *Jenoside*. Kigali, Rwanda: Kigali Memorial Centre, 2004.

Ki-Moon, Ban. "Remarks at the Commemoration of the 20th Anniversary of the Rwandan Genocide." April 7, 2014. https://www.un.org/sg/en/content/sg/statement/2014-04-07/remarks-commemoration-20th-anniversary-rwandan-genocide-english-and.

Kirsch, Philippe. "The Role of the International Criminal Court in Enforcing International Criminal Law." *American University International Law Review* 22, no. 4 (2007): 539–48.

Kleinman, Arthur, and Joan Kleinman. "The Appeal of Experience; the Dismay of Images: Cultural Appropriations of Suffering in Our Times." In *Social Suffering*, edited by Arthur Kleinman, Veena Das, and Margaret Lock, 1–23. Berkeley: University of California Press, 1997.

Koller, David S. "The Faith of the International Criminal Lawyer." *International Law and Politics* 40, no. 4 (2008): 1019–69.

Koskenniemi, Martii. "Between Impunity and Show Trials." *Max Planck Yearbook of United Nations Law* 6, no. 1 (2002): 1–35.

———. "Legal Cosmopolitanism: Tom Franck's Messianic World." *New York University Journal of International Law and Politics* 35, no. 2 (2003): 471–86.

Kothari, Uma. "Visualising Solidarity: Forging Everyday Humanitarianism Through Public Representations of Development." Paper presented at the Institute of Postcolonial Studies, Melbourne, Australia, 8 March 2017.

Kritz, Neil J, ed. *Transitional Justice: How Emerging Democracies Reckon with Former Regimes*. Washington: United States Institute of Peace Press, 1995.

Kwon, O-Gon. "Remarks at Solemn Hearing in Commemoration of the 20th Anniversary of the Adoption of the Rome Statute of the International Criminal Court." July 17, 2018. https://www.icc-cpi.int/itemsDocuments/20180717-asp-speech.pdf.

Leebaw, Bronwyn. "The Irreconcilable Goals of Transitional Justice." *Human Rights Quarterly* 30, no. 1 (2008): 95–118.

Levy, Daniel, and Natan Sznaider. *The Holocaust and Memory in the Global Age.* Translated by Assenka Oksiloff. Philadelphia: Temple University Press, 2006.

———. "Memory Unbound: The Holocaust and the Formation of Cosmopolitan Memory." *European Journal of Social Theory* 5, no. 1 (2002): 87–106.

Lichfield, John. "Sarkozy Admits France's Role in Rwandan Genocide." *Independent*, February 26, 2010. https://www.independent.co.uk/news/world/europe/sarkozy-admits-frances-role-in-rwandan-genocide-1911272.html.

Lohne, Kjersti. "Penal Humanitarianism Beyond the Nation State: An Analysis of International Criminal Justice." *Theoretical Criminology*, https://journals.sagepub.com/doi/abs/10.1177/1362480618806917.

Lorde, Audre. *Sister Outsider: Essays and Speeches.* Trumansburg, NY: Crossing Press, 1984.

Luban, David. "A Theory of Crimes Against Humanity." *Yale Journal of International Law* 29, no. 1 (2004): 85–167.

Maier-Katkin, Daniel, Daniel P. Mears, and Thomas J. Bernard. "Towards a Criminology of Crimes Against Humanity." *Theoretical Criminology* 13, no. 2 (2009): 227–55.

Malkki, Liisa. "Citizens of Humanity: Internationalism and the Imagined Community of Nations." *Diaspora* 3, no. 1 (1994): 41–63.

———. "Commentary: The Politics of Trauma and Asylum: Universals and Their Effects." *Ethos* 25, no. 3 (2007): 336–43.

———. "National Geographic: The Rooting of Peoples and the Territorialization of National Identity Among Scholars and Refugees." *Cultural Anthropology* 7, no. 1 (1992): 24–44.

———. "Speechless Emissaries: Refugees, Humanitarianism and Dehistoricization." *Cultural Anthropology* 11, no. 3 (1996): 377–404.

———. "Things to Come: Internationalism and Global Solidarities in the Late 1990s." *Public Culture* 10, no. 2 (1998): 431–42.

Mamdani, Mahmood. *Beyond Nuremberg: Learning from the Post-Apartheid Transition in South Africa.* Makerere, Uganda: Makerere Institute of Social Research, 2015.

———. "The New Humanitarian Order." *Nation*, September 10, 2008. https://www.thenation.com/article/new-humanitarian-order/.

———. "The Politics of Naming: Genocide, Civil War, Insurgency." *London Review of Books*, March 8, 2007. https://www.lrb.co.uk/v29/n05/mahmood-mamdani/the-politics-of-naming-genocide-civil-war-insurgency.

———. *Saviors and Survivors: Darfur, Politics, and the War on Terror.* Lagos, Nigeria: Malthouse Press, 2010

———. *When Victims Become Killers: Colonialism, Nativism, and the Genocide in Rwanda.* Princeton, NJ: Princeton University Press, 2001.

Manjoo, Rashida, and Calleigh McRaith. "Gender-Based Violence and Justice in Conflict and Post-Conflict Areas." *Cornell International Law Journal* 44, no. 1 (2012): 11–31.

Marlowe, Lara. "Another Rwanda?" *Irish Times*, March 29, 2014. https://www.irishtimes.com/news/world/africa/another-rwanda-1.1741910.

Marston, Sallie A. "The Social Construction of Scale." *Progress in Human Geography* 24, no. 2 (2000): 219–42.

Massey, Doreen B. *For Space*. London: SAGE Publications, 2005.

Maunaguru, Sidharthan, and Neloufer de Mel. "An Exchange on Transitional Justice in Sri Lanka." Research seminar at the University of Melbourne, Australia, February 13, 2018.

May, Larry. *Crimes Against Humanity: A Normative Account*. New York: Cambridge University Press, 2005.

Mbeki, Thabo. "Statement of the President of the Republic of South Africa, Thabo Mbeki at the Commemoration of the 10th Anniversary of the Commencement of the 1994 Genocide in Rwanda." April 7, 2004.

Mbembe, Achille. *On the Postcolony*. Berkeley: University of California Press, 2001.

McCulloch, Jude. "From Garrison State to Garrison Planet: State Terror, the War on Terror and the Rise of a Global Carceral Complex." In *Contemporary State Terrorism: Theory and Practice*, edited by Richard Jackson, Eamon Murphy, and Scott Poynting, 196–212. New York: Routledge, 2010.

McDermott, Yvonne. "Child Victim or Brutal Warlord? ICC Weighs the Fate of Dominic Ongwen." *Conversation*, January 12, 2017. https://theconversation.com/child-victim-or-brutal-warlord-icc-weighs-the-fate-of-dominic-ongwen-70087.

McDonald, Dave. "Ungovernable Monsters: Law, Paedophilia, Crisis." *Griffith Law Review* 21, no. 3 (2012): 585–608.

McEvoy, Kieran, and Kirsten McConnachie. "Victimology in Transitional Justice: Victimhood, Innocence and Hierarchy." *European Journal of Criminology* 9, no. 5 (2012): 527–38.

McMillan, Nesam. "'Our' Shame: International Responsibility for the Rwandan Genocide." *Australian Feminist Law Journal* 28, no. 1 (2008): 3–28.

———. "Regret, Remorse and the Work of Remembrance: Official Responses to the Rwandan Genocide." *Social and Legal Studies* 19, no. 1 (2010): 85–105.

McNamee, Eugene. "Reconciling Rwandan Reconciliations: International Criminal Law Versus National Politics in the Mirror of Humanity." In *Law's Environment: Critical Legal Perspectives*, edited by Ubaldus de Vries and Lyana Francot, 99–118. The Hague, the Netherlands: Eleven Publishing, 2011.

Mégret, Frédéric. "In Whose Name? The ICC and the Search for Constituency." In *Contested Justice: The Politics and Practice of International Criminal Court Interventions*, edited by Christian de Vos, Sarah Kendall, and Carsten Stahn, 23–45. Cambridge: Cambridge University Press, 2015.

———. "What Sort of Global Justice Is 'International Criminal Justice'?" *Journal of International Criminal Justice* 13, no. 1 (2015): 77–96.

Meierhenrich, Jens. "Topographies of Remembering and Forgetting: The Transformation of *Lieux de Mémoire* in Rwanda." In *Remaking Rwanda: State Building and Human Rights*

After Mass Violence, edited by Scott Straus and Lars Waldorf, 283–96. Madison: University of Wisconsin Press, 2011.

Meister, Robert. *After Evil: A Politics of Human Rights*. New York: Columbia University Press, 2011.

Melvern, Linda. *Conspiracy to Murder: The Rwandan Genocide*. New York: Verso, 2006.

———. "France and Genocide: The Murky Truth." *Sunday Times*. August 8, 2008. https://www.thetimes.co.uk/article/france-and-genocide-the-murky-truth-8v22codqrtb

———. *A People Betrayed: The Role of the West in Rwanda's Genocide*. London: Zed Books, 2000.

Merrick, Jane. "Burma Risks Becoming 'the Next Rwanda' as Violence Grows." *Independent*, July 14, 2013. https://www.independent.co.uk/news/world/asia/burma-risks-becoming -the-next-rwanda-as-violence-grows-8707591.html.

Merry, Sally Engle. "International Law and Sociolegal Scholarship: Toward a Spatial Global Legal Pluralism." *Studies in Law, Politics, and Society* 41 (2007): 149–68.

Mertens, Charlotte. "Frames of Empire: Congo and Sexual Violence." PhD diss., University of Melbourne, 2017.

Mertens, Charlotte, and Maree Pardy. "'Sexurity' and Its Effects in Eastern Democratic Republic of Congo." *Third World Quarterly* 38, no. 4 (2017): 956–79.

Michalowski, Raymond J., and Ronald C. Kramer. *State-Corporate Crime: Wrongdoing at the Intersection of Business and Government*. New Brunswick, NJ: Rutgers University Press, 2006.

Minow, Martha. *Between Vengeance and Forgiveness: Facing History After Genocide and Mass Violence*. Boston: Beacon Press, 1998.

Moeller, Susan D. *Compassion Fatigue: How the Media Sell Disease, Famine, War and Death*. New York: Routledge, 1999.

Mohanty, Chandra Talpade. "Under Western Eyes: Feminist Scholarship and Colonial Discourses." *Feminist Review* 30 (Autumn 1988): 61–88.

Moore, Jina. "Rwanda Accuses France of Complicity in 1994 Genocide." *New York Times*, December 13, 2017. https://www.nytimes.com/2017/12/13/world/africa/rwanda-france -genocide.html.

Moreton-Robinson, Aileen. *Talkin' Up to the White Woman: Aboriginal Women and Feminism*. St. Lucia, Australia: University of Queensland Press, 2000.

———. *The White Possessive: Property, Power, and Indigenous Sovereignty*. Minneapolis: University of Minnesota Press, 2015.

Moses, A. Dirk, ed. *Genocide and Settler Society: Frontier Violence and Stolen Indigenous Children in Australian History*. New York: Berghahn Books, 2004.

Movement of Mothers of Srebrenica and Žepa Enclaves. "About Us." Accessed December 17, 2018. http://enklave-srebrenica-zepa.org/english.onama.php.

Musabende, Alice. "Why Libya but Not Rwanda?" *Globe and Mail*. March 31, 2011. https://www.theglobeandmail.com/opinion/why-libya-but-not-rwanda/article574645/

Mushikiwabo, Louise, and Jack Kramer. *Rwanda Means the Universe: A Native's Memoir of Blood and Bloodlines*. New York: St. Martin's Press, 2006.

Mutua, Makau. "Savages, Victims, and Saviors: The Metaphor of Human Rights." *Harvard International Law Journal* 42, no. 1 (2001): 201–46.

Nagy, Rosemary. "Transitional Justice as Global Project: Critical Reflections." *Third World Quarterly* 29, no. 2 (2008): 275–89.

Ndebele, Njabulo S. "The Rediscovery of the Ordinary: Some New Writings in South Africa." *Journal of Southern African Studies* 12, no. 2 (1986): 143–57.

Newbury, David. "Understanding Genocide." *African Studies Review* 41, no. 1 (1998): 73–97.

Nganemariya, Illuminee. *Miracle in Kigali*. Norwich, UK: Tagman Press, 2007.

Ní Aoláin, Fionnaula. "Women, Security, and the Patriarchy of Internationalized Transitional Justice." *Human Rights Quarterly* 31, no. 4 (2009): 1055–85.

Nouwen, Sarah M. H. *Complementarity in the Line of Fire: The Catalysing Effect of the International Criminal Court in Uganda and Sudan*. Cambridge: Cambridge University Press, 2013.

———. "'Hybrid Courts': The Hybrid Category of a New Type of International Crimes Courts." *Utrecht Law Review* 2, no. 2 (2006): 190–214.

Nouwen, Sarah M. H., and Wouter G. Werner. "Doing Justice to the Political: The International Criminal Court in Uganda and Sudan." *European Journal of International Law* 21, no. 4 (2011): 941–65.

———. "Monopolizing Global Justice: International Criminal Law as Challenge to Human Diversity." *Journal of International Criminal Justice* 13, no. 1 (2015): 157–76.

Novick, Peter. *The Holocaust in American Life*. New York: Mariner Books, 2000.

Nussbaum, Martha C. *For Love of Country?* Edited by Joshua Cohen. Boston: Beacon Press, 2002.

"Obama Strikes the Right Note." Editorial. *Toronto Star*, March 31, 2011. https://www.thestar.com/opinion/editorials/2011/03/31/obama_strikes_the_right_note.html.

O'Keefe, Roger. *International Criminal Law*. New York: Oxford University Press, 2015.

Orford, Anne. "Muscular Humanitarianism: Reading the Narratives of the New Interventionism." *European Journal of International Law* 10, no. 4 (1999): 679–711.

———. *Reading Humanitarian Intervention: Human Rights and the Use of Force in International Law*. Cambridge: Cambridge University Press, 2003.

Owada, Hisashi. "The International Court of Justice." In *The Pursuit of International Criminal Justice: A World Study on Conflicts, Victimization, and Post-Conflict Justice*, edited by Mahmoud Cherif Bassiouni, 1:137–42. Antwerp, Belgium: Intersentia, 2010.

Pahuja, Sundhya. *Decolonising International Law: Development, Economic Growth and the Politics of Universality*. Cambridge: Cambridge University Press, 2011.

PBS. "100 Days of Slaughter." Accessed January 12, 2020. https://www.pbs.org/wgbh/pages/frontline/shows/evil/etc/slaughter.html.

Peck, Raoul, dir. *Sometimes in April*. US: HBO Films, 2005.

Peress, Gilles. *The Silence*. New York: Scalo, 1995.

Peskin, Victor. *International Justice in Rwanda and the Former Yugoslavia: Virtual Trials and the Struggle for State Cooperation*. Cambridge: Cambridge University Press, 2008.

Philippopoulos-Mihalopoulos, Andreas. "Law's Spatial Turn: Geography, Justice and a Certain Fear of Space." *Law, Culture and the Humanities* 7, no. 2 (2010): 187–202.

Pierce, Julian R. *Speak Rwanda: A Novel*. New York: Picador, 1999.

Pogge, Thomas. "Priorities of Global Justice." *Metaphilosophy* 32, nos. 1–2 (2001): 6–24.

———. "Real World Justice." *Journal of Ethics* 9, nos. 1–2 (2005): 29–53.

Power, Samantha. *"A Problem from Hell": America and the Age of Genocide*. New York: Basic Books, 2002.

———. "Remember Rwanda, but Take Action in Sudan." *New York Times*, April 6, 2004. https://www.nytimes.com/2004/04/06/opinion/remember-rwanda-but-take-action-in -sudan.html.

Prunier, Gérard. *Darfur: The Ambiguous Genocide*. Ithaca, NY: Cornell University Press, 2005.

Pupavac, Vanessa. "Misanthropy Without Borders: The International Children's Rights Regime." *Disasters* 25, no. 2 (2001): 95–112.

Ra'ad Al Hussein, Zeid. "Keynote Speech by Zeid Ra'ad Al Hussein, United Nations High Commissioner for Human Rights, at the Assembly of States Parties to the Rome Statute of the International Criminal Court." November 16, 2016. https://www.ohchr.org/EN /NewsEvents/Pages/DisplayNews.aspx?NewsID=20873&LangID=E.

Rashed, Haifa, and Damien Short. "Genocide and Settler Colonialism: Can a Lemkin-Inspired Genocide Perspective Aid Our Understanding of the Palestinian Situation?" *International Journal of Human Rights* 16, no. 8 (2012): 1142–69.

Raymont, Peter, dir. *Shake Hands with the Devil: The Journey of Roméo Dallaire*. Toronto, ON: White Pine, 2004.

Razack, Sherene H. "Stealing the Pain of Others: Reflections on Canadian Humanitarian Responses." *Review of Education, Pedagogy, and Cultural Studies* 29, no. 4 (2007): 375–94.

Reichman, Ravit. *The Affective Life of Law: Legal Modernism and the Literary Imagination*. Stanford, CA: Stanford University Press, 2009.

"Remembering Rwanda: The Rwanda Genocide 10th Anniversary Memorial Project." *Pambazuka News*, January 15, 2004. https://www.pambazuka.org/human-security/remembering -rwanda-rwanda-genocide-10th-anniversary-memorial-project.

Republic of Rwanda National Commission for the Fight Against Genocide. Home page. Accessed September 20, 2019. http://www.cnlg.gov.rw/.

Resnik, Judith, and Dennis Curtis. *Representing Justice: Invention, Controversy, and Rights in City-States and Democratic Courtrooms*. New Haven, CT: Yale University Press, 2011.

Rigney, Sophie. "Asylum-Seeker Policy Could Amount to Crime." *Age*, January 24, 2014. https://www.theage.com.au/opinion/asylumseeker-policy-could-amount-to-crime -20140123-31bij.html.

Riles, Annelise. "The View from the International Plane: Perspective and Scale in the Architecture of Colonial International Law." *Law and Critique* 6, no. 1 (1995): 39–54.

RISE (Refugees, Survivors and Ex-Detainees). "Stolenwealth Games Boycott—A First Nations and EX-Detainee Solidarity Statement." March 26, 2018. http://riserefugee.org /stolenwealth-games-boycott-a-first-nations-ex-detainee-solidarity-statement-26-03-2018/.

Roberts, Anthea. *Is International Law International?* New York: Oxford University Press, 2017.

Roberts, Joel. "Sudan: The Next Rwanda?" CBS News. April 9, 2004. https://www.cbsnews .com/news/sudan-the-next-rwanda/.

Robertson, Geoffrey. *Crimes Against Humanity: The Struggle for Global Justice.* 4th ed. London: Penguin, 2012.

Robinson, Duncan. "Dutch Still Grapple with the Shame of Srebrenica." *Financial Times,* July 11, 2015. https://www.ft.com/content/93a5c67a-26d2-11e5-9c4e-a775d2b173ca.

Robinson, Mike, prod. "When Good Men Do Nothing." *Panorama.* BBC, 1998.

Robinson, Mike, and Ben Loeterman, prods. "The Triumph of Evil." *Frontline.* PBS, 1999. https://www.pbs.org/wgbh/pages/frontline/shows/evil/etc/synopsis.html.

Rombouts, Heidy. *Victim Organisations and the Politics of Reparation.* Antwerp, Belgium: Intersentia, 2004.

Rose, Evelyn. "A Feminist Reconceptualisation of Intimate Partner Violence Against Women: A Crime Against Humanity and a State Crime." *Women's Studies International Forum* 53 (November–December 2015): 31–42.

Ross, Eleanor. "UN Urged to Label Isis Crimes Against Yazidi Community as 'Genocide.'" *Independent,* December 21, 2015. https://www.independent.co.uk/news/world/middle-east/un-urged-to-label-isis-crimes-against-yazidi-community-as-genocide-a6781301.html.

Rothberg, Michael. *Multidirectional Memory: Remembering the Holocaust in the Age of Decolonization.* Stanford, CA: Stanford University Press, 2009.

Ruhorahoza, Kivu, dir. *Grey Matter (Matière grise).* San Francisco, CA: Global Film Initiative, 2012.

Rusesabagina, Paul, and Tom Zoellner. *An Ordinary Man: An Autobiography.* New York: Penguin Books, 2006.

Rush, Peter D. "Preface—After Atrocity: Foreword to Transition." In *The Arts of Transitional Justice: Culture, Activism, and Memory after Atrocity,* edited by Peter Rush and Olivera Simić, v–xi. New York: Springer, 2014.

Rwafa, Urther. "Film Representations of the Rwandan Genocide." *African Identities* 8, no. 4 (2010): 389–408.

Rwandan Stories. Home page. Accessed May 22, 2018. http://www.rwandanstories.org.

Sagan, Ann. "African Criminals / African Victims: The Institutionalised Production of Cultural Narratives in International Criminal Law." *Millennium* 39, no. 3 (2010): 3–21.

Said, Edward W. *Culture and Imperialism.* New York: Knopf, 1993.

———. *Orientalism.* New York: Random House, 1979.

Saint-Exupéry, Patrick de. *L'inavouable: La France au Rwanda.* Paris: Arènes, 2004.

Sands, Philippe, ed. *From Nuremberg to The Hague: The Future of International Criminal Justice.* New York: Cambridge University Press, 2003.

Sandström, Emil. "Report on the Question of International Criminal Jurisdiction." UN Doc. A/CN.4/20. In *Yearbook of the International Law Commission 1950,* 2:18–23. New York: United Nations, 1957.

Sassen, Saskia. "Introduction: Deciphering the Global." In *Deciphering the Global: Its Scales, Spaces and Subjects,* edited by Saskia Sassen, 1–18. New York: Routledge, 2013.

Save Darfur Coalition. *Save Darfur.org.* 2006. https://www.loc.gov/item/lcwaN0012552/.

Scalia, Damien. "Legitimacy of International Criminal Tribunals: A Perspective of the Accused." Seminar at Vrije Universiteit, Amsterdam, Netherlands, 2014.

Schabas, William A. "Genocide and the International Court of Justice: Finally, a Duty to Prevent the Crime of Crimes." *Genocide Studies and Prevention* 2, no. 2 (2007): 101–22.

———. *Genocide in International Law: The Crime of Crimes*. New York: Cambridge University Press, 2009.

———. *An Introduction to the International Criminal Court*. 4th ed. Cambridge: Cambridge University Press, 2012.

Schaffer, Kay, and Sidonie Smith. *Human Rights and Narrated Lives: The Ethics of Recognition*. New York: Palgrave Macmillan, 2004.

Schiff, Benjamin N. *Building the International Criminal Court*. Cambridge: Cambridge University Press, 2008.

Schwöbel, Christine, ed. *Critical Approaches to International Criminal Law: An Introduction*. New York: Routledge, 2014.

———. "The Market and Marketing Culture of International Criminal Law." In *Critical Approaches to International Criminal Law: An Introduction*, edited by Christine Schwöbel, 264–80. New York: Routledge, 2014.

Schwöbel-Patel, Christine. "Spectacle in International Criminal Law: The Fundraising Image of Victimhood." *London Review of International Law* 4, no. 2 (2016): 247–74.

Scott, Charles E. *The Question of Ethics: Nietzsche, Foucault, Heidegger*. Bloomington: Indiana University Press, 1990.

Shaw, Martin. "The Snare of Analogy." *Global Dialogue* 15, no. 1 (2013): 6–11.

Shaw, Rosalind. "Memory Frictions: Localizing the Truth and Reconciliation Commission in Sierra Leone." *International Journal of Transitional Justice* 1, no. 2 (2007): 183–207.

Shohat, Ella, and Robert Stam. *Unthinking Eurocentrism: Multiculturalism and the Media*. 2nd ed. New York: Routledge, 2014.

Short, Damien. "Cultural Genocide and Indigenous Peoples: A Sociological Approach." *International Journal of Human Rights* 14, no. 6 (2010): 833–48.

Silver, Steven, dir. *The Last Just Man*. Toronto, ON: Barna-Alper Productions, 2002.

Simpson, Gerry. "Atrocity, Law, Humanity: Punishing Human Rights Violators." In *The Cambridge Companion to Human Rights Law*, edited by Conor Gearty and Costas Douzinas, 114–33. Cambridge: Cambridge University Press, 2012.

———. *Law, War and Crime*. Cambridge: Polity Press, 2007.

Slapper, Gary, and Steve Tombs. *Corporate Crime*. Harlow, UK: Longman, 1999.

Sluga, Glenda, and Patricia Clavin. *Internationalisms: A Twentieth-Century History*. Cambridge: Cambridge University Press, 2017.

Smeulers, Alette, ed. *Collective Violence and International Criminal Justice: An Interdisciplinary Approach*. Antwerp, Belgium: Intersentia, 2010.

Smeulers, Alette, and Lotte Hoex. "Studying the Microdynamics of the Rwandan Genocide." *British Journal of Criminology* 50, no. 3 (2010): 435–54.

Smith, Kerry. "Aboriginal Groups Welcome Refugees." *Green Left Weekly*, August 10, 2013. https://www.greenleft.org.au/content/aboriginal-groups-welcome-refugees.

Social Science Bites. "Doreen Massey on Space." Social Science Space. February 1, 2013. https://www.socialsciencespace.com/2013/02/podcastdoreen-massey-on-space/.

Song, Sang-Hyun. "The International Criminal Court." In *The Pursuit of International Criminal Justice: A World Study on Conflicts, Victimization, and Post-Conflict Justice*, edited by Mahmoud Cherif Bassiouni, 1:142–144. Antwerp, Belgium: Intersentia, 2010.

———. "Statement by ICC President Sang-Hyun Song." July 7, 2011. https://asp.icc-cpi.int/NR/rdonlyres/FED84B71-D7EF-4992-9B12-D93D3BA643B5/0/PresICC070711.pdf.

Spiropoulos, Jean. "Draft Code of Offences Against the Peace and Security of Mankind." UN Doc. A/CN.4/25. In *Yearbook of the International Law Commission, 1950*, 2:253–78. New York: United Nations, 1950.

Stassen, Jean-Philippe. *Deogratias: A Tale of Rwanda*. New York: First Second Books, 2000.

State of Victoria. "Neighbourhood Justice Centre." Accessed December 17, 2018. https://www.neighbourhoodjustice.vic.gov.au/.

Stauffer, Jill. *Ethical Loneliness: The Injustice of Not Being Heard*. New York: Columbia University Press, 2015.

Steele, Jonathan. "Darfur Wasn't Genocide and Sudan Is Not a Terrorist State." *Guardian*, October 7, 2005. https://www.theguardian.com/world/2005/oct/07/usa.sudan.

Stolberg, Sheryl Gay. "Still Crusading, but Now on the Inside." *New York Times*, March 29, 2011. https://www.nytimes.com/2011/03/30/world/30power.html.

Stoler, Ann Laura. "Imperial Debris: Reflections on Ruins and Ruination." *Cultural Anthropology* 23, no. 2 (2008): 191–219.

Stolk, Sofia. "A Solemn Tale of Horror: The Opening Statement of the Prosecution in International Criminal Trials." PhD diss., Vrije Universiteit, 2017.

"Stop Another Rwanda in Sudan." Editorial. *Seattle Times*, July 20, 2004. http://community.seattletimes.nwsource.com/archive/?date=20040720&slug=darfured20.

"Stop Rape Now." Accessed May 22, 2018. http://www.stoprapenow.org/.

Stover, Eric, and Harvey M. Weinstein, eds. *My Neighbor, My Enemy: Justice and Community in the Aftermath of Mass Atrocity*. Cambridge: Cambridge University Press, 2004.

Straus, Scott. "Contested Meanings and Conflicting Imperatives: A Conceptual Analysis of Genocide." *Journal of Genocide Research* 3, no. 3 (2001): 349–75.

———. "Darfur and the Genocide Debate." *Foreign Affairs* 84, no. 1 (2005): 123–33.

———. "The Historiography of the Rwandan Genocide." In *The Historiography of Genocide*, edited by Dan Stone, 517–42. New York: Palgrave Macmillan, 2010.

Straus, Scott, and Lars Waldorf. "Introduction: Seeing Like a Post-Conflict State." In *Remaking Rwanda: State Building and Human Rights After Mass Violence*, edited by Scott Straus and Lars Waldorf, 3–22. Madison: University of Wisconsin Press, 2011.

Stromseth, Jane E. "The International Criminal Court and Justice on the Ground." *Arizona State Law Journal* 43, no. 2 (2011): 427–446.

Survivors Fund. "Learn." Accessed January 26, 2020. https://survivors-fund.org.uk/learn/.

Svirsky, Gila. "Local Coalitions, Global Partners: The Women's Peace Movement in Israel and Beyond." *Signs* 29, no. 2 (2003): 543–50.

Tadjo, Véronique. *The Shadow of Imana: Travels in the Heart of Rwanda*. Oxford: Harcourt Heinemann, 2002.

Tallgren, Immi. "The Sensibility and Sense of International Criminal Law." *European Journal of International Law* 13, no. 3 (2002): 561–95.

———. "The Voice of the International: Who Is Speaking?" *Journal of International Criminal Justice* 13, no. 1 (2015): 135–55.

Tasma, Alain, dir. *Opération Turquoise*. Paris: Cipango, 2007.

Teitel, Ruti G. "For Humanity." *Journal of Human Rights* 3, no. 2 (2004): 225–37.

———. "Humanity's Law: Rule of Law for the New Global Politics." *Cornell International Law Journal* 35, no. 2 (2002): 355–87.

———. *Transitional Justice*. New York: Oxford University Press, 2000.

———. "The Universal and the Particular in International Criminal Justice." *Columbia Human Rights Law Review* 30, no. 2 (1999): 285–303.

Theidon, Kimberley. "Histories of Innocence: Post-War Stories in Peru." In *Localizing Transitional Justice: Interventions and Priorities After Mass Violence*, edited by Rosalind Shaw, Lars Waldorf, and Pierre Hazan, 92–110. Stanford, CA: Stanford University Press, 2010.

Thiam, Doudou. "Fifth Report on the Draft Code of Offences Against the Peace and Security of Mankind." UN Doc. A/CN.4/404. In *Yearbook of the International Law Commission, 1987*, vol. 2, part 1: 1–10. New York: United Nations, 1989.

———. "First Report on the Draft Code of Offences Against the Peace and Security of Mankind." UN Doc. A/CN.4/364. In *Yearbook of the International Law Commission, 1983*, vol. 2, part 1: 137–52. New York: United Nations, 1985.

———. "Fourth Report on the Draft Code of Offences Against the Peace and Security of Mankind." UN Doc. A/CN.4/398. In *Yearbook of the International Law Commission, 1986*, vol. 2, part 1: 53–86. New York: United Nations, 1988.

———. "Second Report on the Draft Code of Offences Against the Peace and Security of Mankind." UN Doc. A/CN.4/377. In *Yearbook of the International Law Commission, 1984*, vol. 2, part 1: 89–100. New York: United Nations, 1986.

———. "Seventh Report on the Draft Code of Crimes Against the Peace and Security of Mankind." UN Doc. A/CN.4/419. In *Yearbook of the International Law Commission, 1989*, vol. 2, part 1: 81–90. New York: United Nations, 1992.

———. "Third Report on the Draft Code of Offences Against the Peace and Security of Mankind." UN Doc. A/CN.4/387. In *Yearbook of the International Law Commission, 1985*, vol. 2, part 1: 63–83. New York: United Nations, 1987.

———. "Thirteenth Report on the Draft Code of Crimes Against the Peace and Security of Mankind." UN Doc. A/CN.4/466. In *Yearbook of the International Law Commission, 1995*, vol. 2, part 1: 33–50. New York: United Nations, 2006.

Tinsley, Rebecca. "Is Cameroon Gradually Becoming Another Rwanda?" *Journal du Cameroun*, January 9, 2019. https://www.journalducameroun.com/en/cameroon-gradually-becoming-another-rwanda/.

Tomuschat, Christian. "Document on Crimes Against the Environment." UN Doc. ILC(XLVIII)/DC/CRD.3. In *Yearbook of the International Law Commission, 1996*, vol. 2, part 1: 15–27. New York: United Nations, 2008.

Tuathail, Gearóid Ó. *Critical Geopolitics: The Politics of Writing Global Space*. Minneapolis: University of Minnesota Press, 1996.

Umutesi, Marie Béatrice. *Surviving the Slaughter: The Ordeal of a Rwandan Refugee in Zaire*. Translated by Julia Emerson. Madison: University of Wisconsin Press, 2004.

UN News. "UN Officials Recall 'Horror' of Srebrenica as Security Council Fails to Adopt Measure Condemning Massacre." July 8, 2015. https://news.un.org/en/story/2015/07/503712-un-officials-recall-horror-srebrenica-security-council-fails-adopt-measure.

United Nations. "Central African Republic: UN Investigators Urge Establishment of War Crimes Tribunal." *UN News*, January 21, 2015. https://news.un.org/en/story/2015/01/488872.

——. "General Assembly Meets to Mark Day of Reflection on 1994 Rwanda Genocide, Expressing Deep Sorrow for Victims, Determination to Act in Future." UN Doc. GA/10232, April 7, 2004. https://www.un.org/press/en/2004/ga10232.doc.htm.

——. "International Residual Mechanism for Criminal Tribunals." Accessed December 17, 2018. http://unictr.irmct.org/.

——. "On Remembrance Day for Rwanda's Genocide Victims, UN Urges Action on Darfur." *UN News*, April 7, 2006. https://news.un.org/en/story/2006/04/175032-remembrance-day-rwandas-genocide-victims-un-urges-action-darfur.

——. "Outreach Programme on the Rwanda Genocide and the United Nations: About: Preventing Genocide." Accessed September 2, 2019. https://www.un.org/en/preventgenocide/rwanda/preventing-genocide.shtml.

——. "Outreach Programme on the Rwanda Genocide and the United Nations: Background Information on the Justice and Reconciliation Process in Rwanda." Accessed on September 21, 2019. https://www.un.org/en/preventgenocide/rwanda/backgrounders.shtml.

——. "Outreach Programme on the Rwanda Genocide and the United Nations: Commemorations." Accessed September 21, 2019. http://www.un.org/en/preventgenocide/rwanda/commemoration/annualcommemoration.shtml.

——. "Outreach Programme on the Rwanda Genocide and the United Nations: Home page." Accessed May 22, 2018. http://www.un.org/en/preventgenocide/rwanda/.

——. "Presidents of the International Court of Justice, International Criminal Court Present Reports to General Assembly." UN Doc. GA/10652. November 1, 2007. https://www.un.org/press/en/2007/ga10652.doc.htm.

——. "Report of the Independent Inquiry into the Actions of the United Nations During the 1994 Genocide in Rwanda." UN Doc. S/1999/1257. December 16, 1999. https://peacekeeping.un.org/en/report-of-independent-inquiry-actions-of-united-nations-during-1994-genocide-rwanda-s19991257.

——. "Responsibility to Protect." Accessed September 21, 2019. https://www.un.org/en/genocideprevention/about-responsibility-to-protect.shtml.

——. "Rome Statute of the International Criminal Court: Overview." Accessed September 21, 2019. http://legal.un.org/icc/general/overview.htm.

——. "UN Commission Finds Sudanese Government Responsible for Crimes in Darfur." *UN News*, February 1, 2005. https://news.un.org/en/story/2005/02/127392-un-commission-finds-sudanese-government-responsible-crimes-darfur.

——. "United Nations Diplomatic Conference of Plenipotentiaries on the Establishment of an International Criminal Court, Rome, 15 June–17 July, 1998: Official Records." Accessed December 17, 2018. http://legal.un.org/icc/rome/proceedings/contents.htm.

————. *United Nations Diplomatic Conference of Plenipotentiaries on the Establishment of an International Criminal Court, Rome, 15 June–17 July, 1998: Official Records: Volume 2.* Accessed December 21, 2019. http://legal.un.org/icc/rome/proceedings/E/Rome%20 Proceedings_v2_e.pdf.

United Nations International Criminal Tribunal for the Former Yugoslavia. "Global Spread of International Criminal Justice." Accessed on September 21, 2019. http://www.icty.org /en/content/global-spread-international-criminal-justice.

United Nations Secretary-General. *The Rule of Law and Transitional Justice in Conflict and Post-Conflict Societies.* UN Doc. S/2004/616. New York: United Nations, 2004.

United States Holocaust Memorial Museum. "Why We Remember the Holocaust." Accessed May 22, 2018. https://www.ushmm.org/remember/days-of-remembrance/why -we-remember.

Uvin, Peter. *Aiding Violence: The Development Enterprise in Rwanda.* West Hartford, CT: Kumarian Press, 1998.

————. "Reading the Rwandan Genocide." *International Studies Review* 3, no. 3 (2001): 75–99.

Van Schaack, Beth. "The Crime of Political Genocide: Repairing the Genocide Convention's Blind Spot." *Yale Law Journal* 106, no. 7 (1997): 2259–91.

————. "The Definition of Crimes Against Humanity: Resolving the Incoherence." *Columbia Journal of Transnational Law* 37, no. 3 (1999): 787–850.

Verhofstadt, Guy. "Discours du Monsieur le Premier Ministre Guy Verhofstadt à l'occasion de la commemoration du 6e anniversaire du début du génocide Rwandais." April 7, 2000. On file with author.

Vernon, Richard. "What Is Crime Against Humanity?" *Journal of Political Philosophy* 10, no. 3 (2002): 231–49.

Vertovec, Steven. "Conceiving and Researching Transnationalism." *Ethnic and Racial Studies* 22, no. 2 (1999): 447–62.

Voices of Rwanda. "About Voices of Rwanda." Accessed May 22, 2018. http://voicesofrwanda .org.

Waldorf, Lars. "Inhumanity's Law: Crimes Against Humanity, RtoP and South Sudan." *International Politics* 53, no. 1 (2016): 49–66.

————. "Instrumentalizing Genocide: The RPF's Campaign Against 'Genocide Ideology.'" In *Remaking Rwanda: State Building and Human Rights After Mass Violence*, edited by Scott Straus and Lars Waldorf, 48–66. Madison: University of Wisconsin Press, 2011.

————. "Mass Justice for Mass Atrocity: Rethinking Local Justice as Transitional Justice." *Temple Law Review* 79, no. 1 (2006): 1–87.

Wallis, Andrew. *Silent Accomplice: The Untold Story of France's Role in the Rwandan Genocide.* London: I. B. Tauris, 2014.

Welsh, Jennifer M. "The Rwanda Effect: Development and Endorsement of the 'Responsibility to Protect.'" In *After Genocide: Transitional Justice, Post-Conflict Reconstruction and*

Reconciliation in Rwanda and Beyond, edited by Phil Clark and Zachary D. Kaufman, 333–50. New York: Columbia University Press, 2009.

Werner, Wouter G. "The Reckoning: Advocating International Criminal Justice and the Flattening of Humanity." In *Documenting World Politics: A Critical Companion to IR and Non-Fiction Film*, edited by Rens Van Munster and Casper Sylvest, 166–82. New York: Routledge, 2015.

White, Rob, ed. *Global Environmental Harm: Criminological Perspectives*. Collumpton, UK: Willan Publishing, 2010.

Williams, Sarah. *Hybrid and Internationalised Criminal Tribunals: Selected Jurisdictional Issues*. Oxford: Hart Publishing, 2012.

Wilson, Richard A., and Richard D. Brown. Introduction to *Humanitarianism and Suffering: The Mobilization of Empathy*, edited by Richard A. Wilson and Richard D. Brown, 1–28. Cambridge: Cambridge University Press, 2009.

Winter, Renate. "The Special Court for Sierra Leone, President." In *The Pursuit of International Criminal Justice: A World Study on Conflicts, Victimization, and Post-Conflict Justice*, edited by Mahmoud Cherif Bassiouni, 1:155–61. Antwerp, Belgium: Intersentia, 2010.

Wolfe, Patrick. "History and Imperialism: A Century of Theory, from Marx to Postcolonialism." *American Historical Review* 102, no. 2 (1997): 388–420.

Woolford, Andrew. "Canada's MMIWG Report Spurs Debate on the Shifting Definitions of Genocide." *Conversation*, June 7, 2019. https://theconversation.com/canadas-mmiwg-report-spurs-debate-on-the-shifting-definitions-of-genocide-118324.

Woolford, Andrew, and Jeff Benvenuto, eds. *Canada and Colonial Genocide*. Abingdon, UK: Routledge, 2017.

Wroughton, Lesley. "World Bank Chief Apologises over Rwanda Genocide." *Star*, June 16, 2005. https://www.thestar.com.my/news/world/2005/06/16/world-bank-chief-apologises-over-rwanda-genocide.

Yates, Pamela, dir. *The Reckoning: The Battle for the International Criminal Court*. New York: Skylight Pictures, 2009.

Young, Alison. *Imagining Crime: Textual Outlaws and Criminal Conversations*. London: Sage, 1996.

———. *The Scene of Violence: Cinema, Crime, Affect*. New York: Routledge, 2009.

Young, Iris Marion. *Responsibility for Justice*. New York: Oxford University Press, 2011.

Young, James E. *Writing and Rewriting the Holocaust: Narrative and the Consequences of Interpretation*. Bloomington: Indiana University Press, 1988.

Young, Robert J. C. *White Mythologies: Writing History and the West*. London: Routledge, 2004.

Zorbas, Eugenia. "Aid Dependence and Policy Independence: Explaining the Rwandan Paradox." In *Remaking Rwanda: State Building and Human Rights After Mass Violence*, edited by Scott Straus and Lars Waldorf, 103–17. Madison: University of Wisconsin Press, 2011.

Index

THE CULTURAL LIVES OF LAW
Austin Sarat, Editor

The Cultural Lives of Law *series brings insights and approaches from cultural studies to law and tries to secure for law a place in cultural analysis. Books in the series focus on the production, interpretation, consumption, and circulation of legal meanings. They take up the challenges posed as boundaries collapse between as well as within cultures, and as the circulation of legal meanings becomes more fluid. They also attend to the ways law's power in cultural production is renewed and resisted.*

Jeffrey R. Dudas, *Raised Right: Fatherhood in Modern American Conservatism*
2017

Renée Ann Cramer, *Pregnant with the Stars: Watching and Wanting the Celebrity Baby Bump*
2015

Sora Y. Han, *Letters of the Law: Race and the Fantasy of Colorblindness*
2015

Marianne Constable, *Our Word Is Our Bond: How Legal Speech Acts*
2014

Joshua C. Wilson, *The Street Politics of Abortion: Speech, Violence, and America's Culture Wars*
2013

Irus Braverman, *Zooland: The Institution of Captivity*
2012

Nora Gilbert, *Better Left Unsaid: Victorian Novels, Hays Code Films, and the Benefits of Censorship*
2012

Edited by Winnifred Fallers Sullivan, Robert A. Yelle, and Mateo Taussig-Rubbo, *After Secular Law*
2011

Keith J. Bybee, *All Judges Are Political—Except When They Are Not: Acceptable Hypocrisies and the Rule of Law*
2010

Susan Sage Heinzelman, *Riding the Black Ram: Law, Literature, and Gender*
2010

David M. Engel and Jaruwan S. Engel, *Tort, Custom, and Karma: Globalization and Legal Consciousness in Thailand*
2010

Ruth A. Miller, *Law in Crisis: The Ecstatic Subject of Natural Disaster*
2009

Ravit Reichman, *The Affective Life of Law: Legal Modernism and the Literary Imagination*
2009

Edited by David M. Engel and Michael McCann, *Fault Lines: Tort Law as Cultural Practice*
2008

William P. MacNeil, *Lex Populi: The Jurisprudence of Popular Culture*
2007

Edited by Austin Sarat and Christian Boulanger, *The Cultural Lives of Capital Punishment: Comparative Perspectives*
2005

The authorized representative in the EU for product safety and compliance is:
Mare Nostrum Group
B.V Doelen 72
4831 GR Breda
The Netherlands

www.ingramcontent.com/pod-product-compliance
Lightning Source LLC
Chambersburg PA
CBHW030818270326
41928CB00007B/789